AFRICENTRIC APPROACHES TO CHRISTIAN MINISTRY

Strengthening Urban Congregations in African American Communities

---

Edited by
Ronald Edward Peters
Marsha Snulligan Haney

University Press of America,® Inc.
Lanham · Boulder · New York · Toronto · Oxford

Copyright © 2006 by
University Press of America,® Inc.
4501 Forbes Boulevard
Suite 200
Lanham, Maryland 20706
UPA Acquisitions Department (301) 459-3366

PO Box 317
Oxford
OX2 9RU, UK

Library of Congress Control Number: 2005928364
ISBN-13: 978-0-7618-3264-5 (paperback : alk. paper)
ISBN-10: 0-7618-3264-5 (paperback : alk. paper)

To Our Students

Contents

Preface

The idea for this book emerged from a series of events that began as a small denominational controversy around community oriented ministry, especially in urban communities where large percentages of African Americans live. This series of events had their origin in a debate that erupted more than a decade ago in the Presbyterian Church (USA) although the debate gained little notice in the wider denomination primarily due to the fact that issues impacting the African American community are generally not at the core of the denomination's agenda. This is understandable since the Presbyterian Church (USA) is more than 95% Euro-American in constituency and overwhelmingly a non-urban denomination. The debate was primarily concentrated among African American Presbyterians and focused on community ministry issues impacting these congregations.

With African American communities across the nation facing harsh realities ranging from disproportionately high instances of infant mortality, cardiovascular disease, and incarceration to racial profiling, and troubled school systems in high crime ridden neighborhoods, Black churches clearly face serious ministry challenges. There were African American Presbyterians who felt strongly that the preoccupation of their denomination with procedural and theological issues that did not touch the above realities in any meaningful way was a situation that must be addressed by Black Presbyterian congregations. These Presbyterians felt they had to focus more seriously on African American community needs rather than perpetually be consumed by denominational maneuverings and theological rhetoric that was irrelevant to African American concerns and deflated effective congregational ministry in African American neighborhoods.

In 1993, resistance to denominational insensitivity regarding African American concerns became the focal point for a group of Presbyterians who collectively were known as *Presbyterians for Prayer, Study, and Action*[i] and lifted a challenge to the church in a discussion paper entitled *Is This New Wine?*.[ii] This group had evolved from the denomination's African American Advisory Committee (AAAC) that worked with the national church's office of Racial and Cultural Diversity. The AAAC had been meeting since 1990 on ways to strengthen Presbyterian new church development and communal outreach activities among African American communities. At its December, 1992 meeting, however, several committee members began to considering the practical inconsistencies of attempting to continually forge ministries uniquely targeted toward African American concerns from the base of denominational structures that were out of touch with core needs and aspirations of these communities and did not have an adequate appreciation of the African heritage. The group, in effort to distinguish itself from the denomination's African American Advisory Committee, began to refer to themselves as *Presbyterians for Prayer, Study, and Action.* While the group gave definition and structure to the dialogue, Ron agreed to document the group's thinking on paper so that it could be shared later with wider constituencies of African American Presbyterians for input and response. By March, 1993 the group adopted the final version of the paper.

   In an April, 1993 cover letter to African American Presbyterian congregations introducing the *New Wine Paper,* Presbyterians for Prayer, Study, and Action outlined their intentions in the following manner:

> As we approach the 21st century, how will African-American Presbyterians create viable ministries in their respective communities? ...This is not to suggest that we are unconcerned for the welfare of our sisters and brothers among other racial/ethnic groups, including our White sisters and brothers. We are also not unaware of the current crisis of spirit that is currently forcing the denomination to make drastic cuts of staff and programs that can only result in the further marginalization of African-American concerns. This focus on the African-American community merely reflects our realization that it is inappropriate for us to: (1) attempt to suggest what others should do in their respective communities; and (2) place denominational politics as a priority over the welfare of our own children and communities.[iii]

   White Presbyterians frequently pride themselves on being rooted in scripture and giving serious attention to the theological analysis. Indeed, it was because John Calvin took seriously the social and political realities of his day that he was able to do profound theological analysis (i.e. *Institutes of the Christian Religion*). In the opinion of the Presbyterians for Prayer, Study, and Action, however, the denomination had fallen well short of its theological orientation with regard to addressing the issues of importance to its African American members.[iv]

   The *New Wine* paper suggested that African Americans should consider whether they needed to withdraw from the Presbyterian Church (USA) as a means of achieving more effective ministries within African American communities. The paper offered a brief chronicle of historical reasons for its bold suggestion. It posited that a new *reforming* spirit of *Afrocentric*[v] models of ministry was needed for Black Presbyterian congregations to be effective in community outreach.[vi] The paper called on African-American Presbyterians to engage in a seven-year period of prayerful discussion of these issues.

   Consistent with genuine resistance efforts, the paper created a storm of controversy among Black Presbyterians who largely divided into three major ideological camps around the issue. One group (probably the largest segment) consisted of those who were chagrined by the behavioral apathy of the denomination to their issues, but were not ready to consider full-scale withdrawal as an option. A second group was willing to seriously debate withdrawal, but was not sure if an alternate denominational structure was the answer since all institutions had faults. A third and small, but vocal contingent, mostly young clergy leadership under age forty, was decidedly disgusted with denominational politics and saw withdrawal as a very practical option. Although there are no clear figures as to the actual numbers of African Americans in the Presbyterian Church (USA), estimates generally place the total somewhere around 2.5% of the whole (about 50,000 persons). There are several vibrant and growing African American Presbyterian congregations, but nationwide large numbers of these churches still struggle without pastoral leadership and face the possibility of closure. For many African American Presbyterians, consideration of the viability of the Presbyterian Church (USA) for ministries of reconciliation, evangelism, and nurture in African American communities is still a matter that is very much open for discussion and it remains to be seen how the bulk of African American Presbyterians will respond to the challenge lifted in the *New Wine* paper.

Over time, the focus of the debate shifted from the "whether we stay or go" dialogue (which limited participants to repeated preoccupations with denominational politics) toward finding ways to address African American community issues. The more fundamental issue of how to encourage the implementation of Africentric approaches to Christian ministry became the primary focus of the discussion. African American Presbyterians seeking to emphasize community ministry found that African Americans of other denominations (both in historically Black denominations and in historically white church groups) also were giving more attention to the significance of Africentrism as a resource in Christian ministry. It is from this perspective that *Africentric Approaches to Christian Ministry* was inspired and why this volume includes works from writers who are not Presbyterian, but who value Africentric approaches to ministry, like Professor Richard C. Chapple, Jr. (African Methodist Episcopal Zion), who teaches Homiletics at Pittsburgh Theological Seminary, Emeritus Professor of Theology at Eastern Baptist Theological Seminary, Dr. J. Deotis Roberts, Dr. Fred Smith (United Methodist), Professor of Christian Education at Wesley Theological Seminary in Washington, D.C., and Dr. Cain Hope Felder (United Methodist), New Testament Professor at Howard Divinity School, in Washington, D.C..

That which started as a sideline debate among a few African American Presbyterians, indeed, eventually moved into a more mainstream ministry focus that views the critical issue in community ministry not as a denominational label, but one that is grounded in Christ and is contextually relevant. It is against this backdrop that the discussion of Africentric approaches to Christian ministry is one that has relevance to the much broader topic of how African American churches will effectively come to grips with the social, economic, political, and cultural devastation that continues to consume inner-city African American neighborhoods.

Ronald Edward Peters (Pittsburgh, Pennsylvania)
Marsha Snulligan Haney (Atlanta, Georgia)
April 2005

Endnotes

i   This was actually a conversation group ("a chat-room") of approximately twenty persons nationwide who were active in the Black Presbyterian Caucus and working with the late Mildred Brown, then staff person to the PC(USA)'s national staff on Racial and Cultural Diversity. Frustrated with the denomination's benign neglect of critical social justice issues in African American communities and congregational needs in Black Presbyterian churches, the group assumed an "ad hoc" committee posture in order to identify themselves and their positions with the wider body of Black Presbyterians and chose to call themselves *African American Presbyterians for Prayer, Study, and Action.* They identified their position with the following words: "We join together in Prayer (for the guidance of the Holy Spirit concerning these matters), Study (of options that will assist in alleviating the negative situations now gripping our communities nationwide), and Action (to create Afrocentric ministries to uplift and liberate the oppressed). The group saw their goal as seeking an Afrocentric Proclamation of the Gospel and undertook activities to distribute and defend this methodological approach to congregational ministry via the *Is This New Wine?* study paper.

ii   See Appendix 1.

iii   Letter forwarded to Black Presbyterian congregations April, 1993 included signatures of the late Mildred Brown (then national church staff for the PCUSA, Associate for Racial and Cultural Diversity), Rev. Robert Burkins (pastor, Elmwood Presbyterian Church, Orange, NJ), Professor Ronald Peters (Pittsburgh Theological Seminary), Professor Warren Dennis (New Bunswick Theological Seminary, New Jersey), Rev. Phyllis Felton (Harambe, Baltimore, MD) Dr. Johnnie Monroe (Grace Memorial Presbyterian Church, Pittsburgh, PA), Rev. Jerry Cannon (C.M. Jenkins Presbyterian Church, Charlotte, NC), Rev. Curtis Jones (Madison Ave. Presbyterian Church, Baltimore, MD), Rev. Amitiyah Elayne Hyman (New York Avenue Presbyterian Church, Washington, D.C.), Professor Marsha Snulligan Haney (Interdenominational Theological Center, Atlanta, GA), Dr. Lonnie Oliver (New Life Presbyterian Church, Atlanta, GA), and Marjorie Ward (then Manager, General Assembly Committee on Representation, PCUSA).

iv   See Gayraud Wilmore (1983, Louisville, KY: Geneva Press; and Louisiville, KY: Witherspoon, 1998). Black and Presbyterian: The Hope and the Heritage.

v   *Afrocentrism* and *Africentricm,* are used interchangeably in this section although the latter term is preferred as the more current usage. As is explained later in the book, both refer to the same philosophical, methodological, and spiritual approaches that recognize pre-colonial Africa as the proper starting point for understanding African culture.

vi   By Afrocentric worship in the United States, reference in this context is to an approach to the ordering of congregational life (celebration, education, nurture, outreach, and stewardship) in such a manner as to emphasize the centrality of African people's needs in America that does not begin only with the heritage of American slavery, but with the heritage of pre-colonial Black Africa as well. Many Black churches, while proud of their history, shy away from discussions of Afrocentrism because so many of its leading proponents have been critical of Christianity's role in Black oppression globally and do not define themselves as Christian. For the most part, Afrocentrism has been criticized in academic circles as historical and cultural romanticism rather than substantive scholarly endeavor. However, we believe that care must be taken not to "throw the baby out with the bath water". Seminaries and churches should at least be aware of the Afrocentric dialogue that finds emotional affinity, if not serious critical examination, in many quarters along "city streets". By affirming the pre-slavery period of African heritage, we move beyond the antebellum period as the origin of African American culture. This process embraces information about African antiquity in the same fashion as Europe looks to ancient Greece and Rome or Chinese culture draws its current focus from its antiquity.

Acknowledgments

It has been a privilege to edit this collection of writings authored by the strong group of skilled and dedicated scholars and church and community leaders whose names appear in the table of contents. Others who have been important to this work, but whose written contributions do not appear in this volume include Robert Burkins, Jerry Cannon, Curtis Jones, Lonnie Oliver, and Marjorie Ward. We are indebted to them for their visions and work. Our colleagues at the Interdenominational Theological Center (I.T.C.) and Pittsburgh Theological Seminary (P.T.S.) also deserve special mention. At the I.T.C., special thanks are due to Constance "CJ" Jackson, Edward P. Wimberly and Michael Battle. At P.T.S., special thanks are due to Jermaine McKinley, John Wilson, and C. Samuel Calian.

We thank God for the leadership of Gayraud S. Wilmore, a scholar, friend, and mentor, without whom this volume would not have been written, and the Africentric ministry discussion among Black Presbyterians over the last decade much less substantive. It was Gayraud who, following the initial distribution of the *New Wine Paper,* took the time to challenge and sharpen the analysis of issues outlined in the paper. His gentle spirit and incisive scholarly insights anchored the discussions. Gayraud arranged for us to participate with him in teaching a Doctor of Ministry course at United Theological Seminary in Dayton, OH in 1996 related to the issues of Africentric ministry that had been lifted up in the *New Wine Paper.* It was Gayraud who first suggested that this book should be written and took the time to read and co-edit all the manuscripts with us. Also, the late Mildred Brown and Dr. Rita Dixon were invaluable to the *New Wine* dialogue and the development of this volume, providing encouragement and suggestions to assist participants in keeping issues of practical application for the local church and community in focus. Two other ecclesiastical giants, our dear departed colleagues James H. Costen and Clinton M. Marsh, were extremely helpful in strengthening the caliber of the *New Wine* dialogue with their insightful critiques, thereby encouraging this book's evolution.

We thank University Press and Audrey Babkirk for their assistance in helping us to bring this work to successful conclusion. To Karen Kapsanis, who read portions of the manuscript, Eugene J. Blackwell, Ethel Parris Gainer and Jacqueline Sledge (Ron's secretary), who assisted in typing the final copies, and

Reta Bigham we are eternally indebted. Finally, and most importantly, we are grateful to God for our spouses, Willie C. Haney, Jr. and Mary Smith Peters. Without their incredible love, patience, and support, this book would not have been possible. If this volume has any merit, all those whose contributions have made it possible share the credit. Its faults, however, are attributable only to ourselves.

Marsha Snulligan Haney (Atlanta, Georgia) and
Ronald Edward Peters (Pittsburgh, Pennsylvania)
April, 2005

From Rhetoric to the Reality of Africentric Christian Ministry

Ronald Edward Peters

Africentrism has long been a controversial topic in academic and religious circles, as has its most clear and vocal spokesperson, Molefi Kete Asante,[1] who first coined the term. Like so many other academic and religious debates, the pendulum of time seems to have swung away from the heated dialogues of the 1960s, 70s and 80s that once preoccupied academicians and religious leaders regarding the significance and place of Africentric methodology and the Black consciousness or Pan-Africanist movements from which it sprang in dealing with matters of history and faith. Shall we revisit questions of whether or not Jesus was a Black man once more?[2] Similarly, shall we return to the old debates in this vein such as, "Were ancient Egyptians really Black Africans? Does God see color? Are there Black people in the Bible?" While these are important questions, the fact is for most people of faith (including people of color), such questions are suggestive of a racial or cultural ideology that has more to do with political consciousness than with spirituality or faith in God.

While diverse voices throughout history, from Sojourner Truth and David Walker to Howard Thurman and Malcolm X, have pointed out the inconsistencies of Christianity among Euro-Americans with regard to race and justice issues, today this historic relationship of theology to social justice realities is not so forcefully emphasized in many churches. The black consciousness focus on social justice issues so clearly articulated three decades ago in James Cone's *Black Theology and Black Power* or nearly two decades ago in Jacquelyn Grant's *White Women's Christ and Black Women's Jesus*[3] appears to have receded from the forefront today in many African American congregations in favor of an emphasis on a personal relationship to God and individual piety. Many church leaders today do not seem to perceive as clear a relationship between poverty and racial oppression and the symbols, rituals and dogma of religion that are pervasively European in outlook, liturgy and theological interpretation. In truth, Black consciousness rhetoric has always been generally perceived as somewhat awkward in many Christian settings. Although faith in God as revealed in Jesus Christ of the Holy Scriptures is open to persons of whatever ethnic ancestry, the fact remains that the symbols and theological dogma of Christianity to this day, more often than not, betray a

European bias that takes little account of the experiences of persons outside of Europe. Africentrism is an approach to Christian faith that seeks to correct this misrepresentation for persons of African ancestry.

Race and Religion

It must be acknowledged that racial and ethnic realities have always been part of religious practice. Giving credence to this fact is the Roman Catholic Church's historic pattern of having a majority of individuals of Italian ancestry elected to serve as Pope, rather than persons of Jewish, Ibo, Navajo, or Manchurian descent. Similarly, in Saudi Arabia, the followers of Islam predominate; while in Germany, Lutheran Christians are in the majority. Throughout sub-Sahara Africa, the percentage of people who regularly follow African Traditional Religious practices far outnumber those who are Buddhists, whereas in India and China, this reality is reversed.

In seeking to discern the ultimate and eternal Truths of divine realities, ethnicity should not exacerbate theological, political, and cultural factors inherent in the interplay of faith and heritage. Rather, ethnicity and heritage should be assets to the human potential for discerning Divine realities instead of liabilities. It appears senseless, therefore, to deny the reality of cultural, ethnic, social or political influences that impact religious beliefs and practices. Yet, in much of urban society and in many African American churches, the role of the African heritage (particularly pre-colonial aspects), is still fundamentally ignored as a significant factor in shaping Christian ministry in North America. The pre-colonial African heritage, including its origins in ancient Egypt, should be a significant aspect of contemporary practice of Christian ministry. The fact is, however, that most analyses of the African experience in the Western hemisphere are approached through the prism of the heinous slave industry with little or no serious consideration given to the influence of Africa (history, culture and social organization, and intellectual and religious thought), prior to colonialism. Africentrism, as a philosophical and methodological understanding of reality for persons of African descent, seeks to correct this deficiency by taking into account the significance of pre-colonial African history and culture as a contributor to modern life. More will be said about this in Chapter Two of this book where I discuss Africentrism with special attention to its relevance to so-called "mainline" denominations and Christian ministry.

Challenges to be Addressed

A book on Africentric approaches to Christian ministry is especially needed during these times when much public attention is being given to faith-based public ministries in African American communities. Much of the political and secular social service rhetoric about government partnerships with religious entities that provide faith-based social service ministries, especially in predominately African American communities, still approaches these ministries from a Eurocentric socio-cultural and religious grounding. As such, this political, secular and religious rhetoric tends to view African American inner city communities as "mission fields" devoid of cultural, intellectual, social or spiritual assets that can be utilized to rectify the challenges to be faced. However, the pluralism of the urban context of ministry (ethnically, culturally, religiously and ideologically) demands an inclusive approach to ministry that recognizes African American communities for their strengths and values their spiritual and cultural heritage. It is here that an Africentric perspective can be helpful. The aim here is to enable religious leaders, social scientists and other academicians to move beyond the realm of acrimonious discussion and debate about problems in African American communities toward practical steps for ministry (and the teaching and learning of ministry) in ways that will address painful realities in urban centers where people remain economically, socially, culturally, politically and spiritually disenfranchised.

This book is not merely interested in Africentric approaches to ministry as an academic exercise, but as one plausible solution for enabling congregations to better address serious challenges in of African American communities. The reality in most inner city communities is that public health and safety are precarious, at best, and economic survival is a daily challenge. Substantive issues are at stake. It should not surprise anyone that by the time they reach pre-school (ages 3 to 5), many African American children have already begun to develop poor self-images; and by their pre-teen years, these youngsters have become well aware of the racism and economic disenfranchisement that has stigmatized their existence from birth. Statistics regarding academic achievement, domestic violence, children in foster care, incarceration, employment, substance abuse, homicide rates, diabetes, hypertension, or HIV/AIDS, all reveal that being African American can be dangerous to one's health and welfare. How can an Africentric approach to Christian ministry affect people suffering with HIV/AIDS; the quality of public school education in inner city communities; or the fact that most of the people who are responsible for the loss of billions on Wall Street are not prosecuted the way petty shoplifters are?

Few will quarrel with the premise that the manner in which people live their lives is profoundly influenced by what they believe about God. It has been widely acknowledged that faith in God has been critical for survival and liberation efforts that have characterized the African American experience in this country. Yet, one constant in the oppression of Africa's descendants in the "New World" has been efforts to eliminate or minimize the significance of their African heritage from all facets of the human experience. Christian religion has provided no exception to this rule.

Much of the discussion about Africentrism and its relationship to Christian ministry has been lodged in academic settings at universities or seminaries. Less frequently has this discussion surfaced in other arenas. Yet, even in these contexts whether in educational institutions, urban congregations, denominational headquarters or seminaries, the importance of an Africentric approach is undervalued or non-existent.[4] This book is written from a perspective that takes African heritage and Africentric methodology seriously as valued resources for gaining a proper understanding of Christian theology by African Americans. As such, the writers of this volume explore Africentrism as an asset to spreading the Gospel in a manner that is not apologetic about its orientation in Pan-African thought, nor glosses over difficult issues that need to be confronted.

While there are several books dealing with Christian ministry from various perspectives (urban, rural, liberal, conservative, etc.), relatively few take seriously the pre-colonial heritage of Africans and African Americans as a means for doing practical ministry. Despite the vast spiritual, cultural, and social impact of historic Black churches on American life, the thirty-year presence of Black Theology, and the twenty-plus year presence of Womanist Theology in the academy, there remains a grievous disconnect among African Americans about the place and significance of African thought and culture in Christianity. Although there is clear recognition of black culture and experience in Christian circles, there is no small degree of skepticism regarding the usefulness of Africentric thought and consciousness for the doing of effective Christian ministry. At the beginning of the twenty-first century, the "double consciousness"[5] of which DuBois wrote a century earlier is still a reality for African American Christians who feel that affirmation of their pre-colonial African heritage and culture somehow negates their Christian faith. Africentrism, for many, is still perceived as being at odds with faith in God as revealed through Jesus Christ. For persons of African descent, a forced bifurcation between their Christian faith, on the one hand, and Africentric affirmation of their personhood on the other, must be recognized as capitulation to an old pattern of spiritual, intellectual, and cultural oppression that is not acceptable.

Keeping It Real

Hip Hop artist Grand Master Flash and the Furious Five, back in 1982, said: "Don't push me, I'm close to the edge." This song, entitled *The Message*, became a hit recording because it expressed the challenges and frustrations associated with inner city life and resonated with many poor people in rural as well as urban communities:

> "The man with Prudential repossessed my car," where the bill collectors "scare my wife when I'm not home," where hopes and dreams are reduced to keeping afloat: "It's like a jungle, sometimes it make me wonder, / How I keep from going under... "Don't push me, I'm close to the edge."[6]

For people, young and old, whose lives are preoccupied by concerns with drive-by shootings, bills they cannot pay, or the illicit drug deals in their neighborhoods, weighty theoretical debates about the cultural or ethnic identity of Jesus and arguments about ancient Egypt are a waste of time. J. Deotis

Roberts, in his helpful analysis entitled *Africentric Christianity*, notes that ideological arguments about culture are insufficient to address fundamental human needs or to make a prophetic critique of culture that proves ultimately liberating for human beings:

> What about the prophetic dimension of religion? Religions often stand over against cultures in critical judgment due to a transcendent norm inherent in a religion. What about salvific needs of sinful human beings? Are ancestors, even African ancestors, able to forgive sins and reconcile us to the divine? Does the ability to use a cultural language and call gods by name in these languages provide any assurance that these gods can hear us and also redeem?[7]

Esoteric discussions about culture and religious dogma, so fascinating to academicians and seminary-trained church leaders, unless handled carefully, tend to have no practical relationship to salvation from the reality of everyday "lived-in" circumstances. Similarly, this business of some white-looking Jesus in a church's stained-glass window who will save people their sins, but has nothing to do with alleviating their daily misery is pointless. For African Americans who are oppressed in urban ghettos the quest for hope, help, and liberation from depressing and dangerous realities in a dehumanizing world is a way of life with no emotional or spiritual space for stuff that makes no sense. The cynicism and distrust that understandably have become associated in the minds of poor African Americans with most structures and agencies of society (education, law enforcement, media, healthcare, social service, business and finance) including the churches. If meaningful change is to come, it will come from approaches to Christian ministry that emphasize the humanity of oppressed persons and that seek to develop meaningful relationships that concretely demonstrate the importance of all people over institutions and material assets. It is this type of ministry that truly connects people in holistic fashion (economically, socially, culturally, educationally, politically, and spiritually) to God, because they become connected to *each other* by what the Scriptures define as *agape* (Mark 12:29-31; John 13:34-35; 1 Corinthians 13:1-13; 1 John 4:7-8), that is, love concretely demonstrated through justice.

The writers included in this volume are drawn from seminary faculties as well as from pastors whose approach to congregational ministry and the teaching of ministry is informed by Africentric methodology. It is the premise of these writers that a more candid acknowledgement of the Gospel's true history rather than its recasting in a European culture and theological dogma that are considered universally applicable, has the potential of empowering oppressed African Americans in urban ghettos to take charge of their lives and communities in ways that can enhance the quality of life for everyone. The point here is not to unilaterally castigate all Eurocentric theological formulations, but rather to recognize that their value is limited for people other than Europeans. As theologian James Cone pointed out years ago:

Because Christian theology is *human* speech about God, it is always related to historical situations and thus all of its assertions are culturally limited... Theology is not a universal language; it is *interested* language and thus is always a reflection of the goals and aspirations of a particular people in a definite social setting."[8]

Applying an Africentric perspective to Christian faith requires, therefore, that the theological assumptions of Western culture will be re-evaluated in light of the information that an Africentric perspective reveals concerning God. Such an analysis cannot alter the reality of God, for the Bible readily acknowledges that our human reasoning is finite in its capacity to comprehend the Divine: *"we see through a glass darkly..."* (I Corinthians 13:12). An Africentric perspective can assist devout Christians, however, who are serious about ministry in urban ghettos created by social, economic, political and cultural systems riddled with racism, sexism, classism, and injustice, to engage in ministry that heals, helps, and empowers rather than anesthetizes. In this way, the rhetoric of faith as revealed in the life, ministry, and resurrection of Jesus Christ and Africentric affirmations no longer compete with each other, but become complementary realities that unify ministry in the church and in communities.

Topic Outline
In looking backward, like the Sankofa bird, we can better understand our present context and, armed with this insight, we are adequately empowered to think about the future. Accordingly, this book is arranged into three sections, each dealing with one of three modalities. *Part I: Setting the Context; Part II: Practical Realities in Ministry; and Part III: Looking Forward.*

Part I: *Setting the Context* includes Chapters One to Three. In chapter one, Gayraud Wilmore justifies the entity we commonly refer to as the Black Church. Written by Marsha Snulligan Haney along with Tumani Mutasa Nyajeka, and Rosetta E. Ross, chapter two examines quality of life issues for Africans and the African diaspora. These reflections are based on conversations with West African theologian Mercy Oduyoye regarding the question *What Has Happened to Us?* In chapter three, entitled *Africentrism as a Challenge to Contemporary Christian Ministry,* I explore the significance of Africentricity as a resource for enhanced ministry regardless of denominational labels.

Part II, *Practical Realities in Ministry,* includes chapters four through nine. Issues involving Africentric Christianity and Urban Ministry are analyzed by J. Deotis Roberts in chapter four. The role of preaching in African American pulpits has always been a key factor in shaping congregational outreach into the community. Accordingly, Homiletics Professor Richard C. Chapple Jr. discusses practical and ontological issues involved in the Africentric perspective that informs the construction of African-American sermonic discourse in chapter five, entitled *Make It Plain Preacher.* New Testament Professor Cain Hope

Felder, in chapter six, examines *The Church's Ministry to the Urban Family: Creative Responses to a Continuing New Testament Challenge.* Chapters seven through ten deal with a series of practical issues in congregational ministry. Drawing upon eighteen years of pastoral experience, I discuss the celebration of the African American cultural season of Kwanzaa as a liturgical resource in chapter seven, entitled *Christians Celebrating Kwanzaa.* Johnnie Monroe, Senior Pastor at Grace Memorial Presbyterian Church in Pittsburgh, Pennsylvania's Hill District (the city's oldest African American community) outlines a paradigm for building strong community outreach ministry from an African-centered perspective in chapter eight, entitled *Building an Africentric Bridge From Inside Stained Glass Windows to the Community Outside.* In chapter nine, Fred Smith gives a historical perspective of Africentric Christian Education in the context Black Church. This section concludes with Gloria Tate, Pastor of the First Presbyterian Church of Teaneck, New Jersey (the first African American pastor of this historically Euro-American congregation) who is the author of chapter ten, *Building Community In a Multicultural Context,* in which she explores the implications of an Africentric perspective in a multi-ethnic environment.

Part III, *Looking Forward,* includes chapters eleven through thirteen and considers issues of future ministry utilizing an Africentric perspective. Professor of Urban Ministry at New Brunswick Theological Seminary, Warren L. Dennis, examines the issues in seminary education from an Africentric approach to city ministry in chapter eleven entitled *The Challenges of Afrocentric Ministry for Urban Theological Education.* Ethicist Katie G. Cannon of the Presbyterian School of Christian Education at Richmond, VA reflects on how Womanist thought has informed her teaching regarding Africentrism through the contributions of her students and how this informs our future ethics in chapter twelve, *Diaspora Ethics: The Hinges Upon Which the Future Swings.* Professor Marsha Snulligan Haney offers some concluding thoughts in chapter thirteen on the missiological realities involved in Africentric ministry. Let us now discover where the journey takes us as we move beyond debate, from rhetoric to reality, in Africentric Christian ministry.

Endnotes:

---

1.   Professor Molefi Kete Asante is the founder of Temple University's African American Studies Department and the author of more than thirty books and hundreds of articles and essays. Some of his most well known works on Africentricity include *The Afrocentric Idea* (Philadelphia, PA: Temple University Press, 1987), *Afrocentricity*

(Trenton, NJ: Third World Press, 1988), and *Kemet, Afrocentricity and Knowledge* (Trenton, NJ: Third World Press, 1992).
2.   Albert B. Cleage, Jr., *The Black Messiah* (New York: Sheed and Ward Press, 1968).
3.   James Cone, *Black Theology and Black Power* (New York: Seabury Press, 1969), Jacquelyn Grant, *White Women's Christ and Black Women's Jesus: Feminist Christology and Womanist Response* (Atlanta, GA.: Scholars Press, 1989). These works are representative of several scholarly treatments of that era concerning the relationship between African American religious fervor and social justice activism.
4.   For a good synopsis of the controversy surrounding Africentrism, academia, and Christian ministry, see J. Deotis Roberts, *Africentric Christianity*, (Valley Forge, PA: Judson Press, 2000). Chapter 3.
5.   W.E.B. DuBois, *Souls of Black Folk* (Chicago, IL: A.C Mclug & Co., 1903).
6.   Alan Light (ed.), *The Vibe History of Hip Hop.* (New York: Three Rivers Press, 1999), 29.
7.   Roberts, 7.
8.   James H. Cone, *God of the Oppressed* (Maryknoll, NY: Orbis, 1997), 36.

CHAPTER ONE

Does the "Black Church" Really Exist?

Gayraud S. Wilmore

An impressive literature on what we now call the Black Church[1] has accumulated since the 1960s, but the term still carries a certain ambiguity. Usually it defines that institution or group of Christian denominations that are "owned and operated" by people of African descent. This is the sociological definition and means that African American congregations, within the predominantly white communions, are normally excluded from this designation, although the practice has been questioned because almost ninety percent of them in, at least the Protestant fold, also "own and operate" themselves to a considerable degree. Moreover, most are in a more or less close contact with each other in the same denomination, and with congregations of all-Black denominations, through various informal religious and secular networks and ethnic caucuses that give them a large measure of historical continuity and separate identity. As several writers in this volume will show, while it is not yet possible to speak of most of these churches as Africentric, an increasing number of congregations identify themselves as Africentric, in the terms by which that particular form of the black church is defined in these pages.

It is, nevertheless, correct to say that there is no monolithic black church in America. But a very conspicuous demography of what persists as a familiar reality in many American villages, towns, and cities, justifies using the term Black Church, if loosely, in most contexts. There are more than 22 million church members in the United States who claim, and/or are recognized by other people, to have sufficient African ancestry to be considered black. A large percentage of these 22 million people (perhaps 85%) are organized in congregations and other religious groupings in which African American membership predominates, and almost all of these congregational units are "in control" of their own affairs under African American leadership at the local church level.[2]

If the first definition of the black church is sociological or demographic, the second is ideological. Some would even say theological. It is weighted toward cultural and theological modalities that are descriptive of the personal stance of many who claim membership in such congregations and who expect their local church, if not their denomination, to have an Africentric or "black" identity and mission. This usage of the term black church first came into vogue in the mid-1960s when the designation "Negro" and "Colored" went out of fashion and "Black" began to connote ethnic pride, an affirmation of the special history, culture, and heritage of the descendants of the African slaves brought to North America. Of course, it also connoted solidarity in the struggle against all forms of white supremacy and racism.

As applied to religious institutions blackness came to mean the renewal and enhancement of the most esteemed values of African American spirituality; the search for the distinctive characteristics of African and African American religions; the refusal to accept Euro-American history, theology, liturgy, and ecclesiastical infrastructures as normative; and a historic vocation to serve and promote the social, economic, and political well-being of the African American community. Since the 1960s, these predispositions for "blackenization" in religion, theology, and church work were often championed by individual congregations. Such congregations supported the Black Power movement on the domestic front and Pan-Africanism on the international front.

One or the other of these two definitions of the term "black church" should be called to mind whenever it appears in this essay. Let it be clear that where we speak of the "Negro Church" a contrast is usually being made with the black church of the second definition. We shall, however, frequently refer to the black church with a small b and c, and with nothing more in mind than those Protestant and Roman Catholic congregations and black Protestant denominations in which persons of African descent are in the majority. Almost always the context will clarify the meaning intended. The terminological confusion which frequently attends discussions about the African American group in the United States points to the significance of the problem of identity in almost every period of its history and, relative to black theology, suggests why questions of faith or "ultimate concern" are just below the surface of the otherwise academic question of African American ethnicity.

Professor Victor Anderson of Vanderbilt University Divinity School has been critical of what he calls the "ontological Blackness" of this perspective. But whites, not blacks, were the first to raise skin color to the level of ontology, and after more than three hundred years of living with a negative appraisal of their being, black Americans decided to make the self-determined and positive transvaluation of their physicality a datum of a theological position and a social strategy of continued resistance to and liberation from dehumanizing racism.[3]

The Black Power movement and the rise of black theology in the late 1960s brought a crisis of identity among all shades of African Americans–from the "light, bright, and damn near white" and the "high yellows," to the "coal black" sisters and brothers, whose blood line could probably be traced back to an African progenitor without any deviation through the genetic pool of the European continent. During the civil rights movement everyone had to decide if, and to what degree, his or her own self-identity and self-understanding needed to be revised according to the commitments of the black cultural renaissance and new political radicalism that accompanied the "long hot summers" of discontent and civil disorder between 1964 and 1968.

To be sure, "Black is beautiful" had *something* to do with skin color. It was a phrase that sought to reverse the preference for light color that had dominated many Negro fraternities and sororities, night clubs, and upper and middle class churches for years. But much more than skin color was involved in that somewhat overweening slogan. It requires no more than a glance at some of the popular leaders of the movement of cultural renaissance, for example, Adam Clayton Powell, Jr., Lena Horne, Mordecai W. Johnson, Anna Arnold Hedgeman, Constance Baker Motley, John Hurst Adams, Angela Davis, Huey Newton, Albert B. Cleage, and Tom Joyner—among many others—to know that Blackness had to do with far more than the color of one's skin or the texture of one's hair. It had everything to do with a hunger for an *ethnic identity* not subordinated to white people; sharing a *collective consciousness about Africa and slavery*; a fierce sense of *independent cultural, economic, and political power*, as demonstrated, for example, by the Black Panther Party, the womanist movement, or the One Hundred Black Men organizations. In short, Blackness had to do with a new awareness and appreciation of everything of worth that belonged to the African American experience. One of my students, a black seminarian, put the matter squarely in this terse poem back in 1973:

> Slappin five
> throwing yr head back and laughin loudly getting excited
> talkin bout somethin
> excitin
> hip slick
> talkin with yr whole body
> be-boppin
> rhythm
> soul food
> rappin and rappin and more rappin
> Corn-rowin plattin
> being fraid of ghosts
> dashikis
> preachin without a manuscript for an hour
> bushes natural fros
> prayin without a prayer book
> cappin
> shoutin
> tall tales
> the boogaloo soul train
> Mahalia BB King Aretha Coltrane![4]

Blackness involved the revalorization of all these meanings, modes, and moods of African American life in America. It connoted a freedom, creativity, and charisma that originated some-where in Africa, survived the Middle Passage, genocide and miscegenation, flowered in the Harlem of Claude McKay and Langston Hughes, and was flaunted in the audacity of the young black revolutionaries who took part in the retaliatory violence of Newark, Watts, Detroit, Washington, D.C., and scores of other cities. The eruption of the 1960s, unlike the stages preceding it, shattered most of the one-sided, outmoded connections with white bohemianism and socialist idealism. Celebrating its disengagement from the culture of white America, it forced a crisis of personal and group identity upon millions of Negroes who, only months before, had marched arm in arm with sincere and trustworthy white comrades toward a racially integrated utopia that was not to be. In the religious rhetoric of the times, we marched toward what the newly created National Council of Churches called as early as 1946, "a non-segregated church and a non-segregated society." It is not that Blackness then or Africentricity now repudiates that long-delayed goal as much as it should be understood that we regarded it then, and still regard it today, as strategically premature and inadequately grounded before the dissolution of the slave mentality of many—not all—Negroes.

An identity crisis is a critical event in the self-development of a person or a people when a decision must be made either to affirm or deny a historical individuality.[5] The development of a subculture within a larger system does not necessarily mean that such a crisis has occurred and a healthy, self-conscious identity is in process. The differentiation between two persons or two groups can be based merely on the mutual acceptance of a status quo of subordination and super-ordination. Instead of a voluntary and constructive decision about the self-identity of a minority, such a situation can demonstrate, sadly, a *lack* of self-identity. An authentic crisis of identity on the part of a subordinated group involves an existential choice of selfhood and the adoption of self-definition–the *naming* of the self. It is a self-election by a liberated person or group to be whom and what one chooses, in participation with one's family and friends—with sisters and brothers who are moving in the same direction. This phenomenon is often at work these days when black parents choose African, or what seems to them to be African-sounding names, for themselves and their children. We sometimes make fun of such names, but though we cannot spell them, we know what they mean.

What is required is a tearing of one's being out of the enveloping husk of another being with whom a fraudulent coalescence, previously elected or imposed and legitimated, has served to stifle individuality and self-consciousness. Such tearing away is more often than not a painful process–and the more slowly it proceeds the more painful, like taking a scab off a wound. A part of the crisis today is that many Negroes and Negro institutions, having made only an ambivalent and painful decision about Blackness, are still going through a slow, fearful and guilt-ridden process of individuation and liberation.[6]

The late C. Eric Lincoln assumed that this transition had already taken place in most African American churches, although he recognized a certain shadow existence of the old church within the new church that was struggling to be born.

Lincoln argued that "the Negro Church died in the 1960s to give birth to a new Black Church which rejects the spiritual humiliation and ethical limitations of Negro-ness . . . Yet the Negro Church which died, lives on in the Black Church that is born of its loins and is inseparable from and continuous with an earlier version of Afro-American religion."[7]

From this angle it is possible to see large segments of the black church in America as still unwilling to accept the full implications of either Blackness or Africentrism, as we understand the latter in this book. Yet the black church today is reluctant to admit that is governed by the presuppositions and norms of white Protestant evangelicalism which, as Lincoln said, "structured and conditioned it [but] are not the norms and presuppositions to which contemporary Blacks . . . can give their asseveration and support."[8] The African American Church, in other words, is still in the throes of its crisis of identity and one of the primary emphases of black theology, viz., that the black Christian struggle for liberation "unconceals" (Frederick Herzog) the essence of the gospel, and is therefore confirmed by it, has not yet been thoroughly assimilated by black Christians and lies on the other side of the crisis which, for most of us, is still a slow and painful experience.

The debate over retaining the term "African" in the names of the two oldest black Methodist denominations, the African Methodist Episcopal Church of Richard Allen (founded in 1816) and the African Methodist Episcopal Zion Church of James Varick and Christopher Rush (founded in 1821), illustrates the anguish over identity experienced by many black Christians in the closing years of the nineteenth century. Bishop Benjamin Tucker Tanner, a notable theologian of the AME Church, believed that theological considerations were involved in holding on to the word "African" in the title of his denomination. What was at stake for Tanner was the humanity of this new African American people, whom God had called into existence for freedom, and who had received from God's own hand the mission of bearing witness to the irrepressible need for the humanization and liberation of Africans, African Americans, and all oppressed and oppressing people, whether black or white.

> What then is the intended force of the title "African"? Is it doctrinal or nation? It is first doctrinal and secondarily national. The doctrinal goal to which the AME Church aspired was the humanity of the Negro . . . It sought to become a church wherein the claim to humanity of this despised class would be practically recognized. The sublime truth means only that men [sic] of African descent are found to be there, and found as men, not slaves; as equals, not inferiors.[9]

The African American churches of the nineteenth century, despite their "client" relationship to white churches in the beginning, by the time of the Civil War and Reconstruction, were clearer about their identity than many of us are today. They knew themselves to be God's judgment on the immorality of American racism and oppression. Their Blackness was, therefore, an expression of their sense of a religio-cultural vocation. By every measure they were amazing institutions. Led for the most part by illiterate preachers, many of whom had been slaves themselves and were just recently freed, these black churches–poverty-stricken and repressed by custom and law, converted thousands, stabilized family life, established insurance and burial societies, founded schools and colleges, and commissioned missionaries to the far corners of the world. And *at the same time*, agitated for the abolition of slavery, conspired to perform illegal actions in behalf of fugitives, fomented slave rebellions, helped to organize the Underground Railroad, promoted the Civil War and the recruitment of black troops, encouraged and sponsored community political education and action, and provided the social, economic, and cultural scaffolding for the entire black community in the United States. Is there anything in this nation to compare with this Black Church–which even before the family was our first underground, proto-institution on American soil?

The solidarity and sense of a common destiny which their leaders and members displayed in both the North and the South, the recognition of each other's ministries, and the free movement of pastors and lay people back and forth between denominations–particularly in rural areas–justifies the composite term, *Black* or *African American* Church—although as has already been said—it should not be regarded as a monolithic institution. This Black Church had a way of identifying itself that symbolized its calling to serve the broad needs of the African American people. Its identity and vocation went hand in hand. The term "African," which formerly had the same force for our ancestors as black or African American has for many of us today, was avowed by black Baptists, Methodists, Presbyterians, Congregationalists, Episcopalians, and Lutherans alike, as a badge of pride in origin and in a common responsibility to vindicate black humanity and the dignity of their *communio sanctorum* through the uniting power of the Gospel of Jesus Christ.

Between the end of Reconstruction and the beginning of the civil rights movement of the twentieth century, the identity of the black church as an institution with the specific mission of liberation for all facets of black life, faded into desuetude in the face of the enervating forces of migration and urbanization. What David M. Tucker discovered about the black congregations of Memphis during the first half of the twentieth century could easily describe the churches and their clergy in many towns and cities across the nation. The traditional institution was shattered and splintered against the hard realities of the urban ghetto.

> The ministry lagged so far behind black business and professional groups in supporting labor unionism and civil rights, that by the end of the thirties a black scholar, Ralph Bunch, could profile the leadership in Memphis without mentioning the clergy, except to criticize their inertia, "The Negro preachers of Memphis as a whole have avoided social questions . . . They have preached thunder and lightning, fire and brimstone, and Moses out of the bullrushes, but about the economic and political exploitation of the Negro of Memphis they have remained silent."[10]

There are important exceptions to this melancholy picture of the African American churches after the turn of the century, but it is close to being accurate about the institution as a whole. It was not simply the triumph of Booker T. Washington's policy of accommodation. The definition of the Black Church as an agent of solidarity and liberation soon collapsed under the weight of a ghettoized version of Christian fundamentalism. Shorn of roots in the militant church of the mid-nineteenth century that enthusiastically welcomed the Civil War as an act of God, African American Christians turned inward to find a white, Americanized Jesus–the mocking image of their own psychic void in the industrial slums of the North. Hence, traditional spirituality became uncoupled from a sense of the historic vocation of black institutions to transform the whole of life for all oppressed peoples. In many congregations, founded in the early years of the twentieth century, a delusive emotionalism became a source of escapist cheerfulness and entertainment on Sunday mornings. Feeling good became the fallacious compensation for an insipid and burdensome life in a scandalously unjust society.

The primary purpose of the black theology movement of the late twentieth century was not to glorify black skin color and promote some religious form of black racism. It was to shake the black church out of it s lethargy. To bring forth a new-old self-consciousness, to instigate a crisis of identity in which black folk would wake up to their own historical individuality as providential. Black theology meant to bind the spiritual power that would be generated by such consciousness to the cultural decolonization and political liberation of the Black Power movements in the United States and South Africa. The history of God's liberating acts--from the Exodus to the ministry of Jesus--provided a paradigm of a gathered nation, a people "who were no people," often faithless and disobedient, yet summoned through suffering and sacrifice, to show the defiant and seemingly autonomous secular movements that it is none other than God, who delivers the oppressed, and "to him who has no might, increases strength" (Isaiah 40:29).

Whether or not Lincoln was correct in his allegation that "the Negro Church is dead" because its own self-image and norms are not those which prevail today in the black community, it is, nonetheless, certain that the ghost of the Negro Church of the early twentieth century still haunts the leadership of the Black Church. If Emmanuel L. McCall is correct when he says that black theologians speak mostly to themselves and that it is a mistake to assume "that black liberation theologians represent the thinking and attitudes of the rank and file,"[11] it is not because black theology is unbiblical, obscure, or lacks an adequate doctrine of the Church, but because many African American preachers, lacking a thorough and honest seminary education, have been getting their church history and theology from the white Christian bookstores, and from some of the Bible colleges: the unenlightened and politically reactionary versions of white Protestant evangelicalism. They have been warned. But because they do not know the rock from which they were hewn, they and their people are oblivious of the inheritance that was passed down to them by people like Maria Stewart, Benjamin Tanner Tucker, William W. Colley, Henry

McNeal Turner, Alexander Walters, Nannie Helen Burroughs, and Francis J. Grimke,[12] to mention a few names that every American Christian ought to know. These were just a few of the leaders of the black church and the race as a whole during the most difficult years of our history.

Older black pastors and leaders who today reject black theology also quietly avoided Martin Luther King, Jr. Many of them still believe that sin is always personal and individual, and have an understanding of salvation that cannot admit of the sanctification of secular conflict and struggle when it is consonant with the teachings of Scripture. Because so many of us are willing to accept what Lincoln called "Americanity"[13] as normative Christian faith, we are unable to see how our own ethnic experiences authenticate the truth of what the Hebrew Bible teaches about human justice and its ultimate vindication, and how the New Testament illumines and gives meaning to the most profound symbol of the quality and style of existence that some of us are bold enough to call Africentrism or "Blackness."

Black theology with its cultural, political, and economic implications, has not been warmly received in the official circles of several major African American denominations. From its inception in the latter part of the 1960s some traditional leaders have regarded it as an attempt, on the part of the secular proponents of Black Power, to take over the churches for purposes out of line with the church's evangelical mission. Others saw black theology as a threat to amicable relations with benevolent white conservatives. For both clergy and laity it was an unpatriotic, anti-democratic instigator of violent urban uprisings on the way to a Satanic black racism. Still others admired the rhetorical militancy of certain schools of black theology, but lacked the ability to preach its message from their pulpits because of their shallow comprehension and fear of its emphases–particularly its argument with Negro Christianity. The mainline African American denominations, with a few exceptions, stayed in the background of the meetings and conferences that introduced and promoted black theology in the public arena. These churches were slow, on both local and national levels, to make this way of doing theology a part of their preaching and programs of Christian Education and social action.

But that is only part of the story of why the African American Church can be called Black. Younger church leaders, scholars, and seminarians now read the works of James H. Cone, J. Deotis Roberts, Cain Hope Felder, Jacqueline Grant, and the other womanist theologians, such as Delores Williams, Diana Hayes, Kelly Brown Douglas, Katie Cannon, and Melva Costen, who put pressure on the churches that was difficult for them to ignore.[14] In the period between 1969-- the year Cone's pathfinding book, *Black Theology and Black Power*, was greeted with great excitement among militant Black clergy--and 1980, when the second generation of black religious scholars were coming out, official black denominational pronouncements appeared here and there which either affirmed black theology, or cautiously reiterated some of its most important emphases.[15]

It would be a gross error to conclude that contemporary African American middle class churches are so entrenched in Euro-American interpretations of the

Christian faith that it is doubtful that they will ever see any relevance in a theology that creates its own space and platform in the black community rather than in the world at large. It would be equally wrong to take the position of some observers, that black theology is essentially an academic enterprise, primarily studied in black seminaries and universities, and has nothing significant to say to ordinary folks in the pews or worshiping in front of their television sets.

There are still hoops and hollers entreating, "Give me that old-time religion!" that hark back to home-coming sermons in the rural South and the simple beliefs of our partly illiterate great-grandparents. But as the old guard pastors and church officials retire or depart to their just and well-earned reward, younger and better educated women and men are taking over the mainline churches. Their belief in self-determination and the confidence they have in their own intellectual and spiritual capacities are opening up new possibilities for the Africentric perspectives that have developed since the early introduction of black theology by James H. Cone and J. Deotis Roberts. Future generations of Christians, black and white, will have these new perspectives buttressed by authoritative books, articles, and television shows written by African American scholars and sponsored by the theological seminars, the black caucuses of the predominantly white churches, and guilds of scholars like the American Academy of Religion, the Society of Biblical Literature, and the Society for the Study of Black Religion.

Although it is true that American Christianity and Islam seem destined to become increasingly multicultural and future churches and mosques will doubtless be more racially integrated than ever before, there is no evidence that mainline African American congregations will attract many white, Hispanic, or Asian Christians looking for a church home. Nor is it likely that the black denominations will voluntarily close shop and gradually melt away in the next one or two hundred years. All signs point in another direction. Christian churches composed mainly of African Americans are here to stay, surrounded by a sea of religious pluralism and multiculturalism, at least for the foreseeable future, and probably for many years beyond.

This does not mean that these ethnic churches will become bastions of a radical theology that affirms Blackness as the most appropriate symbol for Jesus as the Suffering Servant of God, who takes upon himself the suffering and struggle of a people discriminated against, and oppressed because of the color of their skin. Radical black theology is not likely to become the signature of the African American Church. But what C. Eric Lincoln called "the Negro Church" will not be reverted to by black people in the United States. A preference for the old spirituals and the new urban gospel music, the celebration of the founders and heroes (and heroines) of the historic black churches, and increasing interest in Africa and her problems with HIV-AIDS, economic disparities, and transition from brutal dictatorships to constitutional democracies, and her great potential for the future, will identify the black church as a distinctive form of the institutional Christian church in America. The desire to hold on to what remains of a changing but unremitting black culture in the family, schools, entertainment, and the church; the observance of Dr. King's birthday and of Kwanzaa; the increasing number of people who have money enough to become summer tourists to Ghana, South Africa, or Kenya–all these current developments and tendencies seem to point toward the continuation of a certain self-awareness and solidarity among African American Christians, whether we like it or not. That solidarity will be enhanced by a distinctive way of thinking about the message of Jesus within the contours of what has been the unique experience of black women and men.

Paul Calvin Payne, a prominent white Presbyterian educator during the first half of the last century, was fond of saying to his staff, "If it doesn't happen in the local church, it doesn't happen." Generally speaking, that is true, but not precisely, because we have seen some things happen to black Christianity, locally, regionally, and nationally, which were apparently acts of God in history, but were also, in some measure, *extra ecclesia*. But there is enough truth in Paul Payne's adage for black theologians to be admonished that this way of doing theology, and thinking about unity and mission of the church in its ministry to the poor and oppressed, is not guaranteed perpetuity by national and international conferences and consultations that make eloquent pronouncements and then go home with reams of paper.

Black religion began in the "invisible institution" that was the slave church. The modern inheritor of that tradition continues to name itself as a Black Church. But if black theology is to have enduring value for that church for which it was created, and for all Christians, in what it has to say about justice and liberation through Jesus, the Black Messiah, it must remain with the little folk in the pews who perceive the Lord's "blackness" to be continuous with their own suffering, struggle, and triumph over the demonic power of racism, classism, and sexism. A struggle to cherish and be what God made us to be–human persons who are both citizens of this world and citizens of another, both American born and bred and Africentric, both redeemed and redeeming, both–say it loud–"Black and proud!"

Endnotes

1. I am capitalizing both words in this opening sentence to indicate that I am referring to a massive, though highly differentiated, ethnic institution that has maintained a distinct historical individuality and relative sociological solidarity in the United States since the middle of the 18th century. That is, of course, the main argument of this essay.

2. C. Eric Lincoln and Lawrence H. Mamiya, *The Black Church in the African American Experience* (Durham: Duke Univ. Press, 1990) 407. I have taken the liberty of adjusting their total to correct what I think may be an undercount in the number of blacks within white American denominations, including the Roman Catholic Church.

3. Victor Anderson, *Beyond Ontological Blackness: An Essay on African American*

Religious and Cultural Criticism (New York: Continuum Press, 1995).

4. "Blackness Is," by Fred Lucas, Jr. An African Methodist Episcopal minister; written for a Boston interseminary class while he was a student at Harvard Divinity School.

5. A full discussion of identity crisis appears in a published lecture I gave to the black caucus of the Reformed Church in America in 1976: "Identity Crisis: Blacks in Predominantly White Denominations."

6. William E. Cross has described the stages of this process by which Negro adults move from Euro-American determinants to an anxiety-free, constructive commitment to Blackness. "The Negro to Black Conversion Experience," *Black World*, 120:9 (July 1971), 13-27. Cecil W. Cone has an excellent discussion on the problem of identity crisis along different but related lines in his book, *The Identity Crisis in Black Theology* (Nashville: AMEC Press, 1975). Cone perceives it as an epistemological and methodological problem. Black theologians do not know who they are, not because they have rejected the pre-Emancipation black religious traditions, but because they misunderstand them and have mistakenly assumed that the secular and apologetic principles of biblical interpretation, which they appropriated from white theologians on the right or from the Black Power theorists on the left, can give them a point of departure for doing black theology. Only the older black religion, says Cecil Cone, properly understood as a transcendent, personal experience of the "Almighty Sovereign God," can provide the data for an authentic black theology. So far, I agree with Cone, but would suggest that his understanding of the "essence" of black religion truncates what black Christians already know of God and the richness of black church worship, theology, and action. There is much more light to illuminate our path. The crisis is not in black theologians and their attempt to unveil more light so much as it is in the conservative black churches. My position is more fully stated in "The Crisis of the Black Church in America," *The Lott Carey Herald*, 48:7 (July 1978), 3–11.

7. C. Eric Lincoln, *The Black Church Since Frazier* (New York: Schocken Books, 1974), 106.

8. Ibid.

9. Benjamin T. Tanner, *An Apology for African Methodism* (Baltimore: n.p., 1867), 115. Tanner was elected bishop in 1888. His influential position was that the word "African" could unite all black people in the world. Thus the theological significance of the term justified its nationalistic implications. See Daniel A. Payne, *Recollections of Seventy Years* (New York: Arno Press and the New York Times Books, reprint 1968), 261.

10. David M. Tucker, *Black Pastors and Leaders:Memphis, 1819–1972* (Memphis: Memphis State University Press, 1975), 102.

11. Emmanuel L. McCall, in a review of Allan Boesak's *Farewell to Innocence*, in the *Occasional Bulletin of Missionary Research*, 2:3 (July 1978), 110.

12. All strong advocates of a black liberationist theology during the 19th century. Maria Stewart (1803-1879), was a brilliant Christian womanist who challenged the backwardness of black church men and women; Tanner (1835-1923), was a black nationalist AME bishop and editor; William W. Colley (1847-1909), was a pioneer of African missions and promoter of black Baptist unity; Henry M. Turner (1834-1915), was an AME bishop who represented a different version of black nationalism than Tanner, but was a radical, Africentric theologian; Walters (1858-1917), was a fearless AME Zion bishop who fought for African freedom and American civil rights; Francis J. Grimke (1850-1937), was a fiery black Presbyterian pastor and writer who struggled against racism in his denomination; and Nannie

Helen Burroughs (1878-1961), was a progressive womanist educator and the founder of the Woman's Convention of the National Baptist Convention, U.S.A., Inc. In her time Burroughs led the largest organization of black women in the world.

13.   C. Eric Lincoln, "Black Sects and Cults and Public Policy," in Joseph R. Washington, Jr., (ed.) *Black Religion and Public Policy: Ethical and Historical Perspectives* (Philadelphia: University of Pennsylvania Afro-American Studies Program, 1978), 2.

14.   The sharp critique of black theology by African American women theologians does not, by any stretch of the imagination, exclude them from the circle of black male and a few white scholars who saw value in a new theological systematic that reinvigorates the struggle against racism and the study of the largely unexamined but still powerful relationship between ethnicity and faith.

15.   See Gayraud S. Wilmore and James H. Cone, *Black Theology: A Documentary History, 1966–1979* (Maryknoll, N.Y.: Orbis Books, 1979), for an example of some of these statements.

CHAPTER TWO

What Has Happened to Us?
Conversing with Scholar Mercy
Oduyoye on the Quest for Life

Marsha Snulligan Haney
Tumani Mutasa Nyajeka
Rosetta E. Ross

In her plenary address at the 1997 meeting of the All Africa Conference of Churches (AACC) in Ethiopia, East Africa, Mercy Amba Oduyoye posed (to persons attending and to people of African descent generally) the piercing question: "*Den mmusu na yaabo?*" "What has happened to us?" This question (which also may be translated "What has caused this?") has implications for the "what" deriving from internal (*mmusu*) and external (*esian*) causes. On one hand, Oduyoye answers her own question. In her address she noted difficulties experienced by "peoples of Africa and of African descent" deriving from "alienation from our roots," "hatred toward ourselves," and the inability "to become fully integrated into the Western world which we so...yearn to be a part of."[1] On the other hand, Oduyoye leaves open the burden of a response to her question. Calling on Africans to address the difficulties, whether *mmusu* or *esian*, in her address she further asks "[W]hy are we unable to provide quality education for our children?" "Africa is not poor; so why are Africans poor?" "[W]hy have we not developed and utilized [Africa's] resources for ourselves?"[2]

In spite of Africans' difficulties, and the complexities which cause them, Oduyoye says Africans are "troubled, but not destroyed," "bent but not broken," (*Akyea na emmu*). She bases this assertion in two things: the theological hope deriving from the faith of Africans as believers in God and the material reality of Africa's human and mineral resources. Central to Oduyoye's work, in this address and others, is the hopeful perspective that Africans need not resign themselves to their current circumstances. Calling for changes in structures and practices that obstruct movement away from the difficulties of African peoples, Oduyoye challenges African Christians to act out the faith and hope which grounds her assertion. Further, Oduyoye's theological work challenges the Church Universal, and especially the church outside Africa, to re-imagine the meaning of mission. This latter challenge has particular significance for tearing away the missiological ideology that supported colonization, one major factor in African oppression and dependency. For Africans in the diaspora, there is in Oduyoye's work a further challenge: to understand and respond to the colonialist interconnections of difficulties faced by African peoples around the globe.

This essay engages Oduyoye's question, "What has happened to us?" in three ways. First, by examining Oduyoye as an African Christian theologian the paper explores her challenge to Africans to confront the difficulties and to use indigenous and other resources at their disposal to heal Africans' wounds. Second, by exploring Oduyoye's work as a contribution to the field of missiology, the paper presents her as calling for Christian engagement with Africa to have cultural relevance, theological authenticity, and significance for current social and material realities. Finally, by engaging issues lifted up in her address with concerns of African Americans, generally, and Womanist theologians, in particular, the paper asserts that Oduyoye seeks to develop a theology that is meaningful to and supports the flourishing of all life. A final section of the article examines implications of Oduyoye's work for religious scholars of African descent and for the work of all persons who support justice in Africa and the world. While her address provides the central focus for our discussion, issues in other texts by the author are also engaged in this essay.

Mercy Amba Oduyoye: An African Theologian Who Addresses Gender

Oduyoye's major contribution to doing theology in the African church is her ability to merge the spirit of the scholar with that of an activist. As we enter the 21st century, she is one of the African women theologians whose voice clearly calls for reconciliation between the religion of the temple and the religion of the market place within the African context. In *The Will to Rise* and *With Passion and Compassion*, she explores issues around the historic questions of the church's mission particularly where women, the poor, and the suffering are concerned. From its inception during the era of slavery and colonization, and in the 19th an 20th centuries, the African church has been plagued by the historic question of whether the mission of the church is building and maintaining opulent and powerful temples and institutions, or birthing communities and individuals who are healthy and wholesome enough to reach out to others in whatever form of need. Oduyoye argues that the African church has by and large chosen to interpret the mission of the church as that of power and institution building. She alleges that for too long the African church has followed the superimposed Western hierarchic, male-dominated, elitist model which is impervious to the cries of pain and suffering of women, the poor, children and the marginalized. Throughout her work, Oduyoye searches for and names elements that can heal. She agrees with other African scholars that in a lot of cases, Africa's future might be in the past. This is the time for the church, mosque and traditional religion to rebuild healthy traditions that have nourished the African continent, and to overcome inherited or indigenous practices that prevent flourishing of Africans. In relationship to her search for elements that heal, Oduyoye attends, especially, to gender issues.

African women continually speak of being traumatized physically and emotionally. Writers such as Tsitsi Dangarembga, Shula Marks, and Buchi Emecheta have attempted to communicate this condition of African women. In her novel *Nervous Conditions*,[3] Dangarembga conveys the message that the mission of educating the African woman for liberation has failed. According to Dangarembga, education of the African woman was all a part of the "colonial trappings" of the Africans.[4] African peasants are trapped in poverty. Educated African women are trapped in miseducation and elitism. Elite African men are trapped in miseducation and their predecessors' (colonial masters') greed and power. This revelation comes to Dangarembga's character Nyasha, the mission principal's daughter, after years of silent emotional and physical agony over the "nervous condition" of her family, made up of her parents and brother and the extended family in the village.

Because of her father's education and training, Nyasha and her family live in the most opulent house on the mission campus. At the mission and in the village she, in vain, looks for tranquility. One character who baffles her regarding Western education and African women is her mother, Maiguru. Maiguru is an African woman who, like her husband, is Christian and earned a master's degree from a highly reputable institution in London. At the mission, her academic achievements are not compensated by an appropriate position equivalent to her husband's. Socially, at the mission and in the village, everybody places Babamukuru, her husband, on a pedestal, where they fear and worship him as a hero. Kinswomen in the village see Maiguru as aloof and irrelevant. At home she worships, obeys and waits on Babamukuru. Babamukuru belittles her, and uses every tactic to ensure that she remains subordinate to him both in private and public. It is important to note that the tactics he uses are psychological, but beneath these he subtly communicates the message that he will resort to physical violence if necessary.

In *"Not Either an Experimental Doll,"*[5] Shula Marks, using letters of correspondence as primary source material, constructs a biography of Lily Moya, a young Xhosa woman, who, in colonial South Africa was determined to get an education. Unfortunately, her promising potential, triumphs, and trials, over a number of years, gave way to anxiety and depression. Lily Moya eventually was committed to a mental asylum.

In her novel, *The Joys of Motherhood*,[6] Buchi Emecheta, presents a colonial/post-colonial woman, Nnu Ego, who thinks the answer to her seemingly unappreciated life is to have as many children as she can possibly bear. She sacrifices herself in every respect for this dream to materialize. Through a family arrangement, Nnu Ego moves to the city, marries a man she is not in love with, has children and employs every means to keep them alive. Some of her children attain the highest levels of Western education and training, but at the end of her life, Nnu Ego is left unappreciated and alone. By the time of her death, all she really wants is to be taken back to her people in the village for burial.

As these authors demonstrate, issues of African women are complex and relate both to colonial and traditional practices. Oduyoye notes in her address that the Western colonial myth, which is still prevalent in most academic and mass media sources, portrays the unhealed social wounds of African women as having been inflicted by their indigenous cultures and traditions which often have been interpreted as sexist and barbarous. This colonial misrepresentation of African culture was one of the factors Europeans used to justify the colonization and civilization of Africans. The superimposition of European culture and civilization on Africa was given as the only way African womanhood could be rescued to freedom. Without knowledge of African languages or history, Western travelers, explorers, anthropologists, and others flooded libraries with myths which sought to link African customs and traditions to barbarism and to identify this as cause of the tragic condition of African women.[7] In Southern Africa such misguided European research and scholarship yielded source material for a colonial judiciary system known as "customary law." This law was specifically designed by Whites to govern Black, or "native-affairs," as they were called. Under this law designed by colonialists, women could not own property and were to be legal minors from birth to death.

In its zeal to justify the evangelization of African communities the Western church adopted this myth of the negative impact of African customs and traditions on women. The church failed to acknowledge that in its historical consciousness, the women's question presented an ongoing dilemma. Throughout Southern Africa the church's mission to African women became an extended arm of the colonial schemes of dispossessing Africans. Here, we can say, the church's mission to the African woman sought to exchange her hoe for a broom. Thus, the church became an agent of colonial governments to coerce economic and social transformation. In this process, through its mission to women, the church "domesticated" African women who, as a result, lost their land, and their men's loyalty and labor to the colonial system.

Like Dangarembga, Marks, and Emecheta, who starkly portray African women's traumas, Oduyoye speaks boldly, calling for the African church and mosque to lead in creating and implementing a mission and ministry that will engage and work together with the peoples of God who are seeking deliverance. Along with her own voice, Oduyoye sees these others as voices speaking in the wilderness to a people who have ears to hear but choose not to hear and eyes to see but choose not to see. The African church and mosque are basking in an inherited glory of elite male power and privilege, Oduyoye says. This also is true of African public institutions. African women's quest for liberation has often been belittled and dismissed or reduced to public and private humorous comments and jokes about women's questions and demands. Having assumed the power and privileges of the male-dominated colonial church (like the mosque and public institutions) the African church overwhelmingly refuses to either hear or critically analyze the root causes behind contemporary African women's experiences of pain and marginalization. In rejecting accountability and responsibility for the condition of African women, the church often has adopted the colonial myth that African culture and tradition bear the responsibility for this tragic situation. Oduyoye is asking for the African church to come down from its pedestal and opulent institutions so it can walk in the footsteps and talk the language of women and the poor.

Oduyoye has joined the voices of other African theologians and philosophers who are demanding that the African church expunge itself of the colonial Christian fetishes.[8]   African thinkers argue that the post-colonial African church, like African governments, has continued to invest too much energy in the preservation of inherited Western structures, forms, content and systems which originally were not created to liberate African peoples. Among these scholars there is the perspective that African churches' continued link at whatever level with the West is suspicious at best. For them the question is this: Does an examination of the nature of ties between African churches and Western churches leave any suspicion that the African church is serving Western interests? Historically Western interests are based on material greed and lust for power and control. Western interests continue to be the behind the source of African misery and death. How can the African church extricate itself from this legacy of a lust for power and greed that socially translates into elitism, racism, sexism and environmental toxification?

Oduyoye and others are alerting the African church to the fact that the balm to the pain of its people has always been in the African soil. The soil that birthed African peoples points to a beginning with Godself. The African church needs to journey with Africans back to a complete reunion with this beginning. It needs to sing a new song that tells the story that God is and always has been at each African child's birth and will always be there at the time of its death. The song also should proceed to proclaim that it is through community that each person, tree, and animal experiences God. The African church is being called to build communities that empower, nourish, sustain, nurture and heal. A call is going out for the church and mosque to descend from lofty thrones to do meaningful work as defined by the village or the crowded urban conditions, and not by evil political and global systems.

There is pain in every context of a woman's life on the continent. This is an answer to what African men have often feigned ignorance about and out of curiosity and self-interest have asked: "Where are African women really oppressed? Is it just a cop out from Western, white feminist movements?" In response to such questions, Oduyoye gives an opportunity to African women across the continent to speak, if only men would listen. Such speaking out on gender in post-colonial Africa in and outside the church is a major contribution. Many African women pay heavy penalties in terms of social marginalization for speaking out. African women have been misquoted, misrepresented, and misinterpreted in many contexts beyond their control. Western churches and publishers have demanded and portrayed what they wanted to hear about gender in Africa. In spite of this, Oduyoye has been bold not only as a scholar, but she has been an activist as well. In addition to teaching and writing, Oduyoye has sought to make beneficial changes as an active participant in African and global church life. Along with her scholarship, her work with African church bodies and with the World Council of Churches point toward new paradigms for the mission of the Universal Church.

Oduyoye As Missiologist Addressing the Disconnect of Mission and the African Church

Mercy Oduyoye has been extremely helpful in creating a missiology for Africa that is both socially relevant and culturally authentic. Hers is the story of an African Christian leader with missiological vision for new life and liberation in the African church. Throughout her ministry as an international lecturer, researcher, author and World Council of Churches leader, she has attempted to give some understanding of the Church's purpose and mission in the context of tradition and modernity in Africa. Her keynote address to the All Africa Conference of Churches (AACC) 7th General Assembly plenary (the first time in history an address was presented by a woman) entitled "Troubled But Not Destroyed" and her resource paper also presented during the assembly entitled "The Church of the Future, Its Mission and Theology," along with her previous books[9] contain the mature and creative reflections of a woman of singular achievement calling for "unchaining our minds" as relates to issues of mission, church and ministry. By raising the fundamental question, *"Den mmusu na yaabo?"* (What has happened to us?), Oduyoye presents paramount reasons why it is necessary for the church to deliberately and urgently address key concerns related to the identity and purpose of the church in Africa if it is to stay alive, and become well enough to adequately meet both contemporary as well as future challenges. This ability to engage in an introspective self-examination is required of every church in every location on planet earth, and of every generation. Oduyoye's voice therefore is critical and crucial today in terms of the particular challenges facing the African Church internally as well as in relationship to other Christian and religious communions within the larger global landscape.

Oduyoye has several goals in mind in putting forth the need for missiological consideration of the Assembly's theme, "Troubled, But Not Destroyed." These goals serve as a frame of reference for discussing concerns related to the need of the African Church to (1) provide a platform for the voices of those whose backs are bent in relations to the current socio-economic and political crisis facing the continent; (2) challenge theological understandings of church teachings and religious practices that oppress African people; (3) develop a theological method that takes seriously the religious understanding and practice of Africans as a source of theology; and (4) uncover and undo the network of privileges that keep the church absent or marginalized in African communities.

Mercy Amba Oduyoye attempts to meet these goals in two ways. First, she presents areas of struggles and strategies related to clashing ideals, and the necessary compromises between practical politics and religious traditions. According to her, the current marginalization of Africa is the result of power and privilege rules and controls within the international world order that view Africa negatively. She has no hesitancy in describing the exploitation of the natural and human resources of Africa – from the period of the slave trade, through the colonial and neo-colonial periods, to the era of what she refers to as the present day "complying local elites."[10] It is Oduyoye's contention that the African Church, if it is to respond to the questions of life and living, must engage theologically in ministries that are balanced, communal, realistic and biblically based enough to provide Christian responses to practical issues.

Second, by presenting themes which are an elaboration on the issues which ordinary women, men, youth and children face on a daily basis (themes which they discuss among themselves) Oduyoye gives public space and voice to persons who often are overlooked. These concerns are not only expressed in the African values presented in traditional ways of life, and prayers and songs, but are also evidenced in contemporary resources. She makes reference[11] in particular to Miguna Miguna's book entitled *Africa's Volcanic Song: Poems of Liberation and Cultural Renewal*, and lifts up the phrase "the unchaining of our minds." Equally important, however, is her ability to make the connection between current challenges facing African church leaders and their need to actively engage in an exploration of the role of the committed church in the ongoing worldwide mission of God. It is because Africans can see God as the One revealed within their culture, as the God of Hosea and as the God of the New Testament, that they can say "we are at work with Jesus, tending Africa's development (referring to Matthew 18:18 and Luke13).[12] Boldly Oduyoye declares, "We are not destroyed because we believe ourselves to be people called to work with God in overcoming our affiliations and in atoning for our *mmusu*."[13]

Together these aspects of African theological reflection, which appear so diverse, yet are intricately interwoven, serve to point to the need to develop a missiological understanding by which Africans can express their consciousness, as well as find ways to have others pay attention to the African Church and its contributions to the mission of the Universal Church. Oduyoye challenges the church as a God ordained institution and human organization, "to make justice and compassion operative" so that the African Church can participate fully in the mission of the God.[14] The four missional concerns identified above will serve as a framework for discussing the contributions of Mercy Oduyoye as a leading African missiologist.

(1.) Oduyoye provides a platform for the voices of those whose backs are bent due to the staggering socio-economic and political crisis of the continent.
In a second presentation, and as an AACC resource paper, Oduyoye raises the question, "Does the Church have a future in Africa's future?"[15] It is only as the African Church responds to the poor and marginalized of Africa that this question will be answered authentically and with integrity. What it means to be a relevant church in mission in Africa, according to Oduyoye, can only be ascertained as the church provides a platform to address the social, economic and political aspects of life's crisis and related issues facing Africans. Oduyoye confronts this concern first by examining the relationship between economics and religion, and second by lifting up the problem of language.[16] She indicates how entities have impacted the plurality and ambiguity of Christianity in Africa. Concerning the former issue, Oduyoye suggests that the question "Does the African Church have a future?"[17] is a legitimate one, particularly when one considers whether or not the African Church is currently positioned to remain a relevant factor in transforming African communities. While the tendency may be to dismiss this type of question as unnecessary, the following observation by Oduyoye cannot be dismissed:

> In the absence of the force of law or compulsion, the Church in Africa depends on two basic factors: 1) the gifts and the economic capability of its adherents, 2) the institutional infrastructure of the Church. Can the Christian people of Africa afford the structures of the institutionalized Church? However much they may need the ministrations of the Church, it cannot be expected that poor people can pay for them. African Religion was paid for from "state taxes" and the voluntary offerings of its adherents. Western Christianity in Africa has been paid for by a combination of missionary gifts and local contributions.[18]

The problem of language is a difficult one due to the linguistic, material-social, political-economic, and religious-educational spheres of theological study related to Christian ministerial preparation. Socio-political and economic influences based on the culture, communication, and languages of French and English, as well as the inherited philosophy of education of the colonialists do not provide Africans with the tools to address or shape the crisis they are confronted with. Hence, the question, *"Den mmusu an yaabo?"*
Current realities dictate the urgent need for speaking and writing by persons like Oduyoye. She is one who is able with clarity and accuracy to acknowledge that the relational structures existing between churches in Africa and their Euro-

American counterparts often is not very different from that relationship existing between and the so-called debtor nations and the International Monetary Fund and the World Bank. She writes, "while African Churches did not become financially indebted to Western Churches, ecclesiastically, theologically and liturgically they remained tied to their 'benefactors.'[19] The church must be in the forefront in not only critiquing but initiating new economic models to replace troubling ones. This requires that the theoretical dimensions (advocacy, action, and reflection) of missiology must be dealt with in totality, and it is by engaging in such a process that the necessary platform will emerge. Issues of self-hood and self-determination, partnership, globalization, urbanization, and the full effects of colonization must be addressed by the entire African clergy and laity, women and men. Issues such as these that actually or potentially threaten to bend the backs of Africans, must be addressed in light of a post-Pentecost Christian faith practical to life. The churches must take the lead in initiating conversations between the elite class promoted by Western Christianity (the privileged) and the majority of Africans who encounter the poverty of life (the oppressed), as well as across gender and generational differences, and in ways that lead to a constructive common engagement.

(2.) Oduyoye challenges theological understandings of church teachings and religious practices that oppress African people.

In an age of religious, social and identity crisis and confusion, and at a time when social and cultural practices tend to dehumanize people, there is a need for theologians to articulate reasons for continued focus on expanding the Christian faith. Faced with key questions such as "What does Christianity offer that primal (or traditional) religions do not offer?" and "Why should an African become a Christian rather than a Muslim?" The African church must provide responses that are offered not only in word, but also in deed.

What are the churches' teachings and practices toward all the poverties of life?[20] This is an important consideration, particularly given the reality articulated by Oduyoye that though Africa is not poor, there are poor people in Africa. The Church must start asking and responding to the question, "Why are Africans poor?" Furthermore, the churches must grow in their realization that by being poor, Africans (and the church that does not side for liberation and positive reconstruction) are making others rich. While reliance on Western denominations and theological attitudes and practices helped Christianity create the new elite who took over from the colonial regimes, today's religious leaders are required to be concerned with helping local communities to respond to issues of poverty, wealth, and liberation. Status quo maintenance must be viewed in light of Christian themes of justice, sharing, peace and accountability, and how these converge. The hope is that as politicians succeed in weaning Africans away from the dependent mentality of a colonized people, the church will succeed more in stimulating Christian-lived teachings and practices that resound authentically within the African ethos.

Challenges of urbanization, ethnic and religious divisiveness, the modern ease of mobility among young people, and the growing reality of increasing numbers of refugees are examples of just a few more of the pressing concerns the Church must address holistically. An urgent theological concern is centered around the need to reconstruct knowledge of African traditional religion and the role that it has had in shaping the presentation and understanding of Christianity. According to Oduyoye, Christianity cannot afford to undermine the traditional understanding of health care, government, and community. Concerning Islam and the challenge it presents she has remarked that some churches "and the Christian community as a whole was surprised by the vigor of Islam, troubled by its heightened visibility and the intensity of its evangelization which openly co-opts Church language". Notice the following:

> We are in a depressed situation in Africa today, not only because of economic problems, and because of patriarchal structures which we accept as normative, but most radically because we refuse to empower "the other," to be a partner in shaping the changing values of our community life. With the burden/blessing of a triple heritage (African, Christian, Islamic) people in power are able to justify anything. The call to a Church aspiring to be a positive factor in Africa's future, must give continuous and deliberate attention to questions of empowerment, participation and energizing partnership.[21]

How Christians relate to other faiths on issues of salvation, notions of truth, and epistemological orientations in religions must be addressed. In light of the awareness of the strengths, values and histories of other religions, Oduyoye raises these concerns for African Christians who must struggle to make sense out of their faith within pluralistic contexts.[22]

(3.) Oduyoye develops a theological method that takes seriously the religious understanding and practice of Africans as a source of theology.

Perhaps what motivates Oduyoye is what is evident in most African and African diaspora communities worldwide: the need for an authentic African Christian identity. According to some leading African missiologists, there is a tendency to speak of the need to be liberated from the complexes associated with African identity so that they can participate fully in the mission of God.[23] Oduyoye, however, observes that African identity is not something to be liberated FROM, but is the means FOR obtaining true liberation. The transcendency and the immanency of God are discovered only within the particular as we seek knowledge and to be known.

Only as Africans discover Africans as a key source of theology will the need to overcome specific barriers, such as self-hatred, anxiety, apathy and dysfunctional cultural and church practices be actualized. Africa, including her children throughout the world, is at a critical time in history when she can no longer allow others to define herself or determine what role she will have in shaping her self-understanding.

Africa must struggle to be liberated from the prejudices, politics and exploitations of outsiders. However, the struggle does not simply end with liberation, but must include reconstruction – social, moral, political and spiritual reconstruction. Oduyoye reminds us, "Africans and the people of African descent are not slaves; they were enslaved. [African scholar Toyin] Falola insists that without awareness of our pre-colonial history, we shall continue to believe what others tell us about ourselves."[24]

As young people are creating new forms of identity and seek belonging and cohesion through religious perspectives, what kind of a theological method can churches (pastors and other ministry leaders) engage that will enable the church, truly African, to reach out with hope and healing? Recalling that Africans converted to Christianity because they saw an affinity between the Gospel of Jesus and the African worldview, Oduyoye suggests an approach that invites the African church to reconsider both an ecclesiology and spirituality that is dependent upon the development of a dynamic Christology. According to her, "Such a theology will enable Africans experience to that life which is lived in the presence of God and in full view of a spirit world that is in constant communion with the physical and spiritual dimension of life."[25] She continues, "The themes of salvation, liberation, transformation and reconstruction are all filtered through the prism of 'The Jesus Story.'"[26]

(4.) Oduyoye uncovers and undoes the network of privileges that keep the church absent or marginalized in the African communities and in society.

Womanist in her being, Oduyoye has declared, "For as long as we have life enough to be troubled by our troubles, we cannot be destroyed", and yet even as she makes that declaration, she boldly states:

> We have not accepted that power in Africa, as indeed in many parts of the world, has shifted from the nation-state to the transnational corporations. We have not yet acknowledged that these who control the world's economic and financial resources are the real powers determining our destiny. The competition to create a favorable investors climate at times involves the abuse of our own people and our own resources.[27]

Any missiology that claims relevancy will have to critique the relationships that sustain it both internally and externally, past and present. Each relationship must be evaluated by criteria that affirm and support African spirituality, worldview and social organization. While African churches are being revitalized by claiming the symbols, rituals or personifications that best articulate self-identify, (i.e., liturgies liturgists, etc.) these same churches must be committed to uncovering and unmasking the networks of privilege related to colonialization (past) or neo-colonialization (present) and to assimilation and accommodation. African churches must give way to authentic ways of thinking, doing and being the church. While this is readily evident among the African Instituted Churches, it is not so among the majority of the Western churches planted in Africa as a result of the European and Euro-American missionary enterprises.

Because Africa is a continent where economy and governance is tied to the nations of the West, and as Oduyoye acknowledges, this fact has not only unified Africa, but also has deep implications for the ethos of Christianity in Africa, the churches must deal with their life of privilege and of the ways, consciously and unconsciously, churches have acted as oppressor within African culture and society. This is why a new missiology is needed, one that challenges traditionally accepted theology and that seeks to identify with those Jesus identified as "the least of these" – the marginalized, oppressed, and rejected. The destructive consequences of accepting the assertion of Western theology as objective and normative for Africa (and the rest of the world) compel us to see the need for transforming the church so as not to "do" for others, but in order to "be" with others as they seek life, justice and healing. It is within the various arenas of struggles and strategies, of clashing Christian ideals ("in the world, but not of the world") that the church must seek to bridge the gaps between practical politics and economics, religious traditions and theologies, as it embodies the gospel mandates.

It is important to note that a theme most contemporary missiologists seek not to address, is precisely the one that Oduyoye does address and she does so in the context of the question *Den musu na Yaabo*? Here we speak of the relationship between Africans and African Americans.

> We dare not shy away from a hard look at African enslavement which involved three sides of the triangular trade: The African in Africa, Africans in the Americas and the Caribbean, and the Europeans and peoples of European descent who were and are the beneficiaries.... Yes, the trade in human beings is our cardinal *mmusu*. ... God forbid that we should go down in history crying peace, peace where there is no peace.[28]

Oduyoye has clearly provided helpful insights into the cross-cultural implications of working together as Africans and African Americans in mission. There is no salvation that does not involve all persons of African descent with one another. Oduyoye provides an excellent missiological perspective for addressing the task of church development for a relevant renewal of the Universal Church in mission.

As has been demonstrated, Oduyoye, speaking from the standpoint of a Womanist African Christian, is concerned with building a foundation from which the African church can construct a workable, authentic and relevant missiology. The genesis of such a missiological understanding of the church must have the capacity to address the current struggles and hopes of Africa, as well as launch a premise for responding to future challenges. Oduyoye advocates a fuller identification between the African local congregation in its communal and traditional value laden setting, and at the same time being fully aware of its relationship to the Universal Christian Church. Only such a church is able to challenge ministry leaders to redefine their ideas about the meaning of the church and its missional nature. As Oduyoye provides leadership in addressing the complex realities of church life in relationship to prevailing crises in Africa, she painstakingly urges the church not to ignore those who are marginalized, and who are most in need of what the church has to offer. Only as the church is related to the African soil and people, and is willing to confront issues of its heritage and hope, can it consciously choose to actively participate in the quest for life and living. Aware of its role in the continuity of history and in the processes of life, the church in Africa can then position itself to better apprehend the fact of God's unfolding purpose and its contribution to its fulfillment.

Oduyoye's Work in Conversation with Womanist Theology.

Reflecting on Oduyoye's question, "What has happened to us?" provides an opportunity to explore ways that her work intersects with concerns of African Americans and of many Womanist religious scholars. "[T]he Churches' concerns," Oduyoye says, "include all that concerns the people: politics and economics are not excluded".[29] She further observes interrelation of the sacred and the secular, negatively seen in the inequalities within both of these realms permeating each other. "The monopoly of power and lack of inclusiveness that eats up the African state also consumes the churches." she says. These reflections by Oduyoye parallel an important tenet of Womanist theology: that religious thought reflect holistic analysis of life that includes examination and critique of various oppressive hierarchies and exclusion in church and society. "We must ... take concrete steps to exorcize the ghost of this evil, demonstrating to ourselves that as humans, we are meant to be free; we are not meant to be enslaved; enslavement is unnatural."[30]

Correlating with Oduyoye's admonition that "We ... must take concrete steps" is another consideration that undergirds much Womanist religious thought, namely, that theological reflection be meaningful to the material life of black people in particular, and the poor and oppressed in general. As they excavate resources of Womanist religious thought (various documents and texts by and about Black women), Womanist scholars lift up tradition and practice by which religious Black women in the United Stages navigated the ofttimes difficult realities to ensure survival and determine a positive quality of life for their families and communities.[31] Womanism places at center stage the voices and experiences of Black women (which to date primarily has meant Black women in the United States). Womanism arises out of reflection upon the thought and action of Black women. As social activity and social theory, womanism is an evolving political movement and critical theoretical perspective seeking to develop new and renewed social, ecclesial, and political configurations which respond to the complexities, and demonstrate the flexibility central to affirming the diversity of a common humanity. Three areas in Oduyoye's address relate to concerns in Womanist theory, and point back to issues addressed in our discussion of Oduyoye as a theologian and scholar of Christian missiology. These areas are the depletion of diverse resources through various forms of colonialism, the identity issues deriving from colonization and oppression, and colonization's legacy in contemporary economic proscriptions on social life. Moreover, it is possible to describe parallels in the United States that reflect the similarity of the circumstances of "the peoples of Africa and of African descent" to whom Oduyoye addresses her question.

Several times in her address, she refers to the *esian* of historic enslavement of African peoples. "We know we have been in chains to the West for 500 years," she says.[32] This enslavement for Oduyoye includes not only the literal shackles placed on Africans on the continent or transported away from the continent. It also includes various forms of restraint by Western societies that have prevented and continue to prevent positive quality of life for Africans. In fact, these various forms may be spoken of generically as 18th and 19th century resource depletion through colonization which included trafficking in sale of human bodies, Europeans carving up the land and mineral resources of the continent "for themselves as if no Africans were in existence", and contemporary economic colonization through which Africa is part of "the developing world which incurred negative balances in favor of the industrialized countries to the tune of (well over) 9.2 billion U.S. dollars".[33]

Oduyoye describes this contemporary colonization as reflected in the suffering of the majority of Africans when the continent holds "more than half the world's reserve of gold and a third of its diamonds." The solution to Africans' problem, she continues, is not in the gold and diamonds; "for sure … gold and diamonds will not save us." Rather, she says, the possibility for transformation of Africans' lives lies in the potential "moral and ethical strength to refuse to exchange these beautiful gifts for the means of destroying others."[34] Realizing such moral and ethical strength requires re-envisioning social and economic structures. As Oduyoye asserts, this sometimes includes having a wide enough vision to retrieve and reconstruct relevant past traditions that may provide resources for determining a positive future. Here, there is coincidence with Womanist methodologies, which look to historic traditions of religious Black women for models of practice that can enhance the contemporary quality of life in African American communities and beyond.

For Oduyoye, holistic norms should guide such retrieval. "We know that we have to work to promote relationships that recognize and promote the intrinsic value and equality of all people," Oduyoye says. For her, this includes determining norms that attend "to survival and wholeness of an entire people."[35] This perspective in Oduyoye's work and in Womanist theory is diametrically opposed to colonialist traditions which separate persons, support hierarchy, and which ignore or even show disdain for entire groups of people. For African descended theologians and all persons concerned for full human liberation, Oduyoye suggests retrieving those norms "that recognize and promote the intrinsic value and equality of all people."

Unfortunately, the realization of such norms is complicated by the *mmusu* of identity issues. In her address Oduyoye speaks of Africans' difficulty in negotiating ethnic divisions and boundaries of "states created for Africans by Europeans"[36]. Negotiating these and the divisions subsequent to them is relevant to other identities created for Africans by Europeans. The "honorary white" of the former apartheid-governed South Africa, the French colonial practice of granting "honorary" French citizenship to select persons from African colonies, the "house" slave of the U.S. slavery era, and the contemporary "I-made-it-on-my-own-without-the-help-of-affirmative-action-African American-baby-boomer" are all siblings and represent traumatic extreme manifestations of "how we have learnt to hate ourselves so much."[37] Related to and derivative of these identity issues are any number of other challenges to Africa's and Africans' liberation. There is, for example, the ambivalence of some Africans toward African cultural forms. Some "Africans joined Europeans to declare indigenous spirituality and worship as 'paganism'" Oduyoye says. Furthermore, there is even such ambivalence of some African peoples toward each other.[38] In the United States, for instance, Audre Lorde observes this particularly among Black women. Lorde writes: "it is easier to deal with the external manifestations of racism and sexism than it is to deal with the results of those distortions internalized with our consciousness of ourselves and one another."[39] Although she locates origins of identity challenges in colonization, Oduyoye strongly asserts the responsibility for addressing these challenges and influencing currents in the world as belonging to Africans. She says,

> *We* have the capacity to take the reign of God by storm and to undertake bold action. ... The time for self-abnegation is over. *We* have to walk with courage and power. ... *[We]* must 'loosen' our tongues' and articulate our thoughts. *We* must strengthen our hands and provide what we need. We must end dependency and cultivate

true independence. *We* must terminate indebtedness, exterminate
poverty, arrest hunger, detain disease.[40] (italics added).

While she charges African peoples with responsibility to overcome the
problem, for Oduyoye, responding to this identity *mmusu*, cannot occur in a
vacuum. She says, "In addition to the *mmusu* that we perpetrate, there is the
esian that accompanies our membership in the global community."[41] For
Oduyoye, "true independence" involves acknowledging membership in the
global community in two ways. First, there is the need to recognize global
interdependence as part of the same human family, depending on resources of
the one earth, operating within possibilities of the same global ecosystem. This
acknowledgment is recognition of the theological hope to which Oduyoye refers
as the basis for confronting Africans' problems and problems of the disunity of
humanity around the world. In order to act critically on this hope, however,
there is need also to recognize that materially, membership in the global
community means that we are part of a system of inequalities structured against
the global interdependence of human beings. Oduyoye says, there is further
need to acknowledge this aspect of membership in the global community
because the "notion and practice of 'globalization' is not in another esian."[42]
Worldwide economic restraints on political and social life (which are manifest
more intensely in Africa) derive from structures hostile to (or at best not
concerned about) thriving subsistence in African economies. Failure to
recognize the existence and extent of the influence of these structures frustrate
strategies to overcome Africa's dependence. The World Bank and International
Monetary Fund originated in the 1940's after World War II among European
powers to prevent the collapse of European economies. Non-African states (the
G7/8 nations – Canada, the United States, Japan, Germany, France, Italy, and
England) continue to determine policies of the World Bank and IMF and,
thereby, control Africa's and other developing economies through indebtedness
to the World Bank/IMF.[43] Oduyoye observes:

> We have been absorbed willy nilly into an economic system that
> invests in speculation rather than in production; appropriating
> technology requiring minimum labor. So product includes
> unemployed persons. The end result, globally, is the prevailing
> scenario: 'jails for the poor and tours for the rich.' Surveys have
> shown that the construction of jails has become a growth industry.
> Globalization has intensified unemployment and impoverishment;
> perplexed and dismayed we wring our hand crying....[44]

The relationship of this to Africans in the United States is seen in both the
high rate of incarceration of African Americans, the preponderance of lower
incomes among the masses of African Americans, and small amounts of wealth

held by African Americans. Each of these may be seen as deriving from the legacy of U.S. participation in African colonization and enslavement.

For Oduyoye, increasing market economics is neither the pure and simple nor the ethical answer to poverty in Africa or the world. Dependency of Africa and Africans occurred within the context of capitalist market economics. "It was the technological superiority of the West that won the [cold] war," she writes, "not the moral superiority of its economic system".[45] Oduyoye advocates a worldwide interdependence that does not require the dependency of current global economic structuring but which recognizes the common humanity and, therefore, the connections of persons with each other. This recognition calls for persons concerned about a new, just world order to re-envision ways of structuring social and economic life so that members of the global community share the benefits and burdens of our interdependence.

"We are challenged," Oduyoye says, "to search for more just alternatives to SAPs"[46] in Africa. Likewise, we also are challenged to find more comprehensive and more just solutions than affirmative action in the United States. SAPs, or structural adjustment programs (IMF/World Bank conditionalities and prescriptions for regulating debtor-state economies) often increase the burden on already suffering societies and penalize those who have been ravaged by colonialism for the harm done to them. Affirmative action policies are only a preliminary step toward redressing devastation and the continuing oppression caused by over 300 years of U.S. slavery and its legacy of disfranchisement, domination and exclusion. The international Jubilee 2000 movement calling for relief of Africa's indebtedness to the IMF/World Bank and the U.S. reparations debate are possible ways of re-envisioning economic life. Both point to an organic understanding of creation reflected in Womanism's concern for "an entire people" and fully articulated in Oduyoye's concern to "provide security for the vulnerable and pay homage to mother earth,"[47] and to "recognize and promote the intrinsic value and equality of all people."[48] The challenge which Oduyoye and womanism (and others interested in full human liberation) present is that we recognize and use the diverse ideas, imagination, creativity, and ingenuity available through a reciprocal and egalitarian globalism.

Conclusion

In response to the question, "What has happened to us?" Mercy Amba Oduyoye with clarity has explored some of the penetrating internal and external realities facing Africa and African peoples. By leaving open the burden of a response to the penetrating and reflective question posed, the implications of her work religious scholars of African descent and all people who support justice in Africa is obvious. "Silence is no longer an option", proclaims this prominent world theologian who is former deputy general secretary of the World Council of Churches and president of the Ecumenical Association of Third World

Theologians. In light of external destructive forces related to globalization (particularly in light of the August 7, 1998 bombings in Kenya and Tanzania), and internal forces such as the HIV pandemic and its impact of the growing number of orphans, and the decades of civil war within nations such as the Sudan, Liberia and Rwanda, the urgency of engaging the work identified by Oduyoye is extremely critical. The agenda must include the following as fundamental:

> 1. Issues of religion and culture must be addressed by persons, African peoples and others, committed to confronting the difficulties facing Africa by utilizing African resources.
> 2. African missiology, derived from the faith of Africans as believers in God, must replace western missiology transported to the African continent.
> 3. African theology must be committed to and supportive of the flourishing of all of life, especially in the face of major devastations.

The greatest implication of her work, however, lies in her ability to merge the spirit of the scholar with that of the activist. In 1999 Oduyoye advocated for an initiative that placed a priority on the empowerment of women in Africa. As the founder and director of the Institute of Women in Religion (inaugurated at Trinity Theological Seminary, Accra), she assists women in claiming their rights as daughters of God, created in God's own image (Genesis 1:27) through research, seminars, and programmatic initiatives. Based on the values articulated throughout this essay, the institute honors African women's voices and experiences in programs of theological education and in the development of theological curricula inclusive of gender studies and women's perspectives.

Oduyoye's leadership model emphasizes the synergy intersecting the theoretical with the theological, and for her is crucial in addressing holistically the challenges facing the church and the academy in Africa. Her inquiry into the meaning of religious traditions facing African life, is but a reminder of urgency of the choices before us, facing both African peoples and all who support justice in Africa and the world. At a recent speaking engagement (Radcliffe Presbyterian Church, Atlanta, January, 2003) according to Oduyoye "When silence is no longer an option for what happens to women in Africa, then some have to be bad women and say what needs to be said. "The good" women, she said, hold on to the traditions and culture, and will not rock the boat; the "bad" women say that they love the church, but they want to see some changes in the culture and religion.

As an internationally visible African scholar, Mercy Amba Oduyoye provides work, which serves as a beacon and a sign for liberationist scholars around the globe. As a beacon, Oduyoye's work is both a ray of hope and, perhaps, a signal of safety for other voices which either understand themselves as crying in the wilderness, or as about to be overcome by social, economic, and theoretical forces which oppose speaking clearly about and attending to the lives and realities of persons on the underside of economic growth and triumph. Reflecting her engagement with the continent, conceivably, most detrimentally affected by post-colonial continuities of capitalist economy and with the global agenda of the World Council of Churches, Oduyoye's work serves as a sign pointing liberationist and would-be liberationists in the direction of a different global society, which we envision together. For Oduyoye, this envisioning together involves religion and culture, Africans on the continent and Africans in the diaspora, Africans and all others examining and redirecting forces which compel her question, "*Den mmusu na yaabo?*" ("What has happened to us?") Ultimately, this question is a broad interrogation of the contemporary value of every human life.

Endnotes

1. Mercy Amba Oduyoye, "Troubled But Not Destroyed," text of Keynote Address, All Africa Conference of Churches, Addis Ababa, Ethiopia, October 4, 1997, 1.
2. Ibid., 4.
3. Tsitsi Dangarembga, *Nervous Conditions* (Seattle: Seal, 1989).
4. Franz Fanon, *The Wretched of the Earth* (New York: Grove, 1963).
5. Shula Marks, "The Context of Personal Narrative: Reflections on "*Not Either an Experimental Doll*", "The Separate Word of Three South African Women" in *Intrepreting Women's Lives: Feminist Theory and Personal Narratives* edited by The Personal Narratives Group (Bloomington: Indiana University, 1989), 39-58.
6. Buchi Emecheta, *The Joys of Motherhood* (New York: G. Braziller, 1979).
7. V. Y. Mudimbe, *The Invention of Africa: Gnosis, Philosophy, and the Order of Knowledge* (Bloomington: Indiana University, 1988).
8. Eboussi-Boulaga, *Christianity without Fetishes: An African Critique and Recapture of Christianity* translated from the French by Robert R. Barr. (Maryknoll, NY: Orbis Books, 1984); Jean Marc Ela, *My Faith as an African* (Maryknoll, NY: Orbis Books, 1988); and V. Y. Mudimbe, *The Invention of Africa*.
9. While "*The Church of the Future, Its Mission And Theology*" (Resource Paper AACC7AS.2/2) will be frequently referenced in this section of the essay, see also the following books authored by Oduyoye, *Hearing and Knowing, The Will to Arise and Daughters of Anowa.*
10. For an excellent analysis of the process of marginalization, see Frank Chikane's "The Bretton Woods Institutes and The Struggle for Economic Justice" (AACC7AS.2/1, page one).

11.   Oduyoye, "Troubled But Not Destroyed", 8.
12.   Ibid., 3-12.
13.   Ibid., 10.
14.   Oduyoye, "The Church of the Future", 2.
15.   Ibid., 1.
16.   The reality that whenever the AACC, or African government agencies and organizations gather, they rely on Western languages as the primary means of communication was quite vivid and troublesome to this observer.
17.   Oduyoye, "The Church of the Future", 2.
18.   Ibid., 2.
19.   It is significant to quote Oduyoye and her description of Christianity in Africa, for she systematically reminds us of the five types of churches that comprise the African church: (1) "First Century" Christianity in Africa finds current expression in the Coptic and Ethiopia Orthodox Churches; (2) Western churches were planted in Africa as a result of the Euro-American missionary enterprise.   As might be expected, these churches resemble their Western mentors. Today, most ecumenical structures of Africa comprise these two types; (3) a third manifestation of Christianity in Africa is the Roman Catholic Church; (4) the African instituted churches form a fourth manifestation of African Christianity. They have been characterized by a boldness to in cultrate Christianity into the African situation, thanks to direct access to the Bible in local languages; (5) in modern Africa, Christians experiencing a new wave of evangelization, sometimes associated with the so-called "prosperity gospel" which produces another type of church, the full dimensions of which have yet to be studied and discerned. See Oduyoye, "The Church of the Future," 3, 4.
20.   Ibid., 11.
21.   Oduyoye, "The Church of the Future", 2
22.   See Marsha Snulligan Haney, *Islam and Protestant African American Churches: Responses and Challenges of Religious Pluralism* (Lanthan International Scholars Publications, 1999), who recognized the same tendency related to religious pluralism within the African American community, and emphasized the interfaith arena as an area of common dialogical concern facing both Africans, African Americans, and Afro-Carribeans.
23.   Tite Tienou, *"Themes in African Theology of Mission," in The Good News of the Kingdom* (Maryknoll: 1993).
24.   Ibid., 9.
25.   Oduyoye, "The Church of the Future," 7.
26.   Ibid., 9.
27.   Oduyoye, "Troubled But Not Destroyed," 8.
28.   Ibid., 5-6.
29.   Ibid., 4.
30.   Ibid., 6.
31.   See, for example Katie G. Cannon's *Black Womanist Ethics* (Atlanta: Scholars, 1988); Delores Williams' *Sisters in the Wilderness* (New York: Orbis, 1993); Jacquelyn Grant's *White Woman's Christ and Black Woman's Jesus* (Atlanta: Scholars, 1999); Cheryl Townsend Gilkes *"The Role of Women in the Sanctified Church*," The Journal of Religious Thought 43 Spring -Summer, 1986) 24-41, "Going Up for the Oppressed: The Career Mobility of Black Women Community Workers," Journal of Social Issues 39

(Fall 1983) 115-139, and "The Roles of Church and Community Mothers: Ambivalent American Sexism or Fragmented African Familyhood," Journal of Feminist Studies in Religion 2 (Spring 1986) 41-60; Emilie Townes, *Womanist Spirituality* (Nashville: Abingdon, 1994)(?)) Marcia Riggs, *Arise, Awake and Act: A Womanist Call for Black Liberation* (Cleveland: Pilgrim, 1994); Karen Baker-Fletcher, *A Singing Something: Womanist Reflections on Anna Julia Cooper* (New York: Crossroad, 1994); Cheryl Kirk-Duggan, *Exorcizing Evil: A Womanist Perspective on the Spirituals* (New York: Orbis, 1997); Rosetta Ross, *Witnessing and Testifying* (Minneapolis: Fortress, 2003)

32.   Oduyoye, "Troubled, But Not Destroyed", 7.
33.   Ibid., 1.
34.   Ibid., 2.
35.   Walker, Alice, *In Search of Our Mothers' Gardens: Womanist Prose* (San Diego: Harcourt Brace, 1983), ix.
36.   Oduyoye, "Troubled But Not Destroyed", 3.
37.   Ibid., 1.
38.   Ibid., 7.
39.   Lorde, Audre, Sister Outsider: Essays and Speeches by Audre Lorde (Freedom, California: Crossing, 1984), 147.
40.   Oduyoye, "Troubled But Not Destroyed", 9.
41.   Ibid., 5.
42.   Ibid., 5.
43.   Edmund, Doogue, "World Bank to Invite Religions to Summit," Ecumenical News International, www.ur.org/Htngongo.htm (October 31, 1996) [Accessed 16 December 1998].
44.   Ibid., 5-6.
45.   Ibid., 5.
46.   See Gloria T. Emeagwali, *Women Pay the Price: Structural Adjustment in Africa and the Caribbean* (Trenton: Africa Press, 1995).
47.   Oduyoye, "Church of the Future", 9.
48.   Oduyoye, "Church of the Future", 11.

CHAPTER THREE

Africentrism as a Challenge to Contemporary Christian Ministry[1]

Ronald Edward Peters

The hole in the door was covered with a pot, and paper or rags were stuffed around the door's bottom. All of this helped muffle the sound of the singing so it would not disturb Whites in the big house on the Long plantation and alert them to the presence of worship activities taking place among the Blacks on their property. This observation concerning the clandestine nature of a worship service being held on a plantation was given by Ella Harding, a retired North Carolina school teacher.[2] It is well known that what we describe as historic "Black Church" denominational institutions in America originated in what the sociologist E. Franklin Frazier termed "the Invisible Institution."[3] By invisible institution, Frazier referred to the aggregation of Africans in the "New World" who had fallen victim of the European slave trading enterprise and who gathered together periodically to aid in one another's survival efforts, of which worship and the camouflage of celebratory activities were critical elements.

It is out of this context that the Black religious experience in America has largely evolved from a foundation in survival and liberation. The oppression of slavery in the South gave rise to a survival tradition among Black religionists while among free Blacks in the North, efforts centered upon liberation.[4] Until recently, the majority of explanations concerning African elements of American society generally originated with the chattel slave system. In the area of religion, for example, when Benjamin E. Mays wrote his monumental work entitled *The Negro's God* (1933), he drew upon slave songs and narratives as source material for determining the theological perspective of American Blacks concerning God. Numerous authors, writing from a wide variety of perspectives and interests (such as Katie Cannon, James Cone, W.E.B. DuBois, Jacquelyn Grant, C. Eric Lincoln, Peter Paris, J. Deotis Roberts, James Washington, Delores Williams, Gayraud Wilmore, or Carter Woodson), have examined the role of religion in the African American experience. The dominating motif in much of their works has been the survivalist and justice-seeking characteristics intrinsic to African American religion in response to slavery and the resultant evolution of continuing oppression experienced by African Americans. Frazier even claimed that there were no remaining antecedents of religious phenomena among American Blacks that survived slavery (1964).

This approach to understanding the African content in American culture, however, does not plumb all facets of the intricate grid of Africanisms that have become part and parcel of American social, economic, political, cultural, or religious realities today. Using the slave experience as the reference point for examining Africanisms in American culture is like using the period of the "Enlightenment" in European history as a reference point for understanding English or German culture. While significant, English and German roots predate the Enlightenment. Their contribution to America today, therefore, cannot be fully understood apart from examination of their histories during as well as prior to this period. The same is true for understanding African history and culture in American society, including the church. More importantly, approaching the African American experience only from the prism of slavery does not sufficiently take advantage of African insights into human experience or theological understanding so that these assets can enhance the quality of life not only for persons of African descent, but for all people of faith. Worse still, such a historical posture truncates the range of information and means of analysis needed to help people of faith effectively respond to new and more subtle evidences of racism, exploitation, and xenophobia threatening the seeds of human cooperation and mutual affirmation. No one will deny that hosts of racial and cultural groups in addition to those of African descent have experienced cruel indignities in U.S. history. Native American peoples, for example, were nearly exterminated by wars and various broken treaties with the United States and were not universally recognized by law as U.S. citizens until 1924. Also, there are tragic tales of xenophobic reactions by the dominant social, political, and religious culture as defined by "White Anglo-Saxon Protestants" to various other racial, cultural, and religious groups that have become, over time, part and parcel of today's multicultural society. Similarly, many persons from Latin America and the Caribbean are constantly in the news because of their efforts to gain access to U.S. citizenship (Cubans and Haitians have been examples of this) in distinction from the more relaxed access afforded to Europeans. Asians, whether Chinese, Korean, Filipino, Japanese, Indian, or Thai, as well as Pacific islanders experienced more overt forms of discrimination than their European counterparts.

At the beginning of this century, southern European ethnics and persons of various non-mainline Protestant religious groups (Catholics, Jews, Eastern Orthodox, or Muslims) could relate many unfortunate narratives concerning the process of carving out their niches in United States culture. In the post 9/11 era, new waves of abuse and abridgement of civil rights have been heaped upon all persons, but none so severely as those of Arabic descent. Yet, the fact remains that African Americans are the only ethnic or cultural group in America ever to have been denied by U.S. courts of law their status as being *human* (they were recognized as being only three-fifths human) and viewed only as property for nearly half the nation's 226 year history.

In the United States, religious institutions ordinarily referred to as "mainline Protestant denominations" have typically evolved out of and have been shaped by the social, political, economic, and cultural events of American history of which they are a part. It is not surprising, therefore, that these institutions have responded to the African presence in America in the traditional way of using the slavery enterprise and its resultant social consequences as their reference points.

Increasingly, this approach to understanding American society in general and central concerns of African Americans in particular has proved less and less effective for these denominations in their attempts at ministry among this segment of society. As we shall see in this chapter, when taken seriously as a cultural resource for explaining theological realities, an Africentric presentation of the Gospel not only challenges the ineptitude of "old guard" denominational approach, but also corrective for correcting the failings of traditional approaches to Christian ministry within the African American context.

Africentrism, Eurocentrism, and Christian Witness

Africentrism,[5] in the broadest sense, refers to the practice of examining historical evidence as well as current reality by utilizing pre-colonial black Africa rather than European civilization, expansionism, and colonial activity as major points of reference. For years Black and Womanist theologians have been helpful in exposing the misuse of the Bible and the Christian faith as tools in the oppression of African Americans throughout this nation's history. Africentrism assists the Christian community in understanding the cultural and philosophical dynamic that has been employed to justify the cooptation of the churches into the imperialism that defined European colonialism.

While Molefi Kete Asante[6] is generally recognized as the scholar who first used and popularized the term, "Afrocentricity" is now employed in a variety of academic and popular circles with a wide variety of interpretations and nuances. In its most generic form "Afrocentricity" involves the notion that Africa and persons of African descent must be seen as proactive subjects within human history and in the evolution of world civilization, rather than as passive objects mentioned as an aside to the more central human drama of Western history. According to Asante, Afro- or Africentrism regards Africa and its descendants as centers of anthropological value and critical partners in understanding the evolution of world civilization in a way that does not minimize the contributions of other people:

> My work has increasingly constituted a radical critique of the Eurocentric ideology that masquerades as a universal view in the fields of intercultural communication, rhetoric, philosophy, linguistics, psychology, education, anthropology, and history. Yet, the critique is radical only in the sense that it suggests a turnabout, an alternative perspective on phenomena. It is about taking the globe and turning it over so that we see all the possibilities of a world where Africa, for example, is subject and not object. Such a posture is necessary and rewarding for Africans and Europeans. The inability to "see" from several angles is perhaps the one common fallacy in provincial scholarship.[7]

Asante argues that when persons of African descent are able to perceive the world from an African-oriented center (as for Asians, an Asian-oriented center, or Europeans, a European-oriented center), a new consciousness of one's own humanity is fully achieved. This movement toward an Africentric consciousness[8] enables persons of African descent to achieve, from within an African center, what Jesus talked about when he articulated the great commandments: first, love of God and second, love of neighbor as one *loves one's self* (Mark 12:31).

What is not so apparent in much of the public discussion about the term "Africentricity," is that its importance as an anthropological method of examining history and culture, while applicable in a number of contexts, has evolved out of and is of particular significance to the reexamination of United States history and culture. Although inherently global by virtue of its obvious interest not only in Africa, but also in the African Diaspora throughout the world (whether in Brazil, the Caribbean, Australia, or the Philippines), Africentrism is a major component of efforts by North American Africanists to more clearly appreciate their own heritage and its usefulness in a plural society. In this sense, it is important for denominational leaders of so-called mainline U.S. churches to come to grips with the critical value of this concept for doing effective ministry in U.S. culture in the twenty-first century.

Cain H. Felder has identified three distinct streams of thought among Africentrists.[9] Even though I am not sure that there would be unilateral agreement among Africentrists themselves regarding his views, I believe Felder's analysis is useful because it helps us to see that the concept of Africentricity is much less monolithic than is generally perceived. The names I give to these three streams of Africentric thought are not used by Felder, but the descriptions below are based upon his categories.

First, there is Africentrism that is *historical*. Based upon factual data, this approach seeks to correct deficits in most stereotypical Western portrayals of Africa and persons of African descent as passive objects of history. This correction is made without romanticizing African contributions on the one hand or demeaning the contributions of other cultures/peoples on the other. Felder sees himself in this category. Others might include the works of a variety of writers such as Maya Angelou, Haki R. Madhubuti, Toni Morrison, Carter G. Woodson, or Jeremiah Wright.[10]

Second, there is the *cultural* type of Afrocentricity which argues for a common cultural heritage, worldview, and ethos based upon various factors (i.e., rhythm, drumming, harmony with nature, reverence for afterlife, etc.) that are identified as unifying and defining features of what it means to be black or African. Writers like Asante, Karenga, or Van Sertima would be included in this vein.[11]

Finally, there is *elevationist* Africentrism. This is the tendency of some writers to suggest a moral agency or other characteristics that seem to "elevate" Africa and persons of African descent as being various means of cultural or other distinctive qualities to the point wherein they are defined as "better" and/or stronger than others. As such, the African needs to be separated from the damaging and alienating cultures and politics of others, especially Europeans. Albert Cleage, Louis Farrakhan, or Francis Cress Welsing can be viewed as representative of this school of thought.[12]

By Eurocentrism, reference is made to the propensity in Western culture to define all human activity, according to European aesthetic, cultural, social, economic, political, and religious norms. In so doing, Europeans become the psychological standard by which all other contexts are judged. All other cultures are seen as somehow intrinsically inferior rather than merely different since that which is "European" is viewed as the "standard" or "universal" model. A value of "less than" is subconsciously imposed on that which deviates from the European/universal norm. Felder has defined the situation in terms of its effect on the study of theology and biblical interpretation as taught in Christian seminaries today:

> Eurocentrism is a term that denotes the tendency to focus on the contributions, achievements, and significance of Europe dating back to ancient Greece and Rome as the beginning of Western civilization. In this process, the contributions by antecedent non-European groups are marginalized. Eurocentrism has expressed itself tacitly as the presupposed norm for determining value. Since the European Renaissance and Enlightenment, it has provided its own theoretical pseudo-scientific justification.[13]

Most writers on the subject of Africentrism (such as Ani, Asante, Karenga, and Van Sertima) would agree with Felder's definition of Eurocentrism. They join him in describing it as being essentially hierarchical and exclusivist. Of course, Africentrists have been, likewise, accused of having these same tendencies. In any discussion of Africentrism, however, it should be noted that Eurocentrism should not be viewed as its antithesis. Rather, in seeking the benefits to be gleaned from a philosophical perspective that is truly plural, Africentrism and other philosophical foci (such as Eurocentrism or an Asia-centered perspective) should be considered appropriate methods of understanding the histories of respective peoples in ways that are complementary instead of competitive. This is especially important for an avowedly plural society that the United States asserts itself to be.

In understanding the problems posed by Eurocentric dominance in the interpretation of scripture in our churches and their deleterious impact upon Christian ministry in general, Felder puts the matter of biblical reading and interpretation this way:

> ...I have become increasingly concerned about the thorough going Eurocentric translation, reading, and interpretation of the Bible. By "Eurocentric" I mean the recasting of the entire biblical tradition into an ancient religious drama of Eurasian Hebrews who once sojourned in Egypt, which somehow was removed from black Africa, and eventually gave rise to the birth of a European Jesus and Christianity as a Hellenistic religion of the Greco-Roman world. But... this European Jesus was the creation of a post biblical Western culture (especially medieval and Renaissance artists) and its allied religious institutions. It

is not going too far to say that over the centuries there has been a subtle
but steady process by which the Bible has become a captive of Europe
and more recently Euro-American thought.[14]

This situation helps explain the inability of local congregations and their
ecclesiastical networks to close the spiritual divide that continues to alienate larger
segments of the Christian community from vast numbers of African Americans who,
otherwise, might be more responsive to Christian evangelistic efforts. According to
Felder's analysis, seminary education and, by extension, Christian educators,
denominational officials, pastors, and lay leaders, are still shackled by a
thoroughgoing Eurocentric bias that is still very much a part of presentations of the
Gospel in popular culture.

Since a high view of spirituality is part of what Africentrists see as inherent in
the African heritage, European culture is often seen as placing less value on the
metaphysical, regardless of all theological pronouncements to the contrary. Some of
the more strident voices among Africentrists have rejected the Christian faith as no
more than a social or political ideology sacramentalized as a basis for the religious
justification of racial oppression. For example, Marimba Ani argues that in the
European cultural ethos the only thing that even approximates any type of religious
behavior is belief in the scientific method:

> If one looks for a sense of the supernatural, the sacred, or extraordinary
> in European culture, undoubtedly the only area of experience that
> approaches the "religious" in this sense is that of "science." It is only
> (that which) is considered to be scientific that is regarded with the awe
> and humility that in other cultures represents the "religious attitude."
> Scientism... is the institutionalized set of ideas that practices that
> Europeans refer to as "religion" (and) it functions normatively to
> provide the models or paradigms of (what is called) European theology.[15]

While Ani's critique may seem overdrawn to some, the current idolization of
science as represented in the computer/cyberspace technology provides an excellent
contemporary example of her point.[16] The fact that Christians have been so gullible
in supporting imperialistic economic, political, and military ventures throughout the
colonial and modern periods with elaborate theoretical/theological rationalizations
that have, in effect, rendered them co-conspirators against the oppressed has
damaged the credibility of Christian witness today. According to Ani, the role the
church has played frequently has been that of a cultural and political aggressor and
purveyor of European cultural imperialism under the guise of Christian evangelism:

> The church has taken a leading role in cultural aggression, because, of
> all the facets of European expansion, it has easiest access to non-
> European peoples and greatest potential for their ideological
> destruction. Only rarely, and never very effectively, has the Christian

Church attempted to act against what it considered to be the excesses of European nationalism and even in these instances, by virtue of its conversionism, the church still occupies a central position in... (European culture/ideology)... that may be easily grafted onto Christian ideology (theology).[17]

The "Mainline Denomination" in American History and African American Churches

The French sociologist, Alex de Tocqueville (1835), recognized the significance of religious establishments in the social organization of the emerging American society. Indeed, the American Revolution was referred to by some as the "Presbyterian rebellion."[18] Many poor, socially and politically beleaguered European Protestants ventured across the Atlantic to the Americas with hopes of a better life in response to social and political events in Europe. Because Europeans seeking their fortunes in the "new world" relatively quickly acculturated themselves to the concept of Africans as sub-human (three-fifths, according the original wording of the U.S. Constitution), the social acceptance of African enslavement grew into a staple of the colonial culture. Therefore, while pursuing social, religious, and political freedoms of their own, the plight of Africans who were being dehumanized and sold as chattel did not arouse much interest among the Anglicans, Presbyterians, or Congregationalists who were among the earliest of what was to become known as the "mainline denominations" in America. Presbyterians, with their emphasis on academics, were more concerned about the education than the emancipation of the slaves. Indeed, there was an aristocratic elitism about the racism of many White Presbyterian colonial ministers due to their stress on education as compared with either the Methodists or Baptists, who experienced greater success among blacks because of their more favorable attitudes.[19]

Over the years, however, the composition of United States religious institutions, now referred to as mainline denominations, has changed as drastically as has the American society that produced them. Mainline establishment religious institutions in this country now include much more than the exclusivistic arbiters of culture, politics, and moral aesthetics once reserved to those who were termed *White Anglo-Saxon Protestant* denominations. Now the nation's white religious establishment also includes Baptists and Methodists among the Protestants, and Catholics as well as Jews. During the middle of the last century, African-American denominations began to be recognized by the wider society as part of the "mainline" religious establishment, owing in no small measure to the impact made by Martin Luther King, Jr. as one of the most visible spokespersons of the civil rights era. Approximately ninety percent of all African American Christians are affiliated with one of seven historically Black denominational institutions: National Baptist Convention, Incorporated (8.2 million members); the National Baptist Convention of America (3.5 million members); the Progressive National Baptist Convention (2.5 million persons); African Methodist Episcopal Church (3.5 million persons); African Methodist Episcopal Zion Church (1.2 million persons); and the fastest growing denomination among African Americans today, the Pentecostal churches known as the Church of God in Christ (5.5 million persons). Moreover, African Americans are part of historically Euro-American communions. African Americans comprise about two and one half percent of the Presbyterian Church (USA)'s constituent membership or slightly less than 100,000 persons. This compares with 193,861 of the Episcopal Church, 240,000 among United Methodists, 49,705 of the Lutherans, 495,000 American Baptists, and 324,911 Southern Baptists. 1,200,000 of all American Roman Catholics are African American. As such, "mainline denomination" now refers to most "establishment" religious organizations and carries with it certain social class/status connotations, even for congregations and ecclesiastical networks (denominations) that are relatively poor economically.[20]

In all of this discussion of percentages, numbers, and constituent members with reference to Black churches and White mainline denominations, it is important to remember the observation made by Delores Williams that the religious reality commonly referred to as "the Black Church" cannot be unilaterally and uncritically equated with the human entities known as Black denominational institutions. Williams asserts that:

> The black church does not exist as an institution. Regardless of sociological, theological, historical and pastoral attempts, the black church escapes precise definition. ...Some believe it to be rooted deeply in the soul of the community memory of black folk. Some believe it to be the core symbol of the four-hundred-year-old African American struggle against white oppression with God in the struggle providing black people with spiritual and material resources for survival and freedom. Others believe it to be places where black people come to worship God without white people being present. ...I believe the black church is the heart of hope in the black community's experience of oppression, survival struggle and its historic efforts toward complete liberation. It cannot be tampered with or changed by humans to meet human expectations and goals.[21]

While evidencing some latent Platonic imagery, Williams' analysis, nonetheless, serves to underscore the fundamental metaphysical aspect that must accompany any attempt to comprehend the holistic scope of the African American religious experience. Moreover, Williams is correct in emphasizing that the "black church" cannot be defined in terms of some institutional entity, but rather is a spiritual and behavioral reality that defies the limitations of human creations such as denominations.

The Challenge of Community Ministry and the African American Presbyterian Experience
Unless we are careful, much of our discussion about the various "centrist" positions in the cultural panorama of a globally conscious and plural society can become quite esoteric. Such discussions tend to peak the interests of those who

enjoy a measure of economic security and social privilege. Weighty intellectual dialogues hold little interest for people whose daily lives are spent negotiating the means of bare survival against poverty, injustice, ill-health, poor housing, bad education, high crime, and political powerlessness. Ironically, it is among this latter population that an Africentric approach to Christian ministry holds the most promise. This promise does not emanate from a philosophical or methodological approach per se, but from Africentricity's positive approach to African heritage and the most noble cultural values associated with that heritage: community, spiritual affirmation, etc. rather than a mere reaction to European expansionism.

The critical reality prompting interest in the Africentric approach is the challenge to be involved in community ministry. The needs of the African American communities in the inner city differ vastly from those of most parishioners of White mainline congregations either in the city or the suburbs. It is axiomatic today that urban African American congregations are called upon to offer consolation to a steady and growing stream of families whose lives have been tragically altered by violence and death. A few years ago, one Pittsburgh pastor not far from the seminary where I teach had no less than one funeral per week for four consecutive months, all involving African American males who had died as a result of shootings or other violence.

At a time when human suffering has dramatically increased in urban areas where high percentages of African Americans are found, frequently so-called "mainline" congregations are experiencing dwindling numbers, decaying physical plants, and vacant pulpits in significant percentages. Although there is relatively little discussion about the phenomenon, many Black Baptist, African Methodist Episcopal, African Methodist Episcopal Zion congregations are impacted by this reality. The situation is even more critical among congregations affiliated with historically White denominations (i.e. Presbyterians, Congregationalists, or Episcopal). In the Presbyterian Church (USA), for example, many Presbyteries are closing more and more Black congregations and starting none. Over the past thirty years, there has been a dramatic decline among the number of African American congregations within the Presbyterian Church (USA) with little or no interest manifested in starting new ones by Presbyteries containing significant percentages of African Americans within their geographical bounds.[22] By contrast, some of the fastest growing congregations in the nation are those claiming no denominational affiliation.

The problem many so-called mainline congregations experience in African American communities with serious community ministry is further complicated by issues of class. Among African American Presbyterian congregations, for example, many view themselves as being so middle-class in their orientation and imitative of what they view as proper "White Presbyterian" liturgy and ethos, that they do not relate effectively to other African Americans. There is a tendency among African American Presbyterians to expend so much time and energy perpetually trying to relate to the structure of Euro-American Presbyterians, that they are unable to relate to their own heritage or to others within the African American community. Gayraud Wilmore's book, **Black and Presbyterian** (1983) states the matter this way:

> Some of us have been so anxious to prove to our white brothers and sisters that we too are Americans and that we too "belong" that we have deprived them of the gifts God has given to us as a people.... We have been so busy learning how to be "human beings in general" that we have paid little attention to the special qualities of Black humanity that we have to bring when we are true to our own history and traditions.[23]

Wilmore further suggests that this identity crisis among many Black Presbyterians has engulfed them in a situation of dual penalty wherein they are frequently not taken seriously by their White Presbyterian sisters and brothers nor by members of the wider African American community. He states "Black Presbyterians have been criticized by other Blacks for remaining in a predominantly white church where they were under the double jeopardy of having to fight both class consciousness and racism."[24]

Africentric Ministry

By Africentric Christian ministry within the United States, I refer to the ordering of congregational life (celebration, education, nurture, stewardship, public ministry outreach and social service) in such a manner as to emphasize the centrality of African people's needs in America that does not begin with only the heritage of American slavery, but with that of pre-colonial Black Africa as well. By affirming the pre-slavery period of African heritage, we move beyond the antebellum period as the origin of African American culture. This process embraces information about African antiquity in the same fashion as Europe embraces ancient Greece and Rome or Chinese culture embraces its own antiquity. This allows African American culture to focus on a positive historical perspective, emphasizing the full humanity of African people. Such a perspective recognizes Africans as achievers and contributors to world civilization with winners and losers as well as the morally virtuous and the morally corrupt all included within African culture as part of the human drama. There is no suggestion here that African culture possesses some inherent moral superiority simply because it is African.[25] Such a position makes an idolatry of culture and fails to recognize the vulnerability of human reason to become entrapped by its own arrogance as people of all cultures have done over time. Rather, the goal is to avoid the usual deficit model of comprehending the African presence in America which frequently that starts with slaves: "three-fifths human" and unable to help themselves (losers who have nothing to contribute to world civilization with only simple-minded piteous creatures or dangerous heathen involved in the human drama).

Because European cultural influence so thoroughly permeates the current understanding and interpretation of global realities, pre-slavery Africa is still an enigma viewed with skepticism, especially by many non-African descended

Christians. Pre-Christian African religions are still defined in terms of "fetishes" or witchcraft and, as such, are not viewed as fit subject matter for serious theological consideration. Little or no thought is given to attempting to discern how, for example, insights from these early religious practices might inform Christian doctrines concerning Christology or the Holy Spirit. Even dialogue about such matters engenders fears of syncretism in ways never applied to American or European graftings into Christian religious customs (such as the *Thanksgiving* holiday or the ancient Roman return of spring festival that has become *Easter*).

There are four aspects of congregational ministry that are critical to the formation of an Africentric Christian witness: (1) *Theology* (further analysis of Africentrism's implications for God-talk is needed); (2) *Worship* (liturgy and music); (3) *Education and Nurture*; and (4) *Community Outreach or Public Ministry*. It is beyond the scope of this chapter to attempt an in-depth elucidation of all the four factors involved in creating an Africentric ministry. I will mention only one area by way of example: the differences between Africentric and Eurocentric approaches to the use of music in the ***worship*** life of the congregation.

Even though I am not a musician, as a former pastor, I cannot emphasize enough the importance of music as an expression of that which values African heritage. The difference between African-centered and European-centered worship can be seen in the differences that hymns common to both Black and White churches are sung. "Amazing Grace" will typically be sung quite differently in a Black Methodist or Presbyterian congregation as compared to White congregations of the same denominational traditions.

Persons who are in the thirty-something age range or younger generally have much less interest in listening to Bach, Handel, or Mozart in worship than do their parents. The younger potential church-goers have been reared on rap music, music television videos, and Ninetendo. This Hip-Hop generation, born after the death of Martin Luther King, Jr. (post 1968), and many of their parents are frankly not interested in the musical tastes of their grandparent's generation. Their music, and other forms of artistic expression (baggy clothing, exotic hair styles, etc.) reflect much of this sense of frustration, anger, and loss of hope. Entertainers and/or groups like the late TuPac Shakur, Biggie Smalls, Jams Master-J, Eminem, Snoop Doggy-Dog, and Common, Jay-Z, Beyonce, Ja-Rul, Trina and other artists have struck a sensitive cord with many American youth. Much (though by no means all) of this musical genre embodies themes born of rootlessness and hopelessness: violence, machoism, vulgar language, sexual exploitation of females, materialism, and the rhetoric of a warped racial nationalism. Many school youngsters today have embraced what Cornel West has called "nihilistic" behaviors.[26] This is why some youth drive around in cars shooting at other people and have no aspirations for a future. Many do not expect to live past age 16 or 20.

Since I am Presbyterian, I will address the particular situation within my own denomination by way of example. Sadly, many Black Presbyterians (like many United Methodists, Southern Baptists, Episcopalians, Lutherans as well as many National Baptists and African Methodist Episcopal and African Methodist

Episcopal Zion members) have equated classical European liturgy and music with authentic Presbyterian (i.e. *Christian*) worship. Many churches have had difficulty in making the shift to different and more contemporary orders of service and music. Endless worship committee meetings and Session meetings (among Black Presbyterians) deal with the propriety of contemporary "Gospel" (Be Be and Ce Ce Winans or Richard Smallwood) as suitable music styles as opposed to the classical music of American religious culture, the Spiritual. Little thought is given to the utilization of the only pure and indigenous forms of "classical" music native to United States culture, aside from Native American music: the African American spiritual or more recently, jazz, or their contemporary manifestation, rap. The use of the drum, so important in African cultures, is still considered iconoclastic. In this way, worship in Presbyterian and other so-called mainline denominations remains so intricately bound up with the cultural norms of European culture that Christian faith is made inseparable from European aesthetics and values. H. Richard Niebuhr's fifty-year old analysis of Christological assertions[27] about "Christ and Culture" is still true: the God who is worshipped in most churches today is definitely *not* one who transforms culture, but who has been transformed by European culture. The more devastating reality is that, in most cases, the transformation has been so thorough that its mutation of the Gospel into a Euro-cultural aesthetic goes unnoticed as adherents truly perceive themselves to be serving the *One True God*, all the while embracing values and behaviors that, in many ways, reflect a cultural rather than theological orientation.

By contrast, congregations that have been able to embrace an Africentric presentation of the Gospel of Jesus Christ that truly affirms and clarifies central theological tenets of the Christian faith have experienced phenomenal results in membership growth and community ministry, regardless of denominational affiliation. Examples of some Africentric churches that have successfully so to good effect are Baltimore, Maryland's Bethel African Methodist Episcopal Church that views its African heritage as a key theological element of its overall public outreach ministries; Cleveland, Ohio's Mt. Olivet Institutional Baptist Church that has a medical clinic attached to the church; New York City's Abyssinian Baptist Church in Harlem emphasizing community redevelopment, Allen Methodist Episcopal Church of Queens featuring a variety of public ministries from education to medical assistance, and Concord Baptist Church of Brooklyn, which established an endowment fund that sponsors various community outreach programs. Other models of Africentric inspired approaches include the Elmwood Presbyterian Church (East Orange, NJ) that has strong community outreach programs; First African Methodist Episcopal Church (Los Angeles, CA), well known for its public ministries;   First African Presbyterian Church (Lithonia, GA), a fast-growth congregation that has made its African heritage central to its ministries; Hartford Baptist Church (Detroit, MI) has embraced community development as a core facet of its ministry; and New Life Presbyterian Church (Atlanta, GA) with its emphasis on public ministries of service.

In Pittsburgh, Pennsylvania, the Grace Memorial Presbyterian Church has developed a nationally recognized model of educational support for public school children; Macedonia Baptist Church has established its Family and Cultural Enrichment (FACE) with a range of family ministries from HIV-Aids support to family reunification social services; Mt. Ararat Baptist Church has a Tithe Ministry that awards grants totaling ten-percent of the congregation's budget various community organizations. Also, St. Paul Baptist Church (Brooklyn, NY) has focused on strengthening African American men as a central element in its overall ministry and Chicago's Trinity United Church of Christ has a host of public ministries rooted in the congregation's motto "Unashamedly Black and Unapologetically Christian." These are just a few of the growing list of congregations that have found an Africentric perspective on ministry to be a significant enhancement for their witness to the love and liberation of Jesus Christ that embraces cultural, social, and spiritual aspects of life in their ministries.

Conclusion

In summary, European based aesthetic norms in ministry will not suffice among the disillusioned and disaffected masses in urban centers where most African American churches are located. The circumstances giving rise to the cultural, economic, social, and political marginalization from which these communities suffer are so profoundly associated with Euro-cultural values, that solutions associated with these same values typically inspire more doubt than trust among the disenfranchised. On the other hand, congregations that are able to embrace an Africentric presentation of the love and justice that is the Gospel of Jesus Christ are able to experience significant ministries of healing, helping, and growth in community ministry, regardless of denominational or ethnic affiliation.

The Africentric approach to Christianity can enable churches in African American communities to more effectively relate to the full range of economic, ideological, and ethnic diversity in American culture than has previously confronted such congregations. In so doing, local churches will be better prepared to help society, to confront the difficult social, economic, and spiritual challenges of this century. The words of the Rev. Charles Tinley (a Philadelphia cleric) inspire us onward:

> *Trials dark on every hand,*
> *And we cannot understand,*
> *All the ways that God would lead us to that Blessed*
> *Promised Land.*
> *But God guides us with God's eye,*
> *And we'll follow till we die;*
> *For we'll understand it better by and by.*
>
> *By and by, when the morning comes,*
> *When all the saints of God are gathered home,*

> *We will tell the story how we've overcome;*
> *For we'll understand it better by and by.[28]*

This is not to suggest, of course, a "pie-in-the-sky" religious escapism. In the words of James Cone, "the eschatological hope found in black faith... refuses to allow oppressors to define (our realities)."[29] This is the affirmation of faith that ultimately, God's reign will be manifest here on earth (in our society) as it is in heaven and all of God's children, regardless of gender, ethnicity, class, or other superficial hindrance, will be able to proclaim God's victory over evil in our time with the well known acclamation:

> Free at last, free at last!
> Thank God Almighty,
> We're free at last!

Endnotes

1. This chapter is based upon a paper entitled *Africentrism and Mainline Denominations* that I originally delivered Sept. 23, 1994 to the Vanderbilt University Divinity School conference on "Church and Voluntary Organizations."

2. Ella Harding, quoted from a conversation with her son, Rev. Dr. Edward P. Harding, Jr., July 1994.

3. E. Franklin Frazier, *Black Church in America* (New York: Schocken Book, 1964).

4. Gayraud Wilmore, *Black Religion and Black Radicalism* (Maryknoll, NY: Orbis, 1973), 228-29.

5. In this chapter, Afrocentrism and Africentrism are used interchangeably. Since the early 1990s, *Africentricity* increasingly has replaced *Afrocentricity* as the preferred spelling of the word that refers to the philosophical posture that places Africa at the center of its approach to reality. This newer spelling seeks to more clearly identify the concept in a manner that (a) more consciously focuses on the need to assist persons of African descent to be mentally and spiritually liberated from cultural, social, political, and philosophical colonization; and (b) is more obviously associated with the continent of Africa. In this book, the term Africentricity is used predominantly. While in certain instances, various authors may utilize the older spelling in deference to historical context (as I occasionally do in this chapter), except where otherwise noted, the two spellings ordinarily refer to the same philosophical approach.

6. Molefi Kete Asante, *Afrocentricity* (Trenton, NJ: Third World Press, 1988).

7. Molefi Kete Asante, *The Afrocentric Idea* (Philadelphia, PA: Temple University Press, 1987), 3.

8. Asante, *Afrocentricity*, 47-52.

9. Cain H. Felder "Afrocentrism, the Bible, and the Politics of Difference" *Princeton Seminary Bulletin* 15 (1994): 132-138.

10. These authors, writing from a variety of different perspectives, have many works

demonstrating their orientation in the historical approach to culture. Some representative examples include Maya Angelou, *I Know Why the Caged Bird Sings* (New York: Random House, 1970); Haki R. Madhubuti, *Black Men: Obsolete, Single, Dangerous?* (Chicago, IL: Third World Press, 1991); Toni Morrison, *Song of Solomon* New York: Alfred A. Knopf, 1977), Carter G. Woodson, *Mis-Education of the Negro* (Trenton, NJ: Africa World Press, 1993; originally published 1933); and Jeremiah Wright in Jini Kilgore Ross (ed.), *What Makes You So Strong? Sermons of Joy and Strength from Jeremiah A. Wright, Jr.* (Valley Forge, PA: Judson Press, 1994).

11.   See Maulana Karenga, *Kwanzaa: A Celebration of Family, Community and Culture* (Los Angeles, CA: University of Sankore Press, 1998) and Ivan Van Sertima, *They Came Before Columbus* (New York: Random House, 1976).

12.   For further examination of positions reflected here, see Albert B. Cleage, Jr., *The Black Messiah* (New York: Sheed and Ward Press, 1968); also, see Mattias Gardell, *In the Name of Elijah Muhammad: Louis Farrakhan and the Nation of Islam* (Durham, NC: Duke University Press, 1996) and Francis Cress Welsing, *The Isis Papers* (1991).

13.   Ibid., 137.

14.   Ibid., 132.

15.   Marimba Ani, *Yurugu* (Trenton, NJ: New Africa Press, 1994), 110.

16.   In today's information age culture, western society's veneration of information processing technology (scientism) typically implies that the technology itself is almost never deemed to be wrong. Computer malfunctions or "glitches" are usually attributed to human error and "down time" is considered inevitable, usually with no indictment of the technology. Relatively little serious theological analysis has been devoted to the information technology cult by Christian writers. Many are devotees of the new idol themselves and see no reason to question this latest example of the "mainline" religious establishment's continuing practice of the uncritical blessing (worship) of the idols of scientism in western culture. In this instance, the phenomenon of *scientism worship* takes the form of adoring information technology without addressing the host of related implications (for example, the importance of material values over other considerations), such as the wealth required to have access and pay homage to the new idol. All of this is done in the name of "progress."

17.   Ibid., 152.

18.   Gayraud Wilmore, *Black and Presbyterian* (Philadelphia: Geneva, 1973), 60.

19.   Ibid., 60-65.

20.   Figures for the Episcopal, Lutheran, United Methodist, and Roman Catholic churches were supplied by their respective ecclesiastical offices in Pittsburgh. Numbers on the National Baptist, Inc., National Baptist, Unincorporated, Progressive, African Methodist Episcopal, African Methodist Episcopal Zion, and Church of God in Christ churches are from C. Eric Lincoln and Lawrence Mamiya's, *The Black Church in the African American Experience* (Durham, NC: Duke University Press, 1990).

21.   Delores Williams, *Sisters in the Wilderness* (Maryknoll, NY: Orbis, 1993), 204.

22.   Presbyterians for Prayer, Study, and Action, *Is This New Wine?* (Louisville, Ky: Presbyterian Church (USA), 1993), 2.

23.   Wilmore, *Black and Presbyterian,* 35.

24.   Ibid., 55.

25.   This is a criticism that has been made concerning Molefi Asante by Victor Anderson in his book, *Beyond Ontological Blackness: An Essay on African-American Religious and Cultural Criticism* (Continuum, 1999). Also, for a very comprehensive discussion of this

issue, see J. Deotis Roberts, *Africentric Christianity*, (Valley Forge, PA: Judson Press, 2000).
26.   Cornel West, *Race Matters* (Boston, Ma: Beacon Press, 1993), 9-20.
27.   Richard H. Niebuhr, *Christ and Culture* (London: Faber & Faber, 1952).
28.   Quoted in Delores Carpenter and Nolan E. Williams, Jr. (eds), *African American Heritage Hymnal* (Chicago, IL: GIA Publications, 2001), 418.
29.   James H. Cone, *For My People* (Maryknoll, NY: Orbis, 1984), 207.

CHAPTER FOUR

Africentric Christianity and Urban Ministry[1]

J. Deotis Roberts

It was during my professorship at Eastern Baptist Theological Seminary in Philadelphia (1984-1998) that my interest in Africentrism developed. The presence and influence of Temple University Professor Molefi Kete Asante made my participation in the dialogue on African American history and culture compelling because in Philadelphia, discussion of Africentrism had made its impact felt mainly in educational and religious institutions. As one who for years had written and contributed to Black church studies and Black theology discussions and as one who was involved in seminary education and church ministry, I was challenged to respond to the ferment around Africentrism by leaders on campus and in churches in Philadelphia and the vicinity. To meet this challenge, I held conversations with Professor Asante, read behind him and engaged in two public discussions with him. I wanted first to understand the movement and to have dialogue on the subject.

My purpose was to see what I could affirm from Africentrism as a cultural foundation for theological reflection and the practice of ministry. There was a certain urgency that this task be attempted by a theologian interested in ministry. Asante is friendly to the church and its ministry. However, he is a specialist on language usage. His interest is mainly cultural and historical. It became my task to evaluate the Africentric proposal from a confessional stance. The volume I published titled *Africentric Christianity* was a response to this challenge in both church and academy.

Those who have read this book will observe my indebtedness to this cultural movement, but will also view the fact that my use of the Africentric outlook is modified by my commitment to the claims of the Christian faith. Culture may be an instrument to convey a redemptive witness, but the means is not the message. My comparative reflections on Kwanzaa and Christmas illustrate the distinction I make between culture and revelation or redemption. Thus what I have appropriated from the Africentric movement amounts to a "perspective," which is useful for theological reflection and the practice of ministry. For our purpose here we have in view "urban ministry."

Since Africentrism was being discussed in educational programs in urban school systems and being expressed in cultural programs nationwide, providing a theological evaluation of the movement appeared to be a task that I could not ignore. If Africentrism had made an impact on public education and cultural programs, the ministers and their congregations needed to take notice. They needed to evaluate this concept that made such great claims upon Black culture and history. In this context, I will attempt to define Africentrism and describe its positive aspects that may be useful for a more effective witness in the African American church as well as in urban communities that are becoming more culturally diverse and more religiously plural.

The focus of this study is on ministry in a comprehensive sense, to the whole person and to the entire Black community. Various aspects of ministry will be discussed. Both priestly and prophetic dimensions of ministry will come under our purview. Our final concern will be how we are able to reach out to the unsaved in our midst and how we take our place in a situation that is racially and ethnically diverse and committed to religious faiths other than our own.

I. The Meaning and Theological Evaluation of Africentrism

My approach to a definition of Africentrism is descriptive and begins with the understanding that Africentrism is both a means of understanding self and others and a mission for liberation and reconciliation of African Americans.[2] The meaning of this outlook has several insights in view. First, it makes a comprehensive claim for Africa as a continent, which includes all of Africa north and south of the Sahara Desert. Whereas Western scholars have embraced Egypt, they have taken Egypt out of Africa and claimed it as a part of European history and culture. Africentrism has reclaimed Egypt and surrounding territories as a part of classical Africa.

Second, Africentrists have suggested a different way of thinking about Africa. Africa becomes subject rather than object. We want to know all we can about the past and present culture of peoples on that vast continent. We want to claim that history and culture as the background to our peoplehood. "Who we are is who we were" is a summary statement of this Africentric perspective. This different orientation changes the way we think and interpret our experience. Our thinking is more holistic and rational. Reasons of the heart and head are blended. "Both-and" ways of thinking question the Aristotelian "either-or" logic.

Third, Africentrism deepens the roots of the African American heritage. It includes our history during slavery and afterwards, but it affirms that we had a history and culture before slavery or colonialism. Critics of the Africentric movement want to dismiss it as a "myth" that makes us "feel good." Calling upon what they believe to be sound scholarship, they would erase the entire movement as an illusion. Without weighing the evidence, they consider all Africentrists as racist in reverse and as bigots who want to replace Western white racism with a Black expression of racism. They overlook the claim to the hegemony of knowledge and culture of Western thinkers and leaders while dismissing any reality or positive benefits associated with Africentrism.

Fortunately, there are able Black and African scholars who are capable of lifting up the positive aspects of Africentrism without accepting some of the bogus claims of extreme views that have no solid foundation. All human thought is limited and is often bent in the direction of its exponent. What I suggest here is an Africentric perspective that is subject to analysis and careful evaluation. I seek to examine Africentrism as a minister-theologian who has been grasped by a lifetime of encounter, both in thought and life, with the Christian faith. I do not claim a dogmatic or infallible understanding of either Africentrism or the Christian faith. I approach this subject matter with a "believing trust." My constant prayer is, "Lord, I believe, help Thou my unbelief."

In evaluating Africentrism theologically and ethically, those of us who have participated in the Black consciousness/power movement bring considerable hindsight to this discourse. The collective memory of African Americans in both slavery and "freedom" has been carefully recalled and has undergone rigorous scholarly examination. This work started with the work of a few courageous ministers and religious scholars. Now there are many mature leaders and thinkers, women and men, who aid in the search for meaning and the application of the insights of Africentrism to our common life. Our religious life and the mission of Black churches have been enriched and empowered by insights from the Africentric movement. Africentrism is in continuity with all that we know about our past in this country. It has expanded our sense of history into the Africa of antiquity and, at the same time, it addresses the needs and concerns we have for the present. In a previous study, I made this statement, which deserves being repeated here: "Due to ... the negative attitude toward Africa as the Dark Continent, without culture or history, Black and African scholars must bring this field of knowledge up to date."[3]

As a religious thinker, I have researched Western thought for two published volumes.[4] My interest in Africa was from a Eurocentric outlook. As a Black theologian, I am now challenged to take a second look from an Africentric perspective. I no longer allow Euro-American scholars to be my guide. I prefer to let my conclusions flow from the evidence.

Culture is the context in which individuals and groups are socialized. Culture is a vehicle that carries forward history and heritage. It helps to shape our life view and our worldview. It is our *Lebenswelt,* our living world. The significance of culture is intergenerational, sustaining values that parents and grandparents share with each new generation. All people, including African Americans, have a culture.

The World Council of Churches has set the standard in Christian ecumenical circles for the recognition of the cultural contexts of the Christian faith, globally. In recent years I have participated in the project titled "Many Cultures." I recall a visit that several Black theologians and pastors made to Bossey (Switzerland). We fellowshipped and shared Black theology, music and preaching with representative colleagues from the two-thirds world. We all grew intellectually and spiritually in this cross-cultural week of dialogue. We went to Bossey to share our faith, but what we received was more abundant. The cultural context of faith was most revealing of the power of culture as a bridge over which faith must travel to convey meaning, even the experience of redemption. Richard Niebuhr's *Christ and Culture* has much to offer as a perspective on the point we are attempting to make. He offers five typologies on the relation between Christ and culture.[5] The "conversionist" type is most appropriate for our view. This position is affirmative and hopeful toward culture. It holds that Christ is the transformer of culture. Christianity is at its most powerful mode of explanation when faith stands above and over against culture as a transcendent form of judgment. Such judgment is characteristic of the social justice prophets of the Old Testament and the message of Jesus, especially in the Sermon on the Mount.

Theologically, we are seeking a life view and a worldview in which to affirm our faith in Christ and our witness in the Christian community, the church. How may we as a people affirm our African heritage and at the same time be authentic followers of Jesus Christ as we witness and serve in the world?

The Africentric celebration of Kwanzaa and the Christocentric event of Christmas are ideal for illustrating the relationship and the tension between culture and faith in Christ. There is a fundamental difference between culture and redemption. Africentrism is a manifestation of culture while the message of Christmas is salvific: it has to do with the Word made flesh, the advent of the Savior. *Kwanzaa* is Africentric: an important cultural celebration. Christmas is Christocentric. Christmas is not authentic if Christ is not the center of our observation of an event in which God is with us in Christ.

There are values in Kwanzaa that may be added to Christmas in a cultural sense. Kwanzaa, according to Maulana Ron Karenga, a political activist and cultural anthropologist, has seven principles of meaning. It spans the last week of December each year.

Kwanzaa means "first" in Swahili. Reference is to the first fruits of the year. The first harvest has been a time of celebration for Africans since the beginnings of agriculture. The seven principles of *Nguzo Saba* are common among African peoples. Swahili is also a common language. The seven principles are: 1) *Umoja*-unity; 2) *Kujichagulia* –self-determination; 3) *Ujima*—collective work and responsibility; 4) *Ujamaa*— economics; 5) *Nia* —purpose; 6) *Kuumba—creativity;* and 7) *Imani*—faith. The purpose of the event is to build family, community, and culture. It is obvious that many of the principles of Kwanzaa are compatible with the best principles and values of ethics in other cultures, i.e., Euro-American and Asian (Confucian).

I provide a comparative study of Kwanzaa and Christmas in my book *Africentric Christianity.*[6] The summary statement I make there is useful here: "Two conclusions may be drawn from examining Christmas and Kwanzaa. First, the values, ideals and celebration of Kwanzaa do not conflict with the Christian faith, and second, the celebration of Kwanzaa may be useful in ministry to African Americans."[7] As such, we may celebrate Kwanzaa *and* Christmas rather than Kwanzaa *or* Christmas.

II. Africentrism, the Prophetic Witness of the Church, and Issues of Family Life, Education, Economics, and Politics[8]

In the Christian theological tradition, much is said about the "communion of saints." Many do not know that traditional African religion holds a belief similar to this Christian affirmation. This belief is inherent in the intergenerational reverence for ancestors. This is a belief that is held throughout the continent. Therefore, it is a foundational belief directly related to the family system at the heart of African religion.

Family Life. The Swahili word *ujamaa,* "familyhood," is central to an understanding of solidarity in African societies. Julius Nyerere of Tanzania made the concept famous by shaping it into a form of socialism. He asserted that the destiny of humans is drawn from the traditional African view of society as an extension of the basic family unit. Leopold Senghor of Senegal formed a similar ideology from Negritude and developed it into a national program. Thus "family" is central to an understanding of group identity and solidarity in Africa.

The concept of unity, social solidarity, expressed by the Swahili word *harambee*, is essential for the African view of society. The ideal is expressed as a virtue in its own right. It is not just a response to colonialism. Likewise, group loyalty is essential to a sense of peoplehood among African Americans. It may become a matter of survival under harsh oppression. This unity will be short-lived, however, unless it is perceived as an intrinsic good. A positive way of grounding this ideal is to see it as part of a continuous experience of Blacks in Africa and the New World. It is to be viewed in the context of the family or kinship network at the center of African and African American culture. Black churches have a golden opportunity to express unity in the Black community. This is especially true if the Black church understands its own nature and purpose in light of a unity in its own life among its members.

This sense of familyhood needs to be cultivated both in the church and in the home. In this sense, the church becomes an extended family and the family becomes a "domestic church" if *ujamaa* or "familyhood" is representative of communalism. We need to add *harambee* or "unity" as of equal significance for our understanding of a sense of peoplehood. This notion of unity is represented by the image of the "body of Christ" (I Cor. 12:12). St. Paul uses this in reference to the church. But it could also refer to the image of a family. The apostle Paul uses the Greek term *soma* as he views the church as a living entity, over against *sarx*, which is "the body of death." According to this apostle, the body is one, but it has many members or parts. There is interdependence among the members of the body; it is a unity-in-diversity. Thus the African proverb, "Because I am, we are" can be embraced out of a biblical perspective. In a wholesome family, everyone is precious, from the youngest to the oldest, in our collective memory there is, as the Africans put it, a vital relationship "between the living and the living dead." These views have important insights for self-esteem and a concern for the well being of all the children of God who bear the divine image.[9]

Education. We are now 50 years beyond the 1954 *Brown* decision of the U.S. Supreme Court which overturned the 1896 "separate but equal" provision of the *Plessy v. Ferguson* doctrine which gave legal sanction to racial segregation. The *Brown* decision of impacted education, but it went far beyond establishing a legal basis for integrating schools. It touched base in a cluster of societal institutions (racial, ethnic and class). That is to say, it influenced changes in areas of American life beyond public school administrative and instructional systems.[10] The *Brown* decision led to an outlook, especially among Black leadership, of an "integrated" society. However, they were not prepared for the white "backlash" that was to be manifest during the 1960's in the Civil Rights struggle. This tension was dramatized during the "nonviolent" phase of the freedom movement under the leadership of Martin Luther King, Jr.

The Black consciousness/power movement was to put a damper on the desire to integrate the schools. The economic conditions of the Black masses and the location of housing for the poor led to what might be called "busing in reverse." Black children were now bused from their familiar environment to one that was often hostile. We faced a sociological "nightmare" in urban America. Even on the college, university, and seminary campuses, Blacks often found an unwelcome acceptance. With the new mood of the 1970's, which often was filled with a sense of separatism, Blacks clustered among themselves. With a sense of Black pride, they no longer were willing to accept a status of inferiority. The Black power movement was highly political and psychological.

The Africentric movement is mainly cultural. Nevertheless, it is not antithetical to what has gone before. Rather it pushes the "stride toward freedom" forward. Once again, it can be exclusive or inclusive. It can be pro-African American and yet relate to persons in other cultural settings or it can be separatist and be negative to all other cultures. It should be obvious by now that I affirm an inclusive stance. However, it should be clear that I hold for the view that Black culture has its own integrity and has a noble heritage with African roots. Africentrism has gone, historically, beyond Halley's *Roots*. All of Africa, beginning in antiquity (i. e., 10,000 years BC to the present) is now the dimension of the history of the Africentric claim. Thus we take seriously the experience of the period of slavery; we insist that we were "somebody" before we were enslaved. This Africentric perspective has significant potential for the education of the young as well as the re-education of African American adults.

A very important conference on Africentrism was held in Atlanta in 1990. Many scholars in education and other fields were speakers and participants.[11] Upon an examination of the proceedings of this first national conference, I found no religious scholar in a leadership position. This reflects a usual cultural blind spot among Black intellectuals. To do justice to the question of education, we need persons involved who have one foot in the academy and one foot in the church. Religion is such an important factor in African and African American life that education in church and academy needs to be studied together.

This is not something I have observed at a distance. I was a professor of theology at Howard University for 22 years. I was also invited by some church-affiliated secular scholars to be a participant at important conferences on family life and education. Sometimes I was uninvited by committee members who rejected what they considered the "mysticism" of any minister-scholar, especially a theologian.

Professor Janice Hale is an exception and there must be others also. Persons educated in both religion and education who contribute to this dialogue are invaluable. Hale has a degree in religion, is a minister's daughter and a committed Christian, but she also is a full-time professor in education at Wayne State University and has published and provided leadership in both academic and church circles. She studied with Professor Asa G. Hilliard at Georgia State, who has done so much to sensitize public school teachers nationwide to bring an Africentric focus to education. Hale's Ph.D. degree was earned under Hilliard's supervision. However, she has used her knowledge and experience to serve effectively in the field of childhood education. She is also active in the Hartford Avenue Baptist Church in Detroit, where she brought an Africentric perspective to education. Her special focus in the church has been to improve instruction in the Sunday school.

Economics. The economic situation is another area where the Africentric perspective may be useful for survival by opposing the negative effects of racism upon the plight of African Americans. The impact of economics reaches into home life, the excessive imprisonment of Blacks (women as well as men), education, employment and general well being.

The fourth principle of Kwanzaa has reference to economics *(ujamaa)*. This principle focuses on cooperative economics. In a society driven by the profit motive and the vice of greed, it is important to lift up this virtue among African Americans. Other Kwanzaa principles would reinforce the bid for economic uplift. Among these principles are unity, or *umoja; ujima,* or collective works and responsibility; and *imani,* or religious faith. This places economic progress solidly within the Africentric perspective.

It is instructive to look at the last five years of the nonviolent ministry of Dr. Martin Luther King King, Jr. We will observe that his struggle to overcome racist oppression led to his plans for a Poverty March on Washington. He was martyred as he took up the cause of garbage workers on strike in Memphis There is an affinity between freedom and the procurement of means to earn a decent living for oneself and one's family.

African American churches should not follow the "God and prosperity" movement among televangelists. They should identify with the plight of the needy in our midst. A mentee of mine, the Rev. Dr. Albert Avant, now deceased, left a document with us that is valuable. His Ph.D. dissertation on the social ethics of the Progressive National Convention is full of vital information. According to Avant, the founders of this convention adopted as a motto: "A mission to the least, the lost and the left out." Like many human efforts with a noble purpose, we are told that this convention became a comfort zone for the Black middle class. We are here reminded of the summons that our Savior left with the church and its disciples, as follows:

> "The Spirit of the Lord is upon me, because he has anointed me to bring good news to the poor. He has sent me to proclaim release to the captives and recovery of sight to the blind, to let the oppressed go free, to proclaim the year of the Lord's favor." (Luke 3:18-19,RSV)

Politics. In a democracy every adult citizen is entitled to participate in the affairs of state. I recall the suffering and sacrifice Black people endured to gain this privilege denied them due to the stranglehold of racism. For years, our cry was, "Give us the ballot!" It is painful to observe now that many African Americans do not vote.

I was in South Africa in the late 80's before Mandela was released and the new government came to power. My travels in that country were extensive However, I lived with a family for one month in Soweto. There was an obsession among Africans to gain the freedom to vote. We know that they voted in great numbers and that the result was a bloodless revolution in that racist society. Blacks in this country have experienced the same struggle for political freedom. It has been a long time since we have had as much at stake as we have now. It is critical that Blacks in this country weigh all the evidence, consider the issues, make our best judgments. But, by all means, we must vote!!!

Black churches collect a lot of money. If we could keep some of that money in our neighborhoods and take on some collective programs, we could save a lot of youth in our communities and reduce their involvement in the alarming numbers of incarceration and probation statistics. Africentric principles like collective responsibility, if put into practice, would aid us as a people in many ways not only in keeping our youth from being warehoused in prisons, but the Africentric outlook would also direct us to pool and use our wealth to clean up our neighborhoods. Frequently, we are told that in the Jewish community, money is circulated several times before it goes outside the community. By contrast, often Black church money is deposited in banks that discriminate against our members who seek a loan to purchase a house. If we used the Africentric principle of "collective responsibility," we could change this situation to the benefit of our people.

I have often had conversation with leading pastors in major cities. Some of these leaders were once my students and, thus, the conversations have been frank. While often there is a plea for advice, nevertheless, I have been aided more than they by these "echoes from the field." I will share one example. A pastor was gravely concerned about conditions in the neighborhood where his church building was located. He could address the problems in that location, or he could attempt to leave the area and relocate elsewhere. He saw his ministry as being fulfilled where the challenge was greatest. Yet, he would not be able to do what needed to be done by using the resources of his own congregation alone. He asserted that the resources were available to do what was needed if several churches, regardless of denomination, would pool their resources and make a collective witness in the area. But he shocked me by saying that the major problem to be overcome was "the big egos of the pastors." He went on to explain that if we could forget about our status as individual leaders, we would be able to turn this situation around.

III. Africentrism in Diversity

When I first entered the discussion on the Black experience as a theologian, racial considerations in the United States were mainly thought of in terms of Black and white issues. Native Americans, once referred to as American Indians, were here before the colonists arrived, but they had been isolated. They were located on their reservations— out of sight and out of mind. Africans, however, had been near to whites, in the fields and in the master's house. After emancipation, Blacks were still nearby, and something had to be done to establish a proper relation. The consequence was a pattern of discrimination based upon race.

Now the situation is changing. In our nation's ranks are people from different backgrounds and from all over the world. People are seeking permanent citizenship from the global community. Most are coming from the non-Western world. Our neighbors are from Africa, the Caribbean, Asia and Latin America, as well as the islands of the seas. All the races, religions and cultures of the human family are in our urban neighborhood. All these people seek rights and the benefits of our wealthy nation. Even Native Americans are entering into the American mainstream. Spanish-speaking people are replacing Blacks as the largest minority in the country. The crisis in Haiti continues to send thousands of Black people to these shores seeking asylum. What do we do now? The dream of Dr. Martin Luther King, Jr., "Black and whites together," no longer can be the solution to our reality in today's United States.

Some offer "diversity" as the proper response. It is interesting that this concept is offered as a way to overcome racism. I believe Professor Enoch Oglesby to be correct when he describes racism as a mountain in his disturbing account in *O Lord, Move This Mountain*.[2] Nathan Glazer's *We Are All Multiculturalists Now* is a book that we need to read, at least to understand the challenge of diversity in education as well as in other areas of social life.

Diversity can be attractive, but for African Americans it can also be a trap. African Americans must be cautious about the recent emphasis upon diversity, which is offered in place of assimilation, which failed to take place. However, in view of significant demographic changes in society, we must come to terms with the realities that our nation's increased racial ethnic diversity presents to us. Africentrism, if properly understood, can be a useful perspective in this regard. It would imply that we may take our own heritage seriously and yet relate to and respect the culture of others. We would then seek peace and reconciliation amongst equals. It is wholesome to respect the equality and humanity of all of God's children. We should embrace love, justice, and the humane use of power as prime values. In fact, the claims of the Christian faith require that we do so.

As Black people we are not free, however, to ignore our past and present experiences of oppression due to racism. In a real sense, "we are who we were." If we do not accept our past, we lack a sense of direction. Africentrism reminds us that we belong to a *noble* race—not a *superior* race. We take our place among all peoples as equal partners.

It would be wonderful if all whites, Jews, Moslems, Native Americans, Asians, Latinos, and all Africans and African Americans could erase our histories of conflict and enmity and begin a future without any knowledge of the past distrust. Unfortunately such an approach is not realistic. We need to know our past, as painful as it may be. This is not to increase our hatred of others, but to know ourselves and those with whom we need to be reconciled. Cultural experiences are intergenerational. The controversy over the movie, "The Passion of Christ," is so intense due to the fact that its producer, Mel Gibson, apparently overlooked the 2000-year history in which many Christians hated and mistreated Jews, derisively referring to them as "God-killers." In the name of Christianity, people have hated and exterminated Jews supposedly for the cause "of Christ." One only needs to remember Hitler, Nazism and the German Christians. The same evangelical Christians who are so enthusiastic concerning "The Passion" have supported the mistreatment of the Palestinians in the Middle East as well. Black Christians who are biblical literalists need to read their Bibles with the history of Black suffering clearly in view.

As one who has had ministry experiences in the church and on campuses, I have observed what racism has done to both Blacks and whites. However, idyllic our life together is intended to be, one observes that each racial or cultural group brings with it the accumulated experiences of its past. In the interracial or cross-cultural community, the ghosts of the past will reappear, especially in a time of crisis when issues are joined. Dr. King referred to this as "unconscious racism."

By way of illustration, I will refer to a personal experience. As a theologian in a predominantly white seminary with a mixed body of students, domestic and foreign, I observed a serious tension in our peaceful community when the O. J. Simpson decision was announced. We were wearing a mask to cover up our true feelings about each other. Henceforth, we had to find healing for the hurts we brought with us, as we attempted to forge a Christian community. Our foreign students, for the first time, experienced the disease of racism that afflicts American society. The exposure of our open wounds made true healing possible. We found that our wounds were so severe that salves were inadequate. Surgery was required. We had to be honest with each other and for the first time embrace what Dietrich Bonhoeffer described so aptly in his *Cost of Discipleship* as "costly grace." As would-be Christians, we had been thriving on "cheap grace." But now we were challenged to become bearers of the cross of Christ.

When we come face to face with our racial struggles, we get to know where we are in our own hearts and attitudes. We as African Americans find our self-understanding. There is also the dawning of our people-consciousness. Our collective memory comes into our awareness.

Some Blacks have been preprogrammed to reject their African/African American heritage and see only through Euro-American lenses. Some will turn against brothers and sisters. They are unaware that their attitude toward others who look like them reveals a deep-seated hatred of self and lack of self-esteem. These often become like the proverbial "crabs-in-the-basket" (pulling one another down) and seek to be jealous of those who succeed. In a word, instead of turning to each other, we often turn against each other.

This may be manifested as a mild defect among Black intellectuals. However, in the "hood" of urban America, it is experienced as a deadly fever. We observe the pain of parents when one Black male so easily ends the life of another schoolmate. It is the same manifestation of self-hatred and people-rejection, but on two distinct socio-economic levels. In the "hood," this tendency is upgraded to the use of drugs (sometimes a deadly dose) and the easy accessibility and use of lethal weapons.

Conclusion

In this study, we have attempted to present several matters for consideration. First, we have suggested a working definition of Africentrism. Along with the meaning of Africentrism, we stated why it is important for self-understanding and the affirmation of peoplehood for African Americans.

Second, we have presented theological and ethical evaluations of Africentrism. In this section of our discourse, we stated how this concept is being used in this study. We used the events of Christmas and Kwanzaa as a way of bringing Christianity and Africentrism together. What we have is an Africentric perspective.

Third, we sought to apply this Africentric perspective to the challenge of urban ministry. We then discussed some issues in this ministry from an Africentric point of view. Family life, education, economics and politics were discussed from the Africentric perspective. We assert that these concerns can be enhanced by this new outlook. Since Africentrism gathers up aspects of our total experience as a people with an African heritage (both in history and in culture), cultural enrichment, self-esteem and people empowerment are the results.

Finally, we discussed Africentrism in this time of racial and ethnic diversity. Africentrism is a cultural perspective that offers a positive acceptance of the African American cultural heritage. Multiculturalism emphasizes the values of the many cultures that make up the present United States society. Therefore, Africentrism can enter this diverse social situation and be a dignified and equal partner in this pluralistic society. The

Christian ethical position of this author requires both liberation and reconciliation among peoples of many cultural backgrounds in what Dr. King called the "beloved community." The ultimate aspiration of Christians is stated by Jesus in what we know as the Lord's Prayer: "Thy Kingdom come. Thy will be done in earth, as it is in heaven." (Matthew 6:10). Amen.

Endnotes

1. This chapter is taken from a lecture delivered April 2, 2004 at Pittsburgh Theological Seminary for the Metro-Urban Institute's Urban Intensive Weekend Conference on "Africentrism in a Plural Society." The reader will note that the spelling "Africentrism," which is usually rendered as "Afrocentrism," is used throughout this chapter. The usage was suggested by the editors of my book, *Africentric Christianity*, published by Judson Press in 2000. This spelling makes sense in view of the emphasis on "African" in the movement. "Afro" is used in a stronger focus upon more of a Euro-American encounter in the past. This movement claims an anchor in what is described as "Afriology." Africa takes on a more comprehensive meaning geographically, culturally and historically. My embrace of this spelling is not dogmatic. For me it is interchangeable with "Afrocentrism," used by most authors.

2. Much of my reflection upon religion and race has been during the rise of the language of Black consciousness and Black power. I see a continuity between what came forth during that period and what is being lifted up in Africentrism. Thus I will feel free to use "Black" as a point of reference. I will use "African American" also. Along the way, I will put this language in context.

3. J. Deotis Roberts, *Africentric Christianity* (Valley Forge, PA: Judson Press, 2000), 28.

4. See *my A Philosophical Introduction to Theology* (Philadelphia: Trinity Press, 1991) and *From Puritanism to Platonism in Seventeenth Century England* (The Hague: Martinus Nijoff, 1968). Cf. Cornel West, *Prophecy Deliverance* (Philadelphia: Westminster, 1982), 47-49.

5. Richard Niebuhr, *Christ and Culture* (New York: Harper, 1956), 41-45.

6. Roberts, *op. cit.,* p. 76. I apologize for the omission of *ujiamaa* (economics) in this printed volume, 74.

7. Ibid. The remainder of my book attempts to address personal awareness (i. e., self-esteem or "somebodiness"), communal consciousness (our humanity in community), and other valuable human insights. For further discussion, I suggest an examination of the book by Robert E. Hood, *Must God Remain Greek? Afro Cultures and God-Talk* (Minneapolis: Fortress, 1990), 1-10 and Part II.

8. My approach to the prophetic witness of the African American church is deliberate. See my book entitle *Africentric Christianity,* which gives considerable attention to the priestly aspects of ministry. In other writings I have majored in a concern for the prophetic aspect of Christian theology. The titles of two volumes released by me illustrate this interest. They are *A Black Political Theology* (Westminster, 1974) and *The Prophethood of Black Believers* (Westminster, 1994). Also, there are important chapters on the social outreach of Christians in my book, *Black Theology in Dialogue* (Philadelphia: Westminster, 1987). See especially chapters 6, 7, and 8, where I discuss love, justice and power.

9.   There are many important studies that contribute to this discussion upon "family" from an Africentric perspective. Cf. Jawanza Kunjufu, *Restoring the Village Values and Commitment: Solutions for the Black Family* (Chicago: African American Images, 1996); Wallace Charles Smith, *The Church in the Life of the Black Family* (Valley Forge, PA: Judson Press, 1985); K. Brynoll Lyon and Archie Smith, Jr., eds., *Tending the Flock: Congregations and Family Ministry* (Louisville, KY: WJKP, 1998); and Willie Wilson, *The African American Wedding Manual* (Washington, DC: House of Knowledge Publishing, 1994).

10.   For a detailed discussion on the *Brown* decision and its consequences, read Harold Cruse, *Plural But Equal* (New York: William Morrow, 1987), pp. 7-69.

11.   See Asa G. Hilliard III, L. Payton-Stewart and L. O. Williams, eds., *Infusion of African and African American Content in the School Curriculum* (Chicago: Third World Press, 1990).

12.   E. Hammond Oglesby, *O Lord, Move This Mountain: Racism and Christian Ethics* (St. Louis, MO: Chalice Press, 1998).

CHAPTER FIVE

Make It Plain, *Preacher*: Africentrism and Constructing African-American Sermonic Discourse[1]

Richard C. Chapple, Jr.

> Just as a Frenchman needs his Rowland, the Englishman his King Arthur, and the German his Seigfried, Black people also need to know about their heroes and heroines of antiquity. It is a source of strength and encouragement to know that Black people have made contributions to the advancement of world civilizations.
> -Ruben Speaks, the sermon "What Price Freedom"

> You know that it is not from hatred of other races that I seek to be a cultivator of this unique race . . .
> -Aime Cesaire, quoted in *The C.L.R. James Reader*

> We have far too much work to do for us to play the game of rearguard. Europe has done what she set out to do and on the whole she has done it well; let us stop blaming her, but let us say to her firmly that she should not make such a song and dance about it. We have no more to fear; so let us stop envying her.
> -Fanon, *The Wretched of the Earth*

Come on and say something *preacher*! Blackness, when snatched out of the hands of African-Americans and put in the rough hands of the Enlightenment and Romantic movements, forms its identity in a space that is socially limiting. This space represents a racialist social construction -a way to build a society based upon color - that serves to the advantage of whiteness. When the idea of blackness functions in this manner, it becomes the means to produce a way of thinking and acting that does violence to the way black people understand themselves and, thereby, works to limit the experiences of continental African peoples and the African Diaspora (meaning black people in parts of the world other than Africa).

The audience that Africentrism necessarily receives from people of African descent, then, especially among African-Americans, defends the formation of black identity within this white Western social matrix of cultural order and its destructive ideas about being black. Africentrism, as a result, assumes a significant voice that speaks against the disaffirming ideas that the Western world uses for structuring life according to race. As there exists in American society, in particular, a "blackness that whiteness has created," Africentrism uses a black voice to talk about a humanity that looks like a black person's black person.   Molefi Asante, Afrocentrism's architect, writes, "Afrocentrism resembles the black man, speaks to him, looks like him, and wants for him what he wants for himself."[2] Africentrism, then, whether a postmodern discourse, an intellectual movement,[3] a cultural proposal and project, a "dynamic intellectual theory, not a system of thought,"[4] or an ideology of heritage,[5] represents the effort to undo a racialized understanding of blackness that arises from *within* the black community and moves blackness toward a more authentic self-understanding.

"Alright" *preacher*, I'm listening! This chapter, set against the subtle yet harmful presence of Western influence, albeit white influence in the black pulpit, proposes a linkage between Africentrism and black American preaching. This juxtaposition does not adopt, however, the critical move found in Asante whereupon his project implicitly privileges a notion of ontological blackness,[6] accompanied by its modest pretension of polemical sophistry and theoretical slippage.[7] The proposal, here, for a common ground between Africentrism and preaching imbeds greater plasticity in its mode of protest and representation of blackness.

First, this chapter develops a broad understanding of preaching for the African-American pulpit that applies Africentric thinking and forms of cultural inquiry to the preaching task.   Preaching, as I describe it in this way, however, looks to articulate a more general understanding of a "black" sermon. Africentric preaching, despite this critical omission, however, refuses to be embarrassed by its blackness. Unlike James Massey, a dean among African-American homileticians, who adamantly refuses to think in terms of a "black preaching," my proposal does call for a distinct understanding of black preaching, especially when preaching is viewed as a mode of cultural production.   This chapter, secondly, identifies the inherent limitations of Africentric preaching. Intent upon articulating a revolutionary discourse that challenges a white understanding of black existence, Africentrism becomes problematic when situating the implied notion of ontological blackness as its basic premise. Ontological blackness functions ultimately as a reactionary, but still racialized, category for thinking about black identity. Arising from the American racial situation, ontological blackness looks at all African-Americans and expects to see only one type of black person. When thinking about preaching, such a means of envisioning black identity raises concern for what preachers say in the pulpit.

African-American Preaching as Africentric Preaching

Come on *preacher*, talk to me! The theological and political concerns that inform the African-American church's appreciation for what Africentric thinking makes possible unfolds within a theoretical slippage in Asante's representation of blackness. Asante foregrounds the "terroristic" discourse, to borrow from post-structuralism, of Western, white dominance in his thinking. His challenge to the idea of race takes the importance away from the way that whiteness gazes at and describes African-American experience. This challenge to what the West considers appropriate also speaks against the social orders that turn Western racial understandings into an accepted way to talk about blackness, that is to say a rhetoric about blackness. Poised with suspicion toward the way whiteness sees the world, Asante necessarily takes on the racialized, dominant structures and practices that make blackness nothing more than a story about what whiteness desires to exist. African-American Christianity, Asante argues, as it is influenced by Western racialized culture, requires a critical rethinking because the Western Christian God (for Asante a white God) and the cultural situation of African-Americans differs from that of our African ancestry.

Asante argues, here, that African-American Christianity actually contradicts the way that Africentrism ultimately views blackness: The most crippling effect of Islam as well as Christianity for us may well be the adoption of non-African customs and behaviors, some of which are in direct conflict with our traditional values. We out Arab the Arabs as we have out Europeanized the Europeans.[8] This reappraisal of American Christianity speaks to a benevolent hostility that Africentrism expresses toward Christian influences in African-American life. To Asante's displeasure, American Christianity acquaints its devotees with a Euro-American theological and cultural way of seeing the world. When read historically (some say presently as well) through the eyes and imagination of American Christianity, this worldview discounts the worth of blackness. Asante then argues that when African-American Christianity adopts aspects of white American Christianity it unwittingly imbeds benevolent practices that discount, nonetheless, the fullest affirmation of African-Americans.

The slippage in Asante's theorizing occurs, then, in a reflexive gesture that problematizes his reading of African-American Christianity. He locates a constructive materiality -finds something with which to work- when thinking about African-American Christianity despite the critique he makes of the presence of white influence in the worldview of black religious expression. This reflexive critical move in Asante's project suggests that there is common ground between Africentrism and African-American Christianity. This common ground makes it possible to think in terms of not only similar agendas, at points, for the two modes of black cultural reflection but also allows the proposal of a model of Africentric preaching.

"Alright" *preacher*, help me see it! First among the distinctive features of an Africentric model of preaching is the concern for the "sources" the preacher uses when thinking and preaching with an Africentric focus. Preaching that takes place in the context of the black American pulpit, as with all Christian preaching, also emphasizes the importance of finding sources that provide the material for the content of the sermon. Leslie Pollard, in this regard, reminds us of three primary sources that give African-American preaching its content:

scripture, contemporary experience, and history.[9] Contemporary experience and, then, history have importance for this discussion.

Contemporary experience and history both center preaching respectively, but not exclusively, in the legacy and present encounter of the culture of oppression and disenfranchisement inflicted upon America's black citizenry. This understanding of the African-American social situation finds a common interest and use in certain traditional circles of "black" preaching and in the proposal for orienting preaching toward an Africentric perspective.

Whereas the social dimension of black preaching, when speaking of cultural and political issues, most references the historical period of slavery to the present in sermons, an Africentric model of preaching works to discover a blackness *prior* to our arrival in America. The discovery of such a blackness, subsequently, requires also that we complement our prior existence with a concern for our present situation as people *in* America. This methodological shift – meaning the need to think about our lives as Africans, first, and then thinking about our lives as people in America – represents a critical element in Africentric thought. For preaching to be conceived as Africentric, it most reflect this shift in emphasis.

The adoption of this emphasis in method underscores the Africentric principle known as *Nija*. This principle means that we affirm blackness through an ideology of victorious ideas that help psychologically and socially to uplift African-Americans.[10] Preaching that works to underscore the principle of *Nija* also mandates that our pre-American experience as Africans, along with our particular American experience, stands at the center of the values, ideals, and world-view that shape our identity. Preaching, thus understood, places Africentric sources (sources from Africa, black America, and the larger African Diaspora) and materials within first reach on the preacher's study shelf for use when developing sermon. The preacher then, no longer views reality with "inadequate eyes,"[11] the eyes of whiteness. This Africentric gesture gives credibility to Doland Hubbard, who speaking from the perspective of literary theory, claims that the preacher as a "preacher-poet-performer and creator of social values must tap into a linguistic code and its attendant responsive mythology if he [or she] is to be successful as he structures the meaning of blackness."[12] Africentric preaching's self-referencing and affirming impulse, then, invests in naming African and Diasporic African source texts that portray the world through a global understanding of blackness. Conceived this way, preaching not only concerns our encounter with God's redemptive activity amid a particular social circumstance but also preaching becomes a cultural text that speaks against the way a white racial ideology demeans blackness.[13]

Second among the distinctive features of an Africentric homiletic is the deconstructive impulse that Africentric thinking reflexively imbeds in the text of preaching. This distinctive feature surfaces when noting that Africentrism proceeds from the basic claim that its way of viewing the world applies to all forms of expression that state an opinion regarding continental African and

Diasporic blackness. Norman Harris, when constructing his philosophical basis for Africentrism, identifies the desire for freedom and literacy as central to the Africentric understanding.[14] Freedom arises within the living circumstance from which a black person considers his/her relationship to the world in ways consistent with his/her own affirmation of experience. Literacy involves the application of historical knowledge to the concerns both of personal awareness and present knowledge of one's socio-historical situatedness in the world.

J. Deotis Roberts, a significant contributor to Africentric thinking, when distinguished from Harris, argues that Africentrism's basic claim centers attention on the way that Western scholarship develops its knowledge about us as it states that blackness has no glorious past.[15] Slavery is the only African-American past. The task of Africentrism, as the result, requires that we identify a history that predates the enslavement and forced removal of Africans to American soil. Knowledge of this history provides African-Americans and others of African descent with a means of psychological and social affirmation. Cheryl Townsend Gilkes argues that Africentrism provides a way to talk about blackness from within the situation of blackness. The conversation about black personhood as it arises from black people challenges the racialized myths that mark the white presumptuousness of the social sciences.[16]

While Harris, Roberts, and Gilkes assign different points of departure to their thinking about Africentrism, each theorist implicitly operates in a similar way and sets out to achieve the same goal when speaking of the Africentric project. Victor Anderson, in his theological and philosophical discussion of black American identity, identifies this mode of operation identified in the work of the three theorists. He writes: "Afrocentricity is a comparative ideology at the pejorative level of criticism. As a comparative project, Afrocentricity decenters the Eurocentric modes of understanding by exposing the real interests of European intellectuals in justifying and maintaining European imperialist intentions."[17] Anderson, here, accounts for the deconstructive impulse that becomes the goal of the Africentric project. This deconstructive impulse examines the racial strategies found in the spoken and written ideology of whiteness and seeks to attack and to undo the claims that whiteness makes about black personhood. The desconstructive impulse then makes room for constructing anew a more affirming and authentic idea of what blackness means.

When conceived as a form of Africentric discourse, preaching benefits from keeping the deconstructive impulse as a rhetorical property within pulpit expression. The deconstructive impulse – that is the undoing of the negative claims about personhood – has merit for preaching in that it guards preaching from an uninformed and disaffirming use of Western thinking and practice that negates blackness. Gosnell Yorke, a Kenyan theologian, reminds us that the application of Africentric sensibilities to religious inquiry (as is preaching) functions with two intents. As Yorke calls it, an Africentric hermeneutic, meaning the way we interpret blackness, first brings a suspicion to the endeavor to interpret any claim made negatively against our humanity. An Africentric hermeneutic then secondly brings a psychosocial and political hermeneutic of liberation that works to demonstrate the positive and the divine within the humanity of black people. Yorke's Africentric hermeneutic breaks the cultural dominance of interpretations that find only the bad in black personhood. Yorke's Africentrism seeks ultimately to rid the "ideological stranglehold" that Western theology has historically read against a narrowly understood black religious experience.[18]

The deconstructive impulse that Africentrism embeds in its project to undo whiteness merits being included in the way that we think about an Africentric model of preaching. The deconstructive impulse of Africentrism, in this respect, has implications beyond the fight against racial ideology. When considered for developing a model of preaching, this same impulse guards against the black church's giving into an understanding of humanity that arises from the pulpit with the weight of "thus said the Lord" when in fact it reflects "thus said the *preacher*." Writing with Womanist interest in black American preaching, Katie Cannon addresses this potential problematic. Cannon argues that the leadership dominance of black males in the pulpit urgently mandates the need to identify the "socio-ecclesial locations and theological interests" that inform the personhood of the preacher, and, therefore, the sermon.[19] The recognition of the potential to speak with an ideological agenda in preaching allows one to silence the overbearing voice of the preacher while giving greater clarity to distinguishing when, indeed, it is the voice of God that speaks to us.   An Africentric model of preaching, therefore, not only produces a crisis for the way that racialized thinking unwittingly invades the pulpit but also the preaching of African-Americans *to* African-Americans finds itself involved in a similar crisis. African-American preaching can no longer hide its agenda merely by stating that it is the "word of the Lord." Most important to a model of Africentric preaching is the requirement for a more credible standard to govern an authentic biblically and theologically informed sermon that affirms the whole of African-American personhood.

Third among the distinctive features of an Africentric model of preaching is the development of a way of thinking and speaking in sermons that fights the false understanding of blackness that find an audience even in the pulpit. Preaching that adheres to this task adopts Asante's call for "functionality" in shaping a discourse that builds a more positive understanding of blackness, whether African blackness or Diasporic blackness. This way of thinking about preaching accepts the challenge to offer a new way of thinking about blackness once the racialized understandings of blackness have been uncovered and challenged.   Functionality, seen as a way of communicating in Asante's conception of a rhetoric of blackness, participates in the deconstructive agenda given to Africentrism as it makes the meaning-making function of public discourse important.[20] The object of our speaking and writing, in this instance a sermon, discovers meaning and, therefore, significance when both speaker and audience share the same world-view. Related to preaching, two main questions arise when faced with a concern for functionality according to Asante: What does an Africentric model of preaching achieve, produce? What is the attitude conveyed by an Africentric model of preaching? The answers offered to these questions bring to Africentric preaching a merit for its project and give an integrity to preaching that refuses to empty black identity of its fundamental sense of being and cultural value. In this manner, an Africentric homiletic, when speaking against the fictions associated with racial ideology, finds a responsiveness in preaching that aims to produce sermons wherein blackness is affectionately identified, authentically named, and joyously celebrated. This strategy for interpreting black identity brings about a theological and political way to justify the removal of race as a socially approved standard by which to call for an anti-Black world. An Africentric sermon, because of its functionality, resists giving blackness over to social portrayals of pathology and invisibility. Rather, and most crucial, an Africentric model of preaching generates a content that begins with an historic and present knowledge of Africa and, then, an historic and present knowledge of black American and black Diasporic experience. This mode for learning about blackness communicates a more intentional and theologically sound alternative to the way the West historically desires to think about black humanity.

The Limitations of an Africentric Preaching

"Alright" *preacher*, be careful! The application of Africentric modes of inquiry to the cultural discourse of African-Americans, preaching not withstanding, establishes a critical deconstructive and constructive meaning-making agenda for black humanity. Because it works to resist and develop blackness anew, Africentrism, as a means to examine American society, reclaims blackness from the narrow mindset that dictates Western portrayals of African-Americans. Africentrism's meaning-making agenda, however, must not keep an Africentric model of preaching from participating in self-reflection. An Africentric model of preaching cannot afford to hide behind the so-called epistemological privilege of the other or use the race card to neglect considering the effect it has on viewing the world as it does for African-Americans.[21] The specific task of Africentrism, when applied to preaching, does not advocate a "dark essentialism,"[22] as Henry Louis Gates calls it, to replace the dangerous social and political effect of racial ideology. Dark essentialism, simply described, involves the practice whereby black American experience merely replaces white experience as the sole measure of all things and all humanities.

The dark essentialism of Gates draws the discussion of Africentrism into an additional problem as the proposal for an Africentric model of preaching views its work from the perspective of ontological blackness. Ontological blackness, critical to Victor Anderson's theological and philosophical discussion about black identity, speaks of blackness in ways that give only one all-encompassing category for thinking about African-Americans.[23] This description of blackness as it comes out of black experience, though somewhat different from the racialized manner of viewing black persons according to Western ideology, just as narrowly describes African-American identity. The result of this narrow description produces a politics of identity for African-Americans that makes a certain intracultural code of blackness more worthy than others. African-Americans who fail to adhere to a particular code of blackness find themselves potentially marginalized from *within* their cultural community. In reaction to the racialized and opposite categories of blackness and whiteness, ontological blackness creates a new set of social opposites: black versus more black. This new social order created among African-Americans often pits us against one another and ends with one population of African-Americans viewing itself as "blacker" than another. This same group of African-Americans also then views other African-Americans as failing to be "black enough."

The proposal for an Africentric model of preaching must consider this problem an inherent limitation brought about by the presence of a new set of opposites because Africentrism potentially establishes a limit to what it means to be black and what it means to structure a black existence. An Africentric model of preaching, then, if not attentive to its project, potentially stands to limit the very social existence it hopes to expand for black Americans. African-American preaching in Christian contexts, in particular, requires careful attention to the polemical insertion of these opposites for black identity in sermons. Said succinctly, black sermons stand with potential to preach a black cultural ideology that suggests there are some African-Americans who "act more black" than others. Africentric preaching, further still, if maintaining Africentrism's black verses blacker view of personhood creates a discourse that removes ambiguity from the way it describes blackness, thus defining cultural identity in a way that cares little for individual freedom while paying attention more to a communal idea of blackness. Ontological blackness, consequently, as it expresses a dark essentialism, fails to account for present day understandings of blackness that stand in a more polysemic and multi-situated space, a postmodern blackness.[24] The Africentric project, therefore, possibly looses a measure of its value for *all* African-Americans because it remains trapped in a way of thinking about race that is similarly found in the racialized considerations of whiteness.

Africentric thinking places an additional limitation, albeit burden, on the Africentric model of preaching that I pursue. As Asante's project has the potential to limit the experience of blackness that it actually hopes to liberate, this effect of Africentrism shows its consequence when understanding that the sermon represents, among many things, a mode of cultural production. Preaching, said more plainly, develops the support of its divinely appointed message by looking to use everyday sources, in addition to biblical and theological sources, to help articulate the good news of the Gospel. Yet, Asante places a prohibiting condition on the choice of the sources that preachers may use when developing, crafting, and preaching the sermon.

Despite Asante's placement of his "communication person at the center of all social systems, from which information is received from all systems equally,"[25] Asante, strictly understood, imposes a hierarchy and value on the sources available for the preacher's use. The communication person in Asante's work is the person who receives information from the world at large for the purpose of influencing the actions of others. Yet, the earliest conception of Africentrism challenges just what sources are worthy of the preacher's attention. An Africentric preaching model, following the manner by which Asante generates culture, turns first to continental African and, then, Diasporic African sources for illustrating the Gospel. Western religious scholarship, on the other hand, represents the interest and thinking of whiteness; therefore, Western religious scholarship is an oppositional discourse that potentially stifles the progress of blackness. Thus, it warrants being read with suspicion, in fact a hermeneutic of suspicion.

Asante's prohibition on sources, however, limits the preacher in generating sermon ideas and material. Any preacher who labors over sermon development knows the difficulty in finding materials for use in preaching. For Africentrism, however, "the blacker the source the better the source" is a cogent, though negating, mantra. An Africentric model of preaching, as a result, stands to loose its fullest liberating impact when making the restrictive call for no source but a black source and, then, no black source except it support a notion of ontological blackness. If accepting this communicative principle, the very deconstructive impulse underscoring an Africentric preaching model only partially achieves its end because it fails to challenge even a narrow way of thinking relative to its own way of describing the black American humanity it desires to uplift.

The limitation of this partial orientation toward the most encompassing way to understand black humanity inhibits the development of a broadly defined theory of communication related to preaching. In contradistinction to Asante's model for shaping discourse, African-American preachers will more readily embrace the rhetorical tenet from St. Augustine, the North African Patristic Father: "Gold from Egypt is still gold." Similarly, the late Sam Proctor, emeritus pastor of Abyssinian Baptist Church in New York City and preacher extraordinaire, frequently shared that he always looked everywhere for sermon ideas. African-American preachers function best when free to explore all available social texts from which to generate ideas and support for the preaching of the Gospel. This freedom even makes plausible a consideration of texts from the tradition of Western letters, even as Africentric preaching first requires the preacher to examine those sources that reflect an African and African Diasporic world-view. The Africentric method, however, does hasten to caution the preacher's failure to adopt the principle of *Nija* when relying upon Western letters as a sermon source. This ideological principle measures discourse in accordance with its ability to regenerate and to assert communal values that affirm blackness.

An Africentric preaching model, as a last but certainly not final concern, requires a discussion regarding the potential for the sermon to give attention to the social world than the biblical and theological resources that challenge the social world. Doland Hubbard takes note of this dilemma as he sees in African-American preaching a "cultural authority" given to the way in which a sermon is received by its congregational audience. The black sermon, he writes, "is the heroic voice of black America."[26] This conception of preaching envisions the more practical end associated with sermonic discourse and conveys that the symbolic universe of black experience utilizes the speech act of preaching as a "cultural unifying document." As such, preaching must address the implications of a Western discourse that makes blackness a racialized category for thinking about African-Americans.

Conversely, James Earl Massey, the venerable African-American homiletician, cautions us to understand the theological import of preaching. He writes:

> Drawing from the larger statement about God's gracious concern and grace, the sermon is designed and preached to 'open men [and women] upwards,' so that the reality of God's consciousness will affect all who hear, and at those levels where real needs are most acutely known … real preaching … helps the hearer to experience grace, that divine help which deals with human sin and crippling experiences.[27]

While the cultural text present in preaching has its romantic appeal in Africentric preaching, Massey gives testimony beyond the cultural role assigned to the preaching of black experience. Considered for the proposal of an Africentric preaching model, a sermon that fails to distinguish between the cultural and spiritual voice in its preaching stands potentially deficient in its full value to the African-American community. Assigning more significance to the cultural dimension of preaching, on the one hand, infuses preaching with a lack of divine power. Privileging only the religious in preaching, on the other hand, makes its socially irrelevant.

Conclusion

Come on, *preacher*, bring it home! An Africentric preaching model must make an issue out of the Western understanding of race (a fictional social idea) in order to develop a discourse that gives life to the Africentric project. This critical move situates preaching in a more authentic and affirming knowledge about ourselves. Such a way of knowing about blackness, as Asante describes it, finds a tremendous gap in the discourse that affirms blackness over against the discourse of Western racialized ideology that views blackness as a problem. An Africentric model of preaching, then, seeks first to undo the encroachment of Western dominance as it subtly enters the black American pulpit (and other African-American social texts). As a second gesture, an Africentric model of preaching develops a critical voice whereupon the sermon's meaning-making agenda redeems and asserts an affirmed understanding of blackness. The preaching that I propose for an Africentrically informed pulpit keeps two critical questions before it: What are the distinctive features that distinguish the preaching that conforms to the Africentric paradigm? and What are the limitations posed by preaching in an Africentric mode? Within this matrix of inquiry, the preacher stands before the people of God of African descent. I'm with you *preacher*! No one knows what the preacher will say this morning. The congregation simply knows that the preacher is part cultural poet, part heroic voice, and part urbane theologian. The preacher pauses, and the people wait. The preacher leans forth, and the people begin to stand. The preacher gestures outwardly and the people wave him on. The preacher climaxes and the people dance and shout. The words from the preacher usher a brown-skin people into God's presence. The words that the preacher speaks are part biblical text and part theological text. The words that the preacher speaks are part social text and part cultural text. As the preacher speaks and in the way the preacher speaks, the words spoken touch that brown-skin gathering of God's people at their point of spiritual and social yearning. "Walk together children," the preacher said, "don't you get weary." And the church said, "Amen!"

Endnotes

1. Africentric (Africentrism) represents a more etymologically appropriately designation than the term "Afrocentric," as J. Deotis Roberts argues, *Africentric Christianity: A Theological Appraisal for Ministry* (Valley Forge, PA: Judson Press, 2000), vii.
2. Molefi Kete Asante, *Afrocentricity* (Trenton: Africa World Press, Inc., 1988), vii.
3. Gerald Early, "Understanding Afrocentrism," *Civilization* (July/August 1995): 32.
4. J. Deotis Roberts, *Africentric Christianity: A Theological Appraisal for Ministry* (Valley Forge: Judson Press, 2000), 3.
5. Asanti, *Afrocentricity*, 1.
6. Ontological blackness is a critical construct in the theorizing of Victor Anderson in *Beyond Ontological Blackness: An Essay on African-American Religious and Cultural Criticism* (11, 14-17). It refers to the categorical totalizing of black subjectivity identified in the work of most Afrocentric theorists, Asante among them. Anderson prefers to understand the formation of African-American identity (continental and Diasporic African identity as well) by way of bell hooks' "postmodern blackness" in *Colonial Discourse and Postcolonial Theory: A Reader* (421-427).
7. Malinge Njeza, a black South African, offers a constructive discussion in response to the critique regarding the notion of ontological blackness imbedded in Asante's Afrocentrist theory, "Fallacies of the New Afrocentrism: A Critical Response to Kwame A. Appiah," *Journal of Theology for Southern Africa* 99 (November 1997): 47-75.
8. Asante, *Afrocentricity*, 5.
9. Leslie Pollard, "Saga and Song: A Cross-cultural Primer in African-American Preaching," *Ministry*

(May 1995): 5.

10.   Premised in Asante's understanding of *Njia*, Lorine Cummings discusses this concept in her womanist response to Africentrism, Cheryl Sanders, ed., *Living the Intersection: Womanism and Afrocentrism in Theology* (Minneapolis: Fortress Press, 1995), 60.

11.   Molefi Asante, "An Afrocentric Communication Theory," *Contemporary Rhetorical Theory: A Reader* (New York: The Guilford Press, 1999), 554.

12.   Dolan Hubbard, *The Sermon and the African American Literary Imagination* (Columbia: University of Missouri Press, 1994), 9.

13.   Hubbard, writing as a literary theorist, broadens the definition of the sermon in his analysis. The sermon is an aesthetic text whereupon it represents the lived and symbolic context of African-American experience.   The black sermon as a result, he argues, is a culturally unifying document intent upon touching people additionally at the core of their social being, Ibid., 1-25.

14.   Norman Harris, *Afrocentric Visions: Studies in Communication and Culture*, ed. Janice Hamlet (Thousands Oaks: Sage Publications, 1998), 15.

15.   J. Deotis Roberts, *Africentric Christianity*, 27.

16.   Cheryl Townsend Gilkes, *Living the Intersection: Womanism and Afrocentrism in Theology*, ed. Cheryl Sanders (Minneapolis: Fortress Press, 1995), 21.

17.   Victor Anderson, *Beyond Ontological Blackness*, 150.

18 Gosnell L. Yorke, "Biblical Hermeneutics: An Afrocentric Perspective," *University of South Africa Journal* (Unisa Press, 2000).

19.   Katie G. Cannon, *Katie's Cannon: Womanism and the Soul of the Black Community* (New York: Continuum, _____), 113.

20.   Arthur Smith [Molefi Asante], *Language, Communication, and Rhetoric in Black America* (New York: Harper and Row, 1972), 366.

21.   Sue Ellen Case, "Women of Color and Theatre," *Feminism and Theatre* (New York: Meuthuen, 1988), 95-111.

22.   Henry Louis Gates, *Loose Canons: Notes on the Culture Wars* (New York: Oxford University Press, 1992), 98-103.

23.   Victor Anderson, *Beyond Ontological Blackness*, 11-17, 150-155.

24.   Bell Hooks speaks of postmodern blackness in contrast to the modern universalizing agenda of radical black subjectivity that functions as the traditional way that African-Americans speak of identity.   The critique that hooks offers with her postmodern blackness centers concerns for identity formation beyond the essentialsts representations that black culture imposes upon itself, Patrick Williams and Laura Chrisman, eds., "Postmodern Blackness," *Colonial Discourse and Postcolonial Theory: A Reader* (New York: Columbia University Press, 1994), 421.

25.   John Lucaites, et al., *Contemporary Rhetorical Theory*, 552.

26.   Hubbard, *The Sermon and the African American Literary Imagination*, 25.

27.   James Earl Massey, *Designing the Sermon: Order and Movement in Preaching*, ed. William Thompson (Nashville: Abingdon Press, 1980), 16.

CHAPTER SIX

The Church's Ministry to the Urban Family: Creative Responses to a Continuing New Testament Challenge[1]

Cain Hope Felder

In this chapter, I wish to revisit some of the ideas that I put forth more than a decade ago, in chapter none of my first book, *Troubling Biblical Waters " Race, Class and Family* (now in its seventeenth printing). I titled that Chapter, "The Bible and Black Families: a Theological Challenge". There, I put forth the thesis that theologically the New Testament re-defines the notion of family; no longer is the nuclear or the extended family the norm; rather various teachings in the New Testament point to what sociologists call "fictive kinship". This is what emerges as a characterization of the church and communities of believer in both the Gospels[ii] and the Epistles[iii] where one's true relatives are to be determined by the extent to which persons "do the will of God" or understand themselves to be fully yoked to one another as a kind of family (Greek: *ho oikos tou theou*) by and through the blood of Jesus Christ. I then perhaps somewhat idealistically suggested that the modern church needs to take more seriously the reconciling and atoning significance of Jesus' blood sacrifice for us as a means of breaking down the multifarious "diving walls of hostility" within and between racial and ethnic families today. Evidently that is so much easier said than done!

Few churches appear to take themselves that seriously any more and increasingly in America, the spirit of "postmodernism" makes even some NT scholars suspicious about the usefulness of studying ancient texts and trying to discern their contemporary relevance. Here, I am thinking of the Jesus Seminar of the Society of Biblical Literature[iv], several voices within the recent volume, *African Americans and the Bible*[v], or some of the Feminist biblical scholars.[vi] Hapless, fellow that I am. I continue to struggle to be merely modern so I have not "advanced" to the rubric of "postmodernism"!

Thus, my aim in this paper is to re-examine the thesis of Chapter Nine in my Orbis book in light of a few important more recent studies on the Black (largely urban) family, namely Orlando Paterson's *Rituals of Blood: Two Hundred Years of the Consequence of American Slavery* and Andrew Billingsley's *Climbing Jacob's Ladder: The Enduring Legacy of African American Families* and Billingsley's newest offering, *Mighty Like a River: The Black Church and Social Reform*. This latter book is an invaluable resource in documenting specific outreach efforts of Black churches in different parts of the country; such efforts are suggestive of future innovative avenues for urban ministry. As we identify aspects of the modern urban family crisis with a view toward remedies that the church can provide, it is essential that I explain why some of us are giving so much attention to developing resources that emphasize the rich African and multicultural biblical heritage.

Shoring up the Foundations: African American Families and the Bible
Because there often is a disproportionate number of African Americans and other minorities that have sought refuge and job opportunities in the cities of America, the urban church faces a daunting task in identifying and developing effective urban ministries that meet the multiple needs of these urban families. The problem is magnified, inasmuch as the traditional definitions of what constitutes a family is changing. Today, often "family" mean an immediate social network of intimate relatives (not necessarily blood) who presumably share an ultimate concern for one another's welfare. This definition of family allows for a variety of fictive kinship patterns within and allied to modern households. Oddly enough, by NT standard, this definition could also describe the ideal way in which the church has seen itself as "family".

I think that it is fair to say that when the church emerged in the First Century, there family members did not have the burden of race-based social constructs of innate inferiority or superiority of one race or another. Indeed, as some of us have pointed out in various writings, there was no notion of "race" in the more modern sense. This concept is without any scientific basis in term of determining the intelligence or predisposition of one group as opposed to another. Yet, for most of our lives in the United States of America, the Western educational system, public and private, secondary and higher education alike, secular and religious, scarcely has taught, much less emphasized this important fact. Instead, men, women, and children have been provided with reinforcing race-specific images of power, privilege and wealth, buttressed by a view of history that begins with Greece and Rome. Likewise, this same Western educational system often not too subtlety hammers home race-specific images of powerlessness and marginalization; these usually depict the African American as buffoon, athlete, entertainer, or a minor figure with little substantive history.

It is indeed notable that most studies on the Black Family that I have seen begin with the devastating aspects of the Middle Passage and the American slave trade. This suggests that the Black family, wrenched from Africa was willfully destabilized and dehumanized with the implication that it has not recovered since. Part I of Orlando Paterson's study, Rituals of Blood moves essentially in this direction as it attempts to explain the lingering social pathology of the Black family, particularly as it ill-affects Black male-female relations.[vii]

Happily, the work of sociologist Andrew Billingsley moves in another more positive direction. In Billingsley's seminal work, *Climbing Jacob's Ladder*, while acknowledging the tragic impact of slavery on the Black American family, the emphasis is placed on the remarkable resilience, and innovative coping strategies exhibited by Blacks over the years to maintain some sense of stability in the face of almost overwhelming destabilizing socio-economic and political forces.[viii] Billingsley does not hesitate in pointing out a major reason many a Black family survived against the odds, namely The Black Church about which he says:

But, in addition to what it does for its members, the black church as an institution has always reached out to serve important functions for the black community as a whole. It is in this respect both a preserver of the African American heritage and an agent for reform.[ix]

One is therefore not surprised to find an early section of Billingsley book entitled African Renaissance: *The Nile Valley Civilization*.[x] Like others scholarly who focus upon the Nile Valley Civilization as an appropriate subject in the recovery of a heretofore lost ancient African American past, Billingsley quickly moves from the Nile Valley Civilization to the subject of possible Ancient migrations to other parts of Africa, and like other Nile Valley specialists, he fails to note the significance of the early Hebrew/Israelite period of 400 years spent in Egypt (Genesis 15:13-14).

It would appear that if the Black Church would take more seriously studying the neglected, but quite important ancient connection between Nile Valley Civilizations and the shaping of the Bible itself an entirely new broad range of empowering and educational ministries could be launched by the Black Church. In other word, there is a pressing need **to shore up the foundations** of our spiritual and biblical heritage. As some of you know, I have been attempting to establish precisely this ancient connection in several of my published works, since Billingsley's *Climbing Jacob's Ladder*.[xi] We are particularly pleased that our *Original African Heritage Study Bible* has not only sold well over 500,000 copies since 1993, but that it has revolutionized Bible Study among the hundreds of thousands of African American men incarcerated in the United States. These men could have been, and some can yet be transformed in order to return to wholesome roles within their respective families and kinship networks.

Many of these prisoners write to thank us for producing such resources and indicate further that had the preachers shared such knowledge about the extent of their heritage in the Bible they well may never have been caught in the criminal justice trap in America! We have also produced through the American Bible Society, *The African American Jubilee Bible.* Then followed our *Jubilee Legacy Bible,* which for the first time in Bible publishing history, we provide actual archeological data that support the African connections with ancient Israel. We take further pride in having emphasized the Black Family throughout and have expanded this into a curriculum hard back called the "Spiritual Odyssey", study guide for the *Legacy Bible.*

Liberating information is power! The old adage is still true: "the pen is mightier than the sword!" We, as an African people, are a biblical people of the first order; we have a rich and dynamic history that extends far beyond the modern slave period. As we shore up those foundations, we are already moving toward substantial remedies for some of the pycho-social problems that bedevil us as individuals and families in America which continues to practice what Orlando Paterson calls "the secular religion of racism".[xii]

The Urban Family: Biblical Times and Urban America

The urban family in biblical times was often in a state of crisis and despair. Considering the family situations depicted in the Gospel report on the ministry of Jesus, most families not only lived on the edge of survival, but did so in a context of great political constraints, with minimal rights—and those largely held by the *paterfamilias* or male head of household who virtually owned the women, children and slaves of his home. One need only consult a book like *The First Urban Christians* by Wayne Meeks in order to appreciate that urban life in the Greco-Roman ethos of the First Century was not all that pleasant, rarely was there privacy, for example.[xiii] Crowded into candle lit tenements, often with domestic animals not far away, worried constantly about one's "daily bread" and taxes, stress was a virtual presupposition for enduring life's routines.

No doubt, the missionary appeal of Christianity offered one a sense of great worth in the sight of God, despite one's earthly social condition. The church not only held out the possibility of apocalyptic intervention and hope, but she also became a "home for the homeless", especially for displaced women, children, widows, and slaves. Of course, there always were some from the higher classes within the Christian movement, but the preponderance was not of that order. Despite 2000 years of so-called progress and scientific inventions never imagine in the past, large numbers of urban families today are just as stressed and virtually homeless in a culture awash in materialism and selfishness. Although we adduce these parallels between the church of the First Century and now, one fundamental difference remains; the modern church is dying under the weight of its own worldly success.

Theological commentators on the modern church, such as Alister McGrath, tell us that for all practical purposes the European church is a relic from the past, having died a slow death in the wake of secularism and material prosperity.[xiv] He sees the future of Christianity in the Asian and African American contexts where the European Jesus tradition is being adapted creatively. He notes that Christianity thrives in America due to the absence of a State Church and the competition and marketing ethos in America that indirectly causes churches to work harder at pleasing and trying to accommodate the apparent needs of them members.[xv] Thus, the American Church is quite alive, but its identity has been unwittingly shaped by both the dictates of civil religion and market forces within the popular culture.

African American churches have frequently imitated the success models of televangelists and Protestant mega- churches (particularly through the prosperity gospel orientation), putting far more energies into larger and larger sanctuaries (the Georgia Coliseum or the Los Angeles Forum!). For most of these urban churches, the accent is on style, entertainment, and mass appeal rather than on outreach services, educational and cultural enrichment or a spirituality and theology of liberation.

Countering American Forces that Destabilize Urban Families: Possible Remedies to America's "Religion of Racism"

In her provocative book, *When Chicken-heads Come Home to Roost*, Joan Morgan formerly of *Essence* magazine, argues that a significant number of Black Women are raising their daughters to become the idealized Black men that they have wanted for themselves.[xvi] This American Black phenomenon exacerbates the tension in today's Black male female relations in the dating process and role identifications within the contemporary family. Then too, the unisex liberalism of White America has increasingly blurred the so-called heterosexual and homosexual divide; indeed the term "bi-sexual" has become more increasingly acceptable in many quarters of Western society. All of this suggests that the ministering to African American or urban families in general is no simple matter; it requires a commitment to the NT vision of the church as a caring fictive kinship network, but it also requires innovation, determination and creative financing!

In his important resource for countering the destabilizing factors that subvert the African American Family, Andrew Billingsley's Climbing Jacob's Ladder makes five generalizations. First, the African American community is characterized by a large, growing and diverse population in excess of 30 million. Second, the vast majority of these persons live in organized households...where they cooperate the sharing of resources and use of common facilities. Third, while some of these households are occupied by single persons or unrelated groups the vast majority are occupied by persons who are related to each other by marriage, blood or adoption. Fourth, the majority of these family households are married couple families. The total number of black married couples has continued to increase over recent years, even as other family structures have increased even faster. Finally, the 1990 U.S. census data show, that of the 3.8 million black married couple families, a total of 2 million under the age of 18 and nearly as many 1.8 did not have any children.

These data, we are told, support the following scenario: the majority of African Americans live in family households have married couples, the majority of the married couples have young children of their own. This supports the proposition that marriage and family life are still important characteristics. He notes that the African American marriages and family life have been under sever attack in recent years, but wants to stress that most have vitality, adaptability and resilience despite the daunting challenge of it all.[xvii] Billingsley is thus very helpful in clarifying two basic facts. On one hand he shows the black church is for all of its limitations is still at the cutting edge of the African American push to influence the future of its families. Second, self help is fundamental is African American progress in an American climate that is often hostile to African Americans.[xviii]

Beyond this, in his most recent study, *Mighty Like A River: The Black Church and Social Reform*, Billingsley identifies the following churches as well as their practical accomplishments:

(1) **Canaan Missionary Baptist Church, Louisville, Kentucky** demonstrate how black churches can develop economically sound community development programs;

(2) **St. John Baptist Church, Miami, Florida** revitalized a low-income community that was devastated by periodic waves of rioting during the 1980s.

(3) **United House of Prayer for All People, Washington, DC** invested $20 million of its own money in building low-to-moderate income housing;

(4) **St. Paul Community Baptist Church, Brooklyn, New York** assisted in the rebuilding of 5,000 owner-occupied row houses, over a 10-year period;

(5) **Concord Baptist Church, Brooklyn, New York** established the Concord Baptist Church Christ Fund, the endowment sponsors and extensive array of community outreach programs, and church-run operations covered an entire city block;

(6) **Abyssinian Baptist Church, Harlem, New York** developed the Abyssinian Development Corporation which is responsible for the redevelopment of Harlem on a continuous basis;

(7) **Allen African Methodist Episcopal Church, Queens, New York** bought out a run-down one-block commercial district and developed a travel agency, medical and legal professional offices, a barber shop, a restaurant, a drug store, a home-care agency, and a preschool. One third of the church's budget is set aside for the maintenance of these ventures.

(8) **First African Methodist Episcopal Church, Los Angeles, California** is best known for its extensive community outreach.

(9) **Second Baptist Church, Los Angeles, California** renovated two single-room-occupancy hotels in the Skid Row area of Los Angeles;

(10) **Allen Temple Baptist Church, Oakland, California** operates a 75-unit housing development for low-income and elderly citizens, and a 51-unit housing projects;

(11) **Zion Baptist Church, Philadelphia, Pennsylvania** is one of the most innovative economic development programs created by an individual church in the North which grew out of investments from its members.

(12) **Hartford Memorial Baptist Church, Detroit, Michigan** developed a comprehensive plan to revitalize the local community.

(13) **Olivet Institutional Baptist Church, Cleveland, Ohio** practices a brand of ministry that honors the African American heritage, grounds itself in Christian doctrine, and extends itself into the community. Through the teaching methods used, the African American heritage is evidenced.

(14) **Third Shiloh Missionary Baptist Church, New Orleans, Louisiana** is known for not only purchasing two crack houses, but transformed the community and provides on-the-job training in the construction trade for community residents where the unemployment rate is 61%.

(15) **Wheat Street Baptist Church, Atlanta, Georgia** developed a nonprofit corporation that owns and manages two housing developments, several single-family dwellings, and an office building.[xix]

There is good news for families in the city, after all; and Black urban churches around the nation are demonstrating a willingness to help meet the changing needs of families in creative ways. The implication seems to be that the urban context can provide healing in stressful times. Jeremiah 29:7 reminds us that while there is warrant for an "Exodus" from the various "Egypts" that enslave us, we should not rush to exit the city! "But seek the welfare of the city where I have sent you into exile; and pray to the Lord on its behalf. For in its welfare you will find your welfare!" The Urban Church must re-commit herself to the challenged and changing nature of families within the city and become to an even greater measure the symbol of being in the city for good... and the doing of good!

Endnotes

---

1. This chapter was delivered as an address at the Pittsburgh Theological Seminary's Metro-Urban Institute's Urban Intensive Conference on Family Ministry, April, 2002.

ii. "Whoever does the will of my Father in heaven is my brother, and sister, and mother" (Matt. 12:50; compare Mark 3:3-5 and Luke 8:31).

iii. See further *Troubling Biblical Waters: Race Class and Family* (Maryknoll, N.Y.: Orbis Books, 1989) 97, 157. Notably Ephesians 2:14-22, see *TBW; p. 163.* Similarly, Gal.6:10.

iv. Robert W. Funk, Roy W. Hoover and the Jesus Seminar, *The Five Gospels: The Search for the Authentic Words of Jesus* (New York: Mcmillan, 1993).

v. Vincent L. Wimbush, *African Americans and the Bible: Sacred Texts and Social Textures* (New York: Coontinuum, 2000).

vi. Elizabeth Schussler Fiorenza, *Rhetoric and Ethic: The Politic of Biblical Studies:* Minneapolis: Augsburg Fortress, 1999).

vii. Orlando Paterson, *Rituals of Blood: The Consequences of Two Hundred Years of American Slavery* (Washington, D,C.: Civitates:1998j.

viii. Andrew Billingsley, *Climbing Jacob's Ladder: The Enduring Legacy of African-American Families* (New York: Simon and Schuster, 1992).

9. Billingsley, *Climbing Jacob's Ladder*, 350.

10. Billingsley, 87-95.

11. C.H. Felder, Gen, Ed., *The Original African Heritage Study Bible* (Nashville: Winston Derek Publishing Company, 1993); contributing editor, *The African American Jubilee Bible* (New York: The American Bible Society, 1999), Co-Editor with Charles H. Smith, *The Jubilee Legacy Bible* (Nashville: Townsend Press, 2001).

xii. Orlando Paterson, *Rituals of Blood,* 191.

13. Wayne A. Meeks, *The First Urban Christians: The Social World of the Apostle Paul* (New Haven: Yale University Press, 1983) 28-32, 74-78.

14. Alister McRath, *The Future of Christianity* (Oxford: Blackwell Publishers Limited, 2002), 28-30.

xv. McRath, 46-50.

xvi. Jane Morgan, *When Chicken Heads Come Home to Roost* (N.Y.: Simon and Schuster, 1999).

xvii. Billingsley, *Climbing Jacob's Ladder,* 206-207.

xviii. Billingsley, *Climbing Jacob's Ladder,* 349ff, 379ff.

xix. Andrew Billingsley, *Mighty Like A River The Black Church and Social Reform,* 144-169.

CHAPTER SEVEN

Christians Celebrating Kwanzaa: Reflections and Thanksgiving for the African Heritage

Ronald Edward Peters

Scarcely more than thirty-five years after it was first introduced, estimates indicated that over eighteen million people observe Kwanzaa in some fashion.[1] Each year, more and more African Americans celebrate this cultural festival and, for all its significance and increased popularity, many in African American churches nationwide still take little notice of the great educational and spiritual meaning of this occasion. There are a growing number of churches, nonetheless, that have initiated some form of Kwanzaa-related activities as part of their annual programming. For these congregations, there is no question about the relevance of Kwanzaa to the Gospel or its importance in the life of African American Christians. The only issue for these churches is how best to affirm the symbols and rituals of this cultural celebration with traditions long established in the life of the Black Church. The following series of meditations seek to address this issue.

The above notwithstanding Kwanzaa still poses for many Christians troubling questions for their understanding of Christian faith. In one 2001 study of seventy Christian women, it was found that many concerns related to Kwanzaa were due to a lack of clarity about the meaning of the holiday:

> There seems to be a lack of knowledge about Kwanzaa and the celebration. Second, the holiday is perceived as a black holiday, which makes the celebration too exclusive... Third, the concern is voiced that celebrating Kwanzaa is supporting Black Nationalism or separatism. Fourth, some Christians contend that Christians should not celebrate Kwanzaa because the celebration promotes culture over Christ and becomes a substitute for the Christmas holiday.[2]

Ndugu T'Ofori-Atta, Associate Professor of Missiology and Director of the Religious Heritage of the African World at the Interdenominational Theological Center in Atlanta, GA, responded to this lack of clarity in the Christian community with his very helpful book on Kwanzaa, first published in 1991, entitled *ChristKwanza–An African American Church Liturgy*. T'Ofori-Atta analyzed the relationship of Christian themes with the seven principles of Kwanzaa and with African Traditional Religions. His work stands as a strong contribution in this area where theological reflection on this cultural phenomenon remains relatively sparse. Similarly, these reflections on Kwanzaa constitute a pastoral effort to frame the common spiritual themes of the cultural holiday with scriptural themes in Christian teaching.

Originally the meditations that follow were either Bible Study lessons for adults or excerpts from sermons I have preached. They were developed for congregations where I served as pastor or led workshops for other church or community groups that observed the religious importance of this cultural celebration. During these occasions I was always amazed at the tremendous power the message of Jesus Christ has when proclaimed in the context of Kwanzaa. African Americans of all ages and from all walks of life rejoiced and many, as a result of participating in these observances, sought to re-direct their lives toward more altruistic and noble aims regarding other people. Some people might refer to these systemic changes in personal lifestyle and behavior as "conversion" experiences (not to be confused with those who merely "confess with their lips" faith in God, but whose behavior and values remain curiously unaltered).[3] Perhaps it was the fact that during these Kwanzaa-related activities, the Gospel seemed to be set forth in the beauty of its African cultural roots rather than viewed through the prism of European cultural norms, aesthetics, and theological formulations.

In 1966, Maulana Karenga, a Black Studies professor at California State University at Long Beach, began Kwanzaa as a celebration of the cultural roots of Americans with African ancestry. It is observed December 26 through January 1. The word *Kwanzaa* means "the first" and, in this context, is drawn from the phrase *matunda ya kwanza* which literally means "first fruits of the harvest" in the East African language of Swahili. The extra alphabet, *a,* was added to the end of the word later for symbolic reasons (rounding the word out to seven characters). Rooted in the Pan-African movement, affirming the global connections of all persons of African descent, Kwanzaa began as a celebration of African cultural heritage without any particular religious, regional, or political connotations other than its African spiritual origins. Nonetheless, African American Christians observe Kwanzaa to acknowledge that the Almighty God, who has been revealed through Jesus Christ, created African people in the beauty of God's Divine image and to give praise and thanksgiving to God for this. Since Kwanzaa is a celebration of African American culture and heritage, some will ask if it is appropriate for persons who are not of African ancestry to participate in these observances. Unlike the history of many white religious groups and organizations in the United States and Europe, it has not been the practice among African American churches to discriminate against people on racial grounds. Therefore, anyone who sincerely desires to affirm and celebrate African American culture in religious services grounded in Kwanzaa observances is welcomed to do so without respect to skin pigmentation.

This chapter is a brief introduction for church or faith-oriented community groups interested in commemorating this important evolution in African American self-awareness. It is divided into seven segments, one for each of the seven principles of Kwanzaa, with a scripture verse or two related to each respective principle. Basic information on the elements and symbols of the holiday are included in the series for those considering Kwanzaa as part of their religious observances. A sample liturgy is included for worship services related to this season. The series does not pretend to be comprehensive, but is an introduction that aims to prompt more in-depth research concerning this spiritually rewarding time of celebration we call Kwanzaa.

Reflection 1: UMOJA (oo-MOE-jah) / UNITY - Self-Love, the First Step Toward Unity

> Love the Lord your God with all your heart, soul, and mind, and strength... And love your neighbor as (you love) yourself. There is no commandment greater than these. -Mark 12:20-21[4]

Jesus defined the "great commandment" (to love God with every fiber of our being and to love our neighbor as we love ourselves) as the hallmark of our faith. It is important to note that an individual cannot really know how to love his/her neighbor if that person does not first know how to love him or herself. God expects us to love ourselves. If we do not love ourselves, we do not, in fact, appreciate who God created us to be. We cannot really fulfill the requirements, expectations, or potentials that God has placed within us as beings created in God's image unless we are able to accept, affirm, value, and love ourselves.

Self-hatred is one of the worst legacies left by slavery, reconstruction, segregation, racial discrimination, and the continued oppression of persons of African descent in the Americas. It is one of the greatest challenges to true spiritual, intellectual and cultural liberation. It is seen in the shame still culturally associated with almost anything Black: our history, our skin color, culture, religious traditions and habits, and our speech patterns. It is seen in the statistics regarding Black-on-Black crime and in our readiness to accept uncritically Euro-American values or those of other cultures rather than making a serious effort to understand our own. Self-hatred is manifested in the manner in which persons of African descent tend not to trust or appreciate Black-owned businesses, schools, educators, physicians, dentists, or lawyers.

Unless individuals are able to love themselves as God created them, they will be unable to fully realize all the potential that God has given them. If a person has not learned to love or respect her or himself, how can that person be expected to live up to God's expectations that love and respect be shown to others?

Reflection 2: KUJICHAGULIA (koo-jee-cha-goo-Lee-ah) / SELF-DETERMINATION) - Deciding to Learn the Nguzo Saba

> Religiousness... has been an enduring characteristic of Black life not only in the United States, but also in Africa and the Caribbean. Religious institutions, therefore, are of the greatest importance in these societies. To them accrues the primary responsibility for the conservation, enhancement, and further development of that distinctive spiritual quality that has enabled Blacks to survive and

flourish under some of the most unfavorable conditions of the modern world.[5]

Culture consists of the values, traditions, customs, artifacts, and accumulated knowledge and experience of a society that is passed from previous to succeeding generations. This includes beliefs that help people interpret and understand meaning in their lives. Through Scripture, the liberating activity of God is passed down from ancient times to the present.

> Never forget these commands that I am giving you today. Teach them to your children. Repeat them when you are at home and when you are away, when you are resting and when you are working. Tie them on your arms and wear them on your foreheads as a reminder. Write them on the doorposts of your houses and on your gates. - Deuteronomy 13:6-9

The celebration of Kwanzaa reflects a personal decision to recognize and affirm the legacy of communal affirmation, justice, love, resistance to oppression and the self-determining spirit that has African people to survive in hostile environments. This is a means of passing on key survival tools from one generation to the next. For Christians, Kwanzaa is an aid to commemorating the liberating and sustaining power of the God in the life of African Americans. Certainly, Kwanzaa is not the only way to do this, but the Black religious experience in America itself is an expression of the same realities that the value system of Kwanzaa identifies. The only difference is that the African American church places this ethos in the context of praise and worship.[6] Kwanzaa's chief value for African American Christians is its ability to emphasize the unity of God's liberating activity with African culture and heritage for future generations in ways that are devoid of negative impressions of Black life.

The seven principles of Kwanzaa celebrate characteristics and values that have been central to Black survival in the midst of oppression and they should be affirmed and taught to the present and future generations so that the leaders of tomorrow will be able to continue the struggle for a more just world. These principles are presented as general guides for daily living. During each day of the Kwanzaa season, a different principle is stressed. The principles are listed along with Scriptural references from the Old and New Testament for study and meditation on each of the seven days of Kwanzaa.

> *First Day, December 26: Principle 1 = UMOJA (Unity). Scripture References:* Malachi 2:10; Ephesians 4:1-6. Encourage working together to establish and maintain unity in our families, neighborhoods, and among all African people as the first step toward truly affirming the common bond among all people.
> *Second Day, December 27: Principle 2 = KUJICHAGULIA (Self-determination). Scripture References*: Joshua 24:14-15; Matthew 16:13-16. Make our own decisions about what is best for our people

and our children; Stress the need for people to do their own research and think for themselves rather than continuing to allow others to determine their actions.

Third Day, December 28: Principle 3 = UJIMA (Collective work and Responsibility). Scripture References: Psalm 133:1-3; I Corinthians 12:12-26.-To build and keep our neighborhoods together; maintaining our community by working together and making our sister's and brother's problems our problems and solving them together.

Fourth Day, December 29: Principle 4 = UJAMAA (Cooperative Economics). Scripture References: Nehemiah 5:1-13; I John 4:7-21. -To build and support institutions and business enterprises that serve the best interest of all African people and other oppressed peoples rather than supporting businesses that exploit and support oppression.

Fifth Day, December 30: Principle 5 = NIA (Purpose). Scripture References: Isaiah 6:1-8; Luke 4:16-19. To affirm the God-given meaning in your life, recognizing the value of your actions, and working together with others to improve life for African people everywhere.

Sixth Day, December 31: Principle 6 = KUUMBA (Creativity). Scripture References: I Kings 17:8-16; Acts 3:1-10. The God-given ability to make things or to have ideas that can be of help to others; to do as much as we can, in whatever way we can, to make our community better than it was when we inherited it.

Seventh Day, January 1: Principle 7 = IMANI (Faith). Scripture References: Psalm 91:1-16; Hebrews 11:1-6. To be sure of the things we hope for and to be certain of the things that exist, but which we cannot see at present. To believe in our heritage, our parents, our teachers, our leaders and in Almighty God who is the foundation of our struggle for righteousness and our hope of victory.[7]

Reflection 3: UJIMA (oo-JEE-mah) / COLLECTIVE WORK AND RESPONSIBILITY) - Affirming All Life As Sacred

The world and all that is in it belongs to the Lord; the earth and all who live on it are his. -Psalm 24:1

Not everyone who calls me 'Lord, Lord'; will enter the Kingdom of heaven, but only those who do what my Father in heaven wants them to do. When the Judgement Day comes, many will say to me, 'Lord, Lord! In your name we spoke God's message'... Then I will say to them 'I never knew you.' -Matthew 7:21-23

Kwanzaa originated as a cultural celebration with no particular religious, heroic, or political connotations. As such, many people are surprised to find Kwanzaa observances associated with the church. It is important to understand that the often sharp lines drawn within European oriented culture between the "sacred" and the "secular" are not consistent with the African perspective of the universe. Religion, in the African worldview, is not something separate and distinct from other aspects of life. One African scholar, Kofi Asare Opoku of the University of Ghana in West Africa, observed that: "Religion itself is one with life. It is not an isolated aspect of the community's life but permeates every facet of the community's existence."[8]

Throughout the African American experience, from slavery to the present, faith beliefs have always been deeply rooted in the everyday social, political, and cultural experience of Black people. W.E.B. DuBois (*Souls of Black Folks,* first published in 1903) describing the horrors of slavery noted how some African religious practices played such a major role in helping oppressed people that religion was not something separate and distinct from the experience of daily life:

> The old ties of blood relationship and kinship disappeared... It was a terrific social revolution, yet some traces were retained of the former group life, and chief among them was the institution of the Priest or medicine man. He early appeared on the plantation and found his function as the healer of the sick, the interpreter of the Unknown, the comforter of the sorrowing, the one who rudely but picturesquely expressed the longing, disappointment, and resentment of a stolen and oppressed people.[9]

Though radically changed from the days of slavery, the survival and coping needs of African Americans today in the face of continued racism and discrimination must still defy divisive approaches to life that suggest that economic and political affairs have nothing to do with religious practices and beliefs. The reality that Black communities are still plagued by vast unemployment, larger percentages of consumers instead of producers of goods and services, substandard housing stock, and disproportionate poverty, incarceration, and negative health statistics, are realities that *Ujima* calls African Americans to address with religious zeal.

Reflection 4: UJAMAA (oo-JA-ma-a) / COOPERATIVE ECONOMICS) - A Different Way of Sharing the Good News

> Do not conform yourselves to the standards of this world but let God transform you inwardly by a complete change of your mind. Then you will be able to know the Will of God - what is good and is pleasing to him and is perfect. - Romans 12:2

These days, stores begin to slip "Christmas gift ideas" into their advertisements and on store shelves as early as August! Persons who live on the economic fringes of society, as do many African Americans find themselves drawn into the vortex of irresponsible spending that leaves them deeper in debt and more vulnerable to financial crises. This situation affects not only the very poor, but most of us. The irrational spending associated with Christmas shopping is just part of a deeper problem of misplaced economic priorities that functions to keep the flow of dollars going out of rather than into Black communities and Black-owned or controlled businesses.

In typical American Christmas observances, Jesus Christ of Scripture too frequently becomes reduced to the "cultural hero" of consumerism (not unlike to Santa Claus). American theologian H. Richard Niebuhr identified long ago the "Christ of Culture."[10] The commercialization of Christmas and the brazen materialism that has become the center of our society's interest in this holiday has all but eliminated any references to the Christmas message about God's love. Stress, anxiety, and frustration often reflect the "spirit of the season" in American Christmas observances.

For African American Christians, Kwanzaa's emphasis on meditation and learning, as opposed to the materialism of the typical December holiday festivities, has the potential to restore to the commemoration of Christ's birth the spiritual emphasis that should be there. During Kwanzaa, emphasis is placed on personal and communal reflection, learning, and simplicity. The extravagances of today's society are to be avoided. For Christians, Kwanzaa helps strengthen Christmas observances by emphasizing values that are not materialistic, but caring-centered, the way that Christmas was originally intended to be.

Reflection 5: NIA (nee-AH) / PURPOSE - Discovering Purpose By Remembering History

> The Spirit of the Lord is upon me, because he has chosen me to bring good news to the poor. He has sent me to proclaim liberty to the captives and recovery of sight to the blind, to set free the oppressed and announce that the time has come when the Lord will save his people... This passage of Scripture has come true today... -Luke 4:18-19 & 21 (GN)

The Scriptures teach that no one is born whose life does not have a purpose. Many Bible stories include people whose spiritual contributions changed the course of history because they were aware of their divinely-appointed purpose in life. Take, for example, the birth narratives of Moses and Jesus: Exodus 2-3 and Luke 1-2. For Christians, the principle of NIA seeks to assist persons of faith to discern the divine meaning of their lives.

In order to determine a sense of purpose, a clear sense of history must be borne in mind. This is what the symbolism of the Sankofa bird (which faces forward, but looks back) is instructive. The following litany, entitled *The History and the Nguzo Saba,* outlines the story of African American oppression in the Americas as well as the seven God-given characteristics that have enabled survival and liberation. It is set in the pattern psalm to be recited as part of the Kwanzaa religious service and should be read responsively between the leader and the group. This litany is intended to remind participants of their history and God's involvement in their survival and liberation, them to clarify their divine purpose in life today and for the future.

THE HISTORY and the NGUZO SABA: An Affirmation of Faith

LEADER:	Our fore parents were brought to this hemisphere in chains as chattel, united in bondage only because of their color.
PEOPLE:	**WE REMEMBER THE MIDDLE PASSAGE, O GOD.**
LEADER:	The oppression of the gun, the whip, and the chain were used to strip our ancestors of their culture, their family ties, their language, their names, and their spiritual and religious foundations.
PEOPLE:	**WE REMEMBER THE DEATHS OF OUR MOTHERS, O GOD.**
LEADER:	Rape, murder, the selling of children and the killing of fathers did not stop completely with so-called emancipation, but took on new forms called "Jim Crow" laws, lynching, the denial of the ballot and access to equal educational and economic opportunities.
PEOPLE:	**WE REMEMBER THE DEATHS OF OUR FATHERS, O GOD.**
LEADER:	We recognize that even today, new forms of slavery have been forged by the evils of drug trafficking, mis-education, economic deprivation, crime and violence, as well as continued discrimination, overt and covert.
PEOPLE:	**WE REMEMBER THE DEATHS OF OUR CHILDREN, O GOD.**
LEADER:	We recognize that many of us have been made to feel ashamed of ourselves: our African roots, our skin color, our hair texture, and our physical features.
PEOPLE:	**HEAL US, WE PRAY, O GOD.**
LEADER:	We come together this KWANZAA season to affirm our belief in the principles of survival. We come to affirm our belief in God, who has caused us to survive in a hostile environment and who we believe will empower us to overcome all oppression. We affirm our joy and thanksgiving for the blessings we have received even in the midst of a hostile world. We give thanks to God for the Nguzo Saba. We affirm the gift of UMOJA.
PEOPLE:	**FOR THE GIFT OF *UNITY*, WE THANK YOU, O GOD.**
LEADER:	We affirm the gift of KUJICHAGULIA.
PEOPLE:	**FOR THE GIFT OF *SELF-DETERMINATION*, WE THANK YOU, O GOD.**
LEADER:	We affirm the gift of UJIMA.
PEOPLE:	**FOR THE GIFT OF *COLLECTIVE WORK AND RESPONSIBILITY*, WE THANK YOU, O GOD.**
LEADER:	We affirm the gift of UJAMAA.
PEOPLE:	**FOR THE GIFT OF *COOPERATIVE ECONOMICS*, WE THANK YOU, O GOD.**
LEADER:	We affirm the gift of NIA.
PEOPLE:	**FOR THE GIFT OF *PURPOSE*, WE THANK YOU, O GOD.**
LEADER:	We affirm the gift of KUUMBA.
PEOPLE:	**FOR THE GIFT OF *CREATIVITY*, WE THANK YOU, O GOD.**
LEADER:	We affirm your Divine Presence with us in the gift of IMANI.
PEOPLE:	**FOR THE GIFT OF *FAITH*, WE THANK YOU, O GOD. AMEN**

****

Reflection 6: **KUUMBA (koo-OOM-Bah) / CREATIVITY –**
Symbols, Creative Ways to Show Meaning
As Moses lifted up the bronze snake on a pole in the desert, in the
same way the Son of Man must be lifted up, so that everyone who
believes in him may have eternal life. -John 3:14-15 (GN)

Symbols are an important part of worship and celebration. While symbols
are not the actual phenomenon they represent, their imagery calls to mind the
actualities and meanings they portray. The Christian faith is full of symbols. The
most prominent symbol in the Christian faith is the Cross of Christ. It
symbolizes God's selfless and sacrificial love for all human beings and for the
whole creation. While the image of the Cross is not the actual sacrificial and
selfless love of God, this symbol reminds believers of that divine *agape* love and
its focus on justice. Kwanzaa also has symbols. As with other aspects of
Kwanzaa, the names for these symbols are given in Swahili and use of their
Swahili names should be encouraged throughout the Kwanzaa season. The
seven primary symbols of Kwanzaa[11] are:

1. **MAZAO (fruit and vegetables).** *Mazao* (the produce, fruit and vegetables)
   symbolizes the benefits of teamwork and collective labor to be shared
   among those who have worked to produce these rewards. The fruits
   and produce represents the meaning of *Kwanzaa* (first fruits)
   conceived from African agricultural societies which celebrated God's
   give of fruit and vegetables at harvest time.
2. **MKEKA (place mat).** The *Mkeka* symbolizes the basis upon which
   African people's traditions are built. It represents the foundation of
   African culture and history.
3. **KINARA (the candle holder for seven candles).** The seven candles of
   Kwanzaa include one black candle, three red candles, and three green
   candles. Drawn from a Zulu concept, the *Kinara* is symbolic of the
   continental Africans. It should not be confused with the *minorah* used
   in Jewish religious ceremonies that holds eight candles.
4. **VIBUNZI (ears of corn reflective of the number of children in the
   home or communal observance).** The ears of corn are representative
   of future potential and the offspring who will be the producers of
   tomorrow. Therefore, the corn stalks are used to represent our
   children, the hope of the future and elders of tomorrow.
5. **ZAWADI (gifts).** These gifts are tokens of reward and appreciation in
   recognition of the commitments that have been kept within the
   nuclear family. These gifts are intended to encourage and affirm
   personal growth and achievement. They should be of an educational
   nature or created by the giver. Every effort should be made to avoid
   all materialistic overtones when selecting such gifts.
6. **KIKOMBE CHA UMOJA (communal unity cup).** The unity cup
   symbolizes togetherness or unity that is the goal of the community. It
   also symbolizes the sense of bonding with members of the

community who have departed this life to become ancestors as well as with the yet unborn.

7. **MISHUMAA SABA (the seven candles).** The seven candles symbolize each of the *Nguzo Saba* (seven principles) of Kwanzaa. Candle colors are: 1 black, 3 red, and 3 green. The black candle, placed in the center, represents African people; the three red candles on the right represent the shed blood of Africa; the green candles on the left are symbolic of the fertility of the African continent. A different candle is lit each day, beginning with the center candle and going from left to right on successive days, after the center or Umoja candle has been lit.

There are three other symbols involved with Kwanzaa that should be mentioned. First, the display of the *bendera ya taifa* (the Black Liberation Flag) which is also part of Kwanzaa's symbolic representations. The *bendera* is the black, red, and green flag that originated with Marcus Garvey's Universal Negro Improvement Association. The colors of the *mishumaa saba* (seven candles) of Kwanzaa are taken from this flag and its origin in the Garvey movement. Another symbol consists of the display of the *nguzo saba* (seven principles) printed in large letters for all to see during Kwanzaa observances.

Finally, the symbolic representation that is crucial for embracing the whole spirit of Kwanzaa is the *karamu* of feast. During one of the evenings of Kwanzaa the *Karamu* (feast) is held, traditionally on December 31st. The purpose of the Karamu is to allow for communal sharing through cultural expression. If another date other than December 31 seems more practical, it is permissible to hold the Karamu on that date. The church fellowship hall is an excellent site and should be decorated with African artifacts to give the traditional African atmosphere to the occasion. Traditional African clothing is typically worn on such occasions and a variety of foods are shared during the Karamu. Everyone in the church and surrounding community should be invited, with children and young adults especially welcomed.

Reflection 7: IMANI (ee-MAH-nee) / FAITH - A Celebration of Faith In God

Sing to the Lord, all the world! Worship the Lord with joy; come before God with happy songs!... Enter the Temple gates with thanksgiving; go into its courts with praise.
-Psalm 100:1, 2 & 4 (GN)

Kwanzaa observances for African American Christians are an affirmation of God's involvement in their lives through their African culture and heritage. While people of different faith traditions may approach this cultural celebration differently, it is entirely appropriate for African American Christians to celebrate Kwanzaa as a cultural vehicle that is able to carry the weight of their faith heritage through their understanding of God's revelation in Jesus Christ. If possible, worship services should be planned for each of the seven nights of

Kwanzaa. Care should be taken to include as primary participants in these worship services persons outside the congregation since this is a communal celebration that should involve members of the broader community and not only church-members. It is important to stress the idea that this holiday has a strong focus on the community outside the church as much as within. Guests from the wider community may be invited as speakers during some part of the Kwanzaa services in Christian churches.

Below is a sample order of service. Following the same order of service, a suggested *Affirmation of Faith* is included entitled *The History and the Nguzo Saba.*[12] As part of each Kwanzaa worship service, it is suggested that this outline of the African American history and affirmation of the seven principles of Kwanzaa be recited during the service.

SAMPLE KWANZAA CHURCH SERVICE
(Day 1 of 7)

PRINCIPLE OF THE FIRST DAY:

UMOJA (Unity) - Dec. 26
Theme of the Day
(see Reflection 2)
The effort to achieve togetherness in our families, neighborhoods, and among oppressed people is the first step to realizing the common bond among all people.

ORDER OF CEREMONY
OPENING MUSIC
(African traditional music, drummers, and/or Spirituals sung by the congregation)
CALL TO WORSHIP
(Reading from Black literature or Scripture)
PRAYER of THANKSGIVING
(Elder from community)
CEREMONY OF LIGHTING THE CANDLE
Communal Prayer
Lighting of the Candle (A youth assisted by an adult)
Hymn: "This Little Light of Mine"
AFFIRMATION OF FAITH:
THE HISTORY AND THE NGUZO SABA
(Recited responsively each of the seven services of Kwanzaa)
OFFERING
(Optional: to be donated to some communal cause)
SCRIPTURE READINGS
(Reflection 2 above for suggestions)
INTRODUCTION OF SPEAKER
EVENING ORATION

(Reflections on the meaning of today's principle by
someone from the church or wider community)
CLOSING HYMN
Lift Every Voice and Sing (all verses each service)
BENEDICTION

****

Conclusion

For African American Christians, like all PEOPLE OF African descent in
this county, the observance of Kwanzaa is celebration, meditation, and
reaffirmation of the cultural heritage that all people of African origin share in
common. This season calls attention to the ancestors and their contributions to
their descendants and to the world at large. Kwanzaa is a time for Christians of
African descent to give thanks to Almighty God for who we are and for our
ability, by the grace of God, to survive a generally hostile cultural, social, and
political environment through the centuries. This distinctively African American
celebration provides an excellent opportunity for us to share our faith beliefs
with the broader community.

Endnotes

1.   Annette D. Madlock-Jones, "Kwanzaa and Christianity: A Search for Shared Vision"
(master's thesis, Bethel College, Minneapolis, MN, 2001), 11-12. According to Madlock-
Jones, approximately twelve million persons in the United States observe the holiday and
eight million people in Africa, Brazil, Canada, the Caribbean, England, Germany and
other countries.
2.   Annette D. Madlock-Jones, 16.
3.   While these services were designed to enhance appreciation of the African heritage
for descendants of that heritage, it was notable that non-Africans benefited from these
observances as well. Interestingly, persons who were ethnically outside the African
heritage also expressed a more profound sense of faith in God through their own heritage
because of their participation in the Kwanzaa religious observances.
4.   All Scripture references in this section are from the Good News Bible.
5.   Gayraud S. Wilmore, *Black Religion and Black Radicalism* (Maryknoll, NY: Orbis,
1998), 220.
6.   The Black church in the African-American experience originated in slavery as a
resistance movement whose function in society has been defined by the black struggle for
freedom as human beings.   Ample documentation has been made concerning this fact
(James Cone, W.E.B. DuBois, E. Eric Lincoln, Benjamin E. Mays, Henry Mitchell, Peter
Paris, Gayraud Wilmore and others).   While at various times this struggle has taken
differing forms, sometimes evidencing more militancy than at others, the role of the

Black church as an agency of black survival, liberation, and pride is without parallel in American society. For a general overview of the role of the church in this regard, see Peter Paris', *The Social Teaching of Black Churches* (Philadelphia: Fortress Press, 1985), C. Eric Lincoln & Lawrence Mamiya's *The Black Church in the African-American Experience* (Durham: Duke University Press, 1990), or Gayraud S. Wilmore's *Black Religion and Black Radicalism.*

7.   Wilmore (1998), 3-4.

8.   Kofi Asare Opoku, "African Traditional Religion: An Enduring Heritage," *The Journal of the Interdenominational Theological Center* XVI, No. 1 & 2, (Fall 1988/Spring 1989): 14.

9.   W. E. B. DuBois, *Souls of Black Folks* (Chicago, IL: A.C McClurg & Co., 1903), 216.

10.   Richard H. Niebuhr, *Christ and Culture* (New York: Harper & Row, 1951), 11.

11.   Cedric McClester, *Kwanzaa: Everything You Always Wanted to Know But Didn't Know Where to Ask.* (New York: Gumbs & Thomas, 1984), 6-8.

CHAPTER EIGHT

Building an Africentric Bridge from Inside Stained-Glass Windows to the Community Outside

Johnnie Monroe

> *"All too many have been more cautious than courageous and have remained silent behind the anesthetizing security of the stained-glass windows."* –Martin Luther King, Jr., "Letter from the Birmingham Jail"[1]

The only hope for strengthening and regenerating the African American community resides in its faith communities, and overwhelmingly, this means utilizing African the American church. Dr. Martin Luther King, Jr., while arrested in Birmingham, Alabama, during the struggle for Civil Rights in the 1960s criticized white middle-class church leaders for their lack of courage in challenging the legalized racial segregation that characterized society at that time, preferring to remain quietly silent and irrelevant in their quiet sanctuaries while others suffered injustices on the streets outside their churches. For the African American church, Africentrism means Black folk taking seriously the blessings of their African spiritual heritage as a resource for improving the quality of life for all people in society. This concept is not new and its potential for enabling African American Churches to embrace inner city African American communities that are in crisis is as real today as it has ever been.

Historically, the Christian faith that was nurtured among African slaves was engrafted on an African religious base. In spite of all efforts to dilute and or distort these Africanized Christians traditions, they ultimately emerged full-blown into what we now call African American Christianity. It has been this faith as expressed through the antecedents and current incarnations of the African American church that has stood as a bulwark against the forces of oppression that have attacked every facet of life for Africa's descendants in America since their involuntary introduction to the "New World." In my experience as a pastor for more than thirty years, first in Chester, Pennsylvania at the Thomas M. Thomas Memorial Presbyterian Church and now at the Grace Memorial Presbyterian church in Pittsburgh, Pennsylvania, I am convinced that the congregational life and public ministry of the African American Church remains the best hope in the African American community for positive, systemic change and improvement in the life of our people.

C. Eric Lincoln and Lawrence H. Mamiya in *The Black Church in the African American Experience* describe the significance of the church in African American communities.

> Historically, black churches have been the most important and dominant institutional phenomenon in African American communities. The prescriptions of 250 years of slavery, followed by another hundred years of Jim Crow segregation, permitted only the religious enterprise among black people to become stable, cohesive and independent social institutions. As a consequence, black churches have carried burdens and performed roles and functions beyond their boundaries of spiritual nature in politics, economics, education, music and culture.[2]

For many years, the Black church met the needs of the Black community that no other institutions could or would meet. Especially was this true in the segregated south and to a lesser degree in the urban north. In the South, the black church organized helping hands societies, small financial institutions that started with Christmas Saving clubs, home builders groups, fraternal organizations, such as the Odd Fellows and other groups to bring about social and economic change.[3] The black church had the community spirit that came with her from the Motherland of Africa.

Growing up in the segregated South, I recall how we, as African Americans, were relegated to "our place". In segregated communities where we lived, there were schools, clubs and churches. The houses were modest and not all of the roads were paved. There were wooden bridges across streams in rural areas. Signs marked "For Colored Only" invariably pointed to facilities that were inferior to the ones marked "For White Only". This segregated south, therefore, produced an alternative social structure and economy in African American communities that drew upon the skills and entrepreneurial talents of people whose ancestors were brought from Africa. The citizens of these communities bought with them from Africa. This alternative social structure and economy, though less extensive than Southern White communities and less protected from assault by the hostile forces of segregation, nonetheless, produced a healthy environment in which African Americans not only survived, but also managed to prosper to some degree. These segregated Black communities produced Black owned cafes, restaurants, office buildings, construction companies, barber shops, beauty salons, hospitals, banks, insurance and taxicab companies.

I recall when my parents were able to graduate from the old icebox (an insulated storage cabinet "appliance" that kept its food contents cool) to a new electric refrigerator. During the days when our family had the old icebox, we had to purchase a block of ice from the iceman and we wrapped it in newspaper trying to preserve it all week in order to keep our food fresh. Then we got our new refrigerator. This refrigerator was purchased from a group of Black farmers on Manning Avenue in Sumter, South Carolina. They had organized themselves into a co-op, pooled their resources, and worked for social and economic advancement. It was the African American church that called these men together to pool their resources and do for themselves. This was my first introduction to what we now celebrate as the Kwanza principle of UJAMAA, Cooperative Economics.

In the late fifties, sixties and beyond, a shift came in the Black church and society. The shift was toward integration. This happened after the Topeka, Kansas, decision of the US. Supreme Court (1954), Brown vs. the Board of education. Unfortunately, when African Americans began to integrate the so-called "mainstream" white society (i.e., schools and colleges, patronizing previously "White Only" establishments, neighborhoods that were formerly closed to them), we lost much in the process. We forfeited many of our community's institutions, much of the folkways, mores and historic cultural values that we bought with us from Africa and nurtured in community life in spite of segregation. Many Blacks felt that to be "accepted" and "move the race forward" we had to integrate into the larger, predominately white society. Too often this included abandoning communities where Black communalism had been preserved and encouraged and the spiritual rituals of the Black church and its faith in God were valued. As we moved out of our old communities, African Americans living both outside and inside these formerly segregated communities began to take on more of the materialistic and militaristic values of a larger society that had long been insensitive to their needs. The old neighborhoods that once nurtured the oppressed began to take on destructive and hostile characteristics. The importance of the church as the unquestioned spiritual anchor in the life of these communities began to fade for younger generations.

The time has come for the Black church to reunite with the community where it is located and to reintroduce some of the folkways and mores that came with us from Africa. We must seek to build a bridge that connects the African American church and African American community in meaningful ways. The bridge I see being built is not one of the bridges we see construction companies from outside erecting in our neighborhoods, having torn down other important landmarks. We need a different kind of bridge; one built of a different kind of materials. It is a symbolic bridge, but at the same time, very real. I see a strong wooden bridge being constructed with treated wood, not built by huge construction companies from other areas, but built by local people indigenous to our African American neighborhoods who love the local people and environmental landscape for its God-given potential. I see a bridge being built one plank at a time and connected by a strong unbreakable cable that will last for years and years.

This bridge will allow the African American church to walk out from behind the stained glass windows of its sanctuaries, reach into and embrace its own communities and the residents of those communities to affirm black life and the indigenous institutions that reflect divine righteousness and love. We must, however, build our bridge plank by plank. I remember bridges with today their thick wooden planks that I saw in my youth. Analogically, I saw these "bridges" in my community ministry as a pastor in Chester, PA, and I have seen them constructed in a process that works for us today at Grace Memorial Presbyterian Church in Pittsburgh. In the next few pages, I want to list some planks for this bridge that are the characteristics of an Africentric ministry. These planks constitute the infrastructure of the bridge I see spanning the wide-open gulfs that are the needs of our African American communities. I view the Africentric ministry as one of the strong planks that we must put into this bridge between God, our Creator, Redeemer and Sustainer, the black Church, and our brothers and sisters in the African American community that we are called to serve today.

The First Plank: Prayer

In November 2002 we had at least three shootings or murders of young men in the Schenley Heights Community of Pittsburgh. Schenley Heights is where the Grace Memorial Presbyterian Church is located. It is the community to which upwardly mobile African Americans moved in the 1940's, 50's, and 60's, to escape the lifestyles of the "riff-raffs" in the lower Hill District closer to downtown. In those days, Schenley Heights was a quiet community of upscale homes owned by the Black social elite of Pittsburgh. Many remain in this community today. However, the social conditions from which the community's earliest African Americans sought to escape fifty years ago, by the latter quarter of the last century, had caught up to its current residents with full force: drive-by shootings, drug trafficking, declining housing stock, educationally challenged schools, and a higher than average unemployment.

Rev. Carmen Cox-Harwell, my pastoral associate, and I went to visit the Schenley Heights family of one of the murdered young men. As we stood in the family's living room just before they left the house to go to the funeral home for the wake, the young man's mother and father said to us "We need prayer as never before." Then they said, "Reverends, we need to find a way to address the senseless killing in our communities." It was significant that the first thing the parents of this murdered young man recognized was the need for prayer as a means of ending the destructive violence that had taken their son from them and was destroying the fabric of their community.

Faith in God and a profound belief in the power of prayer are not new in the African American community. It is part of the heritage of faith that finds its roots in our African inheritance and it is this belief in prayer that has been a key factor in African American life through slavery, segregation, and until this day. It is often ignored or downplayed in popular culture as emotionalism or an otherworldly self-delusion. However, for people in crisis prayer is the first tool of survival. It is a practice that enables the victims of oppression to regroup and prepare themselves for healing and healthy corrective action.

As we think of building the bridge from stained glassed windows to the community the first plank we need to place in construction the bridge is the *plank of prayer*. Church folks need to understand that prayer is a dialogue and not a monologue. We speak to God and then we settle down long enough to be still and allow God to speak to us. We need prayer to discern God's will for what our mission and ministry should be. The saving grace for the Black church and community has been prayer. Our foreparents knew that power and articulated their beliefs in words of the spiritual:

> *I prayed and I prayed,*
> *I prayed all night long.*
> *I prayed and I prayed,*
> *Until I found the Lord.*

James 5:13 reads, "the prayer of the righteous availeth much." We believe with all our hearts that there is power in prayer. We pray knowing that God hers and answers prayer. We pray in faith, in belief. R. A. Torrey in his book, *The Power of Prayer and the Prayer of Power* writes:

> "Prayer in faith, that is praying with an unquestionable belief that you will receive exactly what you ask; yes, believing as you pray that God has heard your prayer and that you have received the thing that you ask, is one of the most important factors in obtaining what we ask when we pray."[4]

African American Christians often talk about the power of prayer, but fail to practice the act of praying. Yet, the community is looking to the church to call it to a time of prayer, especially in moments of crisis. The African American heritage of faith in God and belief in prayer cannot be ignored if a church is to embrace Africentric ministry. The first plank in the bridge of Africentric ministry is the plank of prayer. It is the foundation of our outreach and organizing in and to the community. As our ancestors used to say, "Folk who won't pray right can't live right."

The Second Plank: Listening

The second plank in the bridge between the church and its community is what I call *Active Listening*. Today we are bombarded with such a variety of sensations (television, radio, computers, computer games, CD players, DVD players, etc.) that we routinely filter out much of what we see and most of what we hear. Because of the quick pace of our lives today, our attention spans have become increasingly shorter. In this media driven culture, where 15 or 30 second commercials appear on our television screens in rapid succession and on radio in the same fashion, we are unaccustomed to listening to each other as was formerly common place. Visual images on MTV now graphically portray the moods and messages of songs that words alone used to convey. Active listening is not as important anymore because so much of society is programmed to depend on visual communication.

The African American church must be attentive to what the community is saying. Active listening means that information is processed and internalized in such a way that it actually changes the listener and his or her intended response. Active listening implies a relationship of sufficient length to facilitate real communication. This is important in African American culture because ours is an oral culture. Indeed, one of the gifts that God gave people of African descent is the gift of *storytelling*. James O. Stallings, in *Telling the Story: Evangelism in Black Churches,* tells us that:

> Stories come in all sizes, shapes, and forms, and all sorts of circumstances. They are really gifts from God speaking to us; allowing us if we listen to hear, see, grow and be transformed.[5]

Without cultivating the skill of active listening, the stories of people in our communities will not be heard and important information on African American life will be lost. There are stories in the community that the church needs to hear: stories of yesterday, stories of today, and stories of hurt, pain, struggles, and successes.

Listening builds relationships. As people share their stories common interests are revealed and contrasting views are clarified. As the community reveals its story, the church listen, learn and connect. If the church does *active* listening jointly designed ministries of power can develop because there is an investment on the part of both partners. Church members may want to engage community members in one-on-one dialogues or projects in order that people may be given the opportunity to share stories and learn from each other. This type of *active listening* is a key to building the sense of *Umoja* (Unity) that once characterized Black community life. It is a indispensable plank for   bridges of an Africentric ministry that spans the stained glass windows and the world outside and hears the real issues, needs, joys, and aspirations of the community.

The Third Plank: Collaboration

If the Church is to bring about real change in the community, it must be done in collaboration *with* the community. While the church is the spiritual mentor of the community, it is the community where the church is located that legitimizes the church. Therefore, it is essential that there be serious collaboration and communication between these two entities. After actively listening to those in the community and hearing their stories, the church is in a better position to know with whom and how to build collaborative relationships in order to participate in ministry with others.

At Grace Memorial Presbyterian Church we operate a number of community outreach ministries under the umbrella of separate corporate structures especially designed to support our 501(c)3 not-for-profit corporations.

One is called the Schenley Heights Community Development Program, Inc. Through it we operate a five-day per week tutorial and enrichment program, a track and field program, and a parents support group. We have also organized the Schenley Heights Collaborative, another 501(c)3, to address the housing and economic needs of our community. We operate a program for teens called *United Teens on a Mission* (UTOM) for teenagers of our community. None of these ministries would have been possible had we not collaborated the local public school system, local schools, social agencies, and community groups such as block clubs. The word collaboration is new for the church. Historically, many churches historically have been accustomed to developing programs *for* the community and not *with* the community.

Collaboration involves becoming embedded in the lives of people who are not members of the local church, developing relationships and listening to the ideas and opinions of the wider neighborhood. In general, in setting up church-based community organizations, the governing structures will include persons who live in the community but may not be members of the church. Working with local community-based groups and agencies (such as local schools, other congregations, colleges, etc.) is a way that the resources of the church can be greatly augmented to provide a better quality of ministry than could be provided by the congregation alone. This is part of the African American heritage of being involved with the community. If the bridge of Africentric ministry is to be built in the city, it must have a plank in it called *collaboration.*

The Fourth Plank: Community Concept

An Africentric ministry that serves as a bridge between the church and community requires a plank that I call *Community Concept.* This is critical, for if this plank is not in place, bridge building between the church and the community cannot happen. This is a plank that the church will stand on apart from the community for a period of time, for it is by reference to this plank that the church will decide how it will react, respond, and minister to and with the community in which it is located.

By *community concept,* I refer to how we *feel* about the community in which God has placed us to do ministry. In order to determine how we feel about a particular community, we must honestly answer several questions. What is our outlook on this community? Is it generally positive or pessimistic? Do we perceive a positive potential there? Is this a community in which we feel we can work and enjoy ministry? Can we minister to a community that is different from the norm which we feel most comfortable? Difference here does not refer to racial difference alone. It may be economic difference, class difference, social difference or people with a different lifestyle than our own. While all communities have their challenges, do we see the strengths of this community outweighing its weaknesses?

More and more, we are finding that African American churches are leaving black neighborhoods because they feel that they can no longer relate to the residents of these communities. In many instances, the areas that are being left behind are being viewed as having too many problems and challenges that overwhelm us. We see them as *hopeless wastelands* instead of fertile grounds waiting to be tilled, fertilized, and planted. In such situations, the departing congregations will not describe the situation in these terms, but will emphasize the advantages of doing ministry in other areas. Sometimes, as the old neighborhood changes and new residents move in, they are not regarded as children of God with potential to be worked with, but only as "problem people."

Deep down within, I am a "farm boy" from South Carolina. My late father and my whole family were sharecroppers in the rural areas of Sumter County, South Carolina. I remember once when my Father wanted to expand his planting capabilities in order to better provide for our family, he could not find cleared land anywhere near us. Therefore, my Dad identified a plot of swampland near our house that he decided to farm. All of our neighbors thought he was crazy, but he was determined to give it a try. He dug out the roots of old decayed trees, underbrush, and the branches of that swamp day after day. It was not easy, but he was determined and in time had cleared that piece of swampland. He then tilled the soil, fertilized it, planted the seed, tended the plants and watched the crop grow. Not long after, our family reaped what farmers called a *bumper crop*. It was a huge success that produced more food than anyone else thought possible. What other people saw as wasteland with absolutely no potential at all, my father saw as fertile soil waiting to be tilled and cultivated.

For too long those of us in the institutional church have seen the communities where God has placed us as wastelands. We have bought into the wider society's negative opinions about areas in which poor people live, where housing is substandard, schools are said to be wretched, crime is high while lawful employment opportunities are low. We begin to believe only the official news reports about our neighbors and accept the bank's assessments of our land values. When challenges come, we feel little responsibility to reach out with love in this environment because we have subconsciously bought into the idea that the neighborhood beyond redemption.

Real estate records are full of examples where African Americans began to move into all-white neighborhoods and the white congregations moved out because they saw such areas as wastelands. That is how Grace Memorial got the building it currently occupies at 1000 Bryn Mawr Road in Pittsburgh. We commonly refer to this as the "White flight" phenomenon. On the other hand, many African American congregations have remained in the city with meager resources, seeking to do the will of God to work with these communities to strengthen them while others have created a *Black Flight* phenomenon. A truly Africentric approach to ministry has to have a *community concept* that recognize and treats the community as fertile ground waiting to be tilled.

That is the *community concept* that shapes our congregation's view of ministry at this point in history. It is our belief that the Schenley Heights community is filled with people with potentials, has numerous resources, and is a fertile field for cultivation. Our *community concept* sees this piece of the earth as an opportunity for ministry that more than justifies our investment of time, talent and money in service to our neighbors. Some of our ministries include:

a) After-school Tutorial and Enrichment Program (ASTEP) that serves over 130 Children daily.

b) Summer Enrichment Program for over 100 Children and youth for six weeks during the summer months.

c) An older youth and teen program, United Teens on a Mission "UTOM", that meets weekly and allows children and youth to deal with issues and opportunities of their own choosing.

d) Four Bible Study groups to help people learn the Word and relate Scripture to daily life and personal spiritual growth.

e) A Men's Ministry (*The Potters*) to help men come to grips and deal with the issues that relate especially to men.

f) Young adult ministry that allows the younger people of the church and community wrestle with the issues of life through Bible Study and discussion groups.

g) The Schenley Heights Collaborative, a housing ministry that works with at least five other community groups concerned with the availability of affordable housing.

h) Grace Church is also a member of the Pittsburgh Interfaith Impact Network (PIIN), an interracial and interfaith network of over thirty congregations working to support systemic change and transform power structures in the City of Pittsburgh and Allegheny County.

I could go on naming ministries of Grace. Suffice it to say that we have invested in groups that are in our community because we feel that the community is God's fertile field that is simply waiting to be tilled, fertilized tilled and prepared to yield harvest.

We believe that the schools and other institutions of our communities can be changed for the better; that our children can learn; that the church can make a difference. Our concept of the community is a positive one and it is an essential plank for building the bridge of Africentric ministry from inside the stained glass toward the community outside.

The Fifth Plank: Risk Taking

I am completely convinced that any African American congregation that is ministering in an urban area must be willing to take risks and lose all for the sake of Christ. Risks sometimes involve dealing with people who, though they are the intended beneficiaries of our efforts, will disappoint and even destroy us. Risks involve incurring the wrath of so-called "power brokers" of the community who exist in local government, the immediate neighborhood, or even in the local congregation. These are people with whom we may not agree from time to time. Risks involve making financial commitments to communities or persons whom the wider society may see as "not worth it."

I realize that the latter statement is bold and perhaps even rash, but effective urban ministry is risky work. We are called to take what I like to call "a faith walk". The Word tells us that "We all by faith and not by sight" (1 Corinthians 5:21). At Grace, we have been walking by faith and taking the risk of meeting the needs in our community. We do not know what the end is going to be, but is this not what we all are challenged to do? Moreover, is this not precisely the call that comes from Jesus Christ? For nearly 135 years, Grace Church has been taking a risk and moving around in the Hill – without a lot of economic resources, but simply trying to make a difference. Taking risks, then, is a plank in the Africentric ministry bridge that will not be easy, but it will be safer than no risks at all, because no risk equals no faith in God.

Conclusion

Our faith heritage as Africentric people has always placed the welfare of the community at the center of the church's concern. Although the economic, political, and social realities of racism still challenge African American life, the African heritage and religious traditions that have enabled African and African American people to overcome obstacles in the past are with us today on both sides of the Atlantic. While many may see our communities as facing ever increasing problems, I believe an Africentric perspective of Christian ministry leads one to see the times in which we live as one of the greatest opportunities for the African American church in our long history. Building the bridge of ministry from stained glass windows into the communities around our churches is for me the key to saving and strengthening our communities. The five planks of *Prayer, Listening, Collaboration, Community Concept,* and *Risk-Taking* are not new inventions, but time-tested hallmarks an African American Christian ministry, *Africentric Christian ministry,* that is certain to provide safe crossing for those who, in faith, desire to make the connections from *inside* to *outside.* Let's be about the business of bridge building!

Endnotes

---

1.   Martin Luther King, Jr. "Letter from the Birmingham Jail" as it appears in James M. Washington's *Testament of Hope: The Essential Writings of Martin Luther King, Jr.* (San Francisco, CA: Harper, 1986), 299.

2.   C. Eric Lincoln and Lawrence H. Mamya, *The Black Chruch in the African American Experience* (Duke University Press, 1990), 92.

3.   This is a fact that has been documented by several writers, among them Peter A. Paris, *The Social Teaching of the Black Churches* (Philadelphia, PA: Fortress Press, 1985) and Andrew Billingsley, *Mighty Like a River: The Black Church and Social Reform* (New York: Oxford University Press, 1999).

4.   R. A. Torrey, *The Power of Prayer and the Prayer of Power* (Grand Rapids Michigan: Zondervan Publishing House), 123.

5.   James O. Stallings, *Telling the Story: Evangelism in Black Churches* (Valley Forge: Juson Press, 1998), 9.

CHAPTER NINE

Africentric Christian Education: A Historical Perspective

Fred Douglas Smith, Jr.

Let us begin our discussion of Africentric Christian Education by first taking into account Molefi Kete Asante's notion of an Africentric epistemology. For Asante, Afrology is the study of African concepts, issues, and behaviors as an amalgamation of the three fundamental postures of feeling, knowing, and acting. This approach to understanding is to be distinguished from what Asante views as a Eurocentric linear method of delineating affective, cognitive, and connotative aspects of a singular phenomenon for study. Given this analysis, an approach to Christian education would necessitate the study of African heritage and culture in a manner that separates cognitive aspects from other aspects of the African experience. According to Asante, the Africentric method involves a more holistic or circular approach. This more holistic or circular Africentric perspective is of vital importance to appreciating the significance of the educational experience in the African American Christianity that has enabled Africans in America to survive and move beyond survival to liberation. Unfortunately, most studies of African American Christian education (when it has been studied at all) have been conducted using an Eurocentric linear method which restricts analysis its cognitive form. Such an approach leaves unexamined other aspects of religious education that takes place within the African American community.

Secondly, the historical study of Christian education in the African American religious experience usually begins with slavery and missionary efforts. Such investigations reports James Tymes in *The Rise of Religious Education among Negro Baptists*[1], generally focus on attempts to tend the soul of the enslaved Africans as their one possession. The question of the Africans" physical situation (i.e., body, selfhood, or personality) was left to his or her master. As a consequence everything thought to be African was despised. Systematic and brutal attempts were made to expunge all remnants of African culture and heritage from the consciousness of the enslaved people. Their very humanity was questioned, challenged and then denied. Survival was the chief task of Africa's descendants in America precisely because they had to endure the most gruesome slavery in human history or they were exterminated.

A Eurocentric approach to African American Christian education, therefore, only addresses the religious teaching that impacted this population cognitively. It does not address other aspects of Christian education that have to do with the culture, personality, or self-empowerment that are inherent in the lives of African peoples. The pre-slave African culture, religious grounding, and social organization that were part of the experience of the enslaved Africans in America were not factored into Eurocentric approaches to religious education among these people. Most records of Christian education for African Americans only document efforts sanctioned by slave masters. However, religious education took place outside the missionary efforts of whites. Enslaved persons of color were forced to draw on cultural resources innate in their African culture, which survived the middle passage, and could not be expunged in spite of slave indoctrination. African Americans engaged their whole being in the task of survival, and in the New World. African beliefs were integrated with American realities to form a hybrid religion that proved to be a key factor spiritual and physical survival.

According to Mays and Nicholson[2] in order to survive, the African in America had to develop survival techniques. The most important significant survival techniques were religious. One religious technique was the songs they sang which became known as the *Black Spirituals*. Another was charismatic preaching and cathartic worship experiences. I contend that both are forms of religious education that have roots in an African-centered culture and spiritual ethos. It is this aspect of Christian education that I argue constitutes the essence of what I understand to be Africentric Christian education.

Well-meaning missionaries used forms of banking education[3] such as slave catechisms (a form of cognitive oppression) in attempts to make the Africans good slaves. However, this was only a small part of the religious education that took place on plantations under the watchful eyes of slave masters and overseers. The Africans developed a form of Christianized folklore, consisting of a spirit of hope and expressed in music of the soul that instructed them in the ways of God and made survival possible under the most brutal of conditions.

There were two forms of Christian education. One took place in Sunday school settings structured by slave masters or under their supervision. The other, more important form of Christian education –the Africentric model—took place in the "invisible institution" (the secret religious meetings) held deep in the woods or in the slave quarters late at night. This second kind of Christian education has been largely invisible and acknowledged because of the Eurocentric method generally utilized in the study of African American religious experience.

A Folk Africentric Christian Education of Survival

A goal of Africentric Christian education is to awaken in oppressed people a sense of transcendence that corrects the tendency of demeaning social and political structures to limit their attention to the dynamics of oppression rather than to draw attention to sources of human dignity. The function of religious education as a response to oppression is to present persons with appropriate metaphors through which they may come to see and understand their condition differently. These metaphors provide a vision by which persons begin to see what should be what they can hope for, and how they ought to act. An Africentric religious education is a metaphorical process by which a person of African descent can see, from the context of his/her cultural heritage, not only how she/he should be, but how the world can be; not just what to hope for, but how to achieve it. Such a person comes to a new understanding of not merely how she or he ought to act in light of the African heritage, but how to change action into a transforming praxis of self and the world.

During slavery, Reconstruction, and Jim Crow segregation, this Africentric hope enabled generations of oppressed people of color to fashion a survival technique of transcendence. These "old folks", as they were sometimes called in deference to their having survived amidst brutal living situations, had a different point of reference outside their historical context. This point of reference enabled them to relativize the historical present. That is what I mean by trans-historical consciousness. It is as if they lived simultaneously in all times. This perspective enabled them to spiritually and intellectually identify with situations outside of their own; situations they drew from biblical stories. As a result, African-Americans caught in the vice of slavery knew how "to make bricks without straw". They "crossed the Red Sea with Moses" in the book of Exodus. At the same time, they endured North American slavery and celebrated the Emancipation Proclamation on June nineteen ("Juneteenth") in Texas. They suffered the indignity of legalized Jim Crow in the South and quietly practiced Jim Crow in the North. They also shared the *Dream* of Martin Luther King, Jr. The old folks" hope was not only for a "this-world" freedom, but also for an "other-world salvation". They had a spirit of hope and knew with uncommon certainty that "trouble don't last always".

During slavery, segregation, and lynching, this perspective provided African Americans with a hope for a transhistorical or otherworldly salvation that made the struggle for a this-worldly liberation not only possible, but worthwhile. The religion of my grandmother and my great Auntie Lily helped them to speak of their oppression and struggle from a perspective that differed from the one, which trapped other family members in their preoccupation with current circumstances. They were able to achieve a "heavenly" or transcendent perspective on life's circumstances enabling them not only to survive, but to plant seeds of liberation in others. Zora Neale Hurston drew upon this reality as she wrote about the function of "the Hope-Bringer" in African American folklore:

> Old Massa met our hope-bringer all right, but when Old Massa met him, he was not going by his right name. He was traveling, and touristing around on the plantations as the laugh-provoking Brer Rabbit. So Old Massa and Old Miss and their young ones laugh with

and at Brer Rabbit and wished him well. And all the time, there was High John de Conquer playing his tricks of making a way out of no-way. Hitting a straight lick with a crooked stick. Winning the jackpot with no other stake but a laugh. Fighting a mighty battle without outside-showing force, and winning his war from within. Really winning in a permanent way, for he was winning with the soul of the black man whole and free. So he could use it afterwards. For what shall it profit a man if he gain the whole world and lose his soul? You would have nothing but a cruel, vengeful, grasping monster come to power.[4]

The question is not whether African Americans will have metaphorical models (real or imagined) that will serve heroically as models of identity formation. Such models, in fact, already exist within African culture and Christian tradition and these heroic metaphorical models that enlist imitation can be prophetic in shaping character, promoting vision, and inspiring transformative action. According to John W. Roberts, professor of folklore and folk life,

The heroes that we create are figures who, from our vantage point on the world, appear to possess personal traits and/or perform actions that exemplify our conception of our ideal self, the self that our personal or group history, in the best of all possible worlds, has prepared us to become.[5]

Roberts argues that a particular culture selects and promotes hero/heroines to fit the historical needs of the group. Slaves needed to survive a system that deprived them of liberty and the most basic human needs such as food and clothing. Thus, slaves retrieved from their African heritage the wily trickster. Under Jim Crow laws African Americans were not only denied the protection of law, but law also served as an instrument for their continued oppression. The outlaw who could beat the system of racially oppressive laws, therefore, became a hero/heroine.

According to Roberts, figures and actions considered heroic in one historical context or by one group of people may be viewed as ordinary or even criminal in another historical context or by other groups, or even by the same groups at different times. Yet, these ordinary and even criminal figures are endowed with charisma by the telling and retelling of their stories in light of a given people's need for heroes and heroines to meet the historical challenge of their time. Africentric Christian education seeks to claim the strengths of the pre-slavery African culture and the African American experience of oppression in such a way that their identity with an ordinary carpenter executed as a common criminal and endowed with charisma becomes for all time the means of hope and transhistorical perspective that empowers survival.

According to Theophus Smith in *Conjuring Culture*[6], Jesus Christ has been such a metaphorical hero/heroine for centuries in the Western World and for a significant portion of humankind:

> ...because of his multiple persona as (1) cosmic lord and divine logos--the word of God by whom all things were created and subsist; (2) an earthly (Davidic) king, heir of an ancient dynasty and of a messianic destiny of imperial power and rule; and (3) a religious leader of miraculous and prophetic powers who represents and mediates divine favor and judgment, beneficence and justice, to the acclaim and prosperity of his people and all Nations.[7]

There is much in traditional Christian education today that fails to provide metaphors of Jesus capable of attracting significant charisma[8]and dignity. An Africentric Christian Education that is capable of portraying Jesus as the liberating force and heroic model through identification with the historical justice seeking models of the African heritage in this country. Hence, the first task of Africentric Christian education is to address the historicity, relevance and seriousness of Jesus" metaphorical persona, transhistorical nature, and relevance. The persona of metaphor for Jesus Christ is endowed with charisma when his metaphors have historicity, relevance and seriousness. This occurs when: (1) In Jesus, we can recognize the transhistorical possibilities in one person who challenged historical structures of oppression and achieved transhistorical salvation; (2) Jesus plays a significant role in an on-going drama of liberation, reconciliation and transformation; (3) Jesus is the ultimate model of dignity and heroic action. One function of Africentric Christian education, then, is to interpret the charismatic reality of Christ[9] in the liberation of African Americans from forces of oppression today.

Christian education in the African American church has a long, but often-unappreciated history because the cultural and political nature of that education in the African American experience is not adequately taken into account. One of the primary historians of Christian Education in the African American experience was Grant Shockley[10]. Shockley attempted a historical sketch of religious education in the African American experience drawing on cultural and political sources and provided a ground-breaking analysis of what we now refer to as an Africentric approach to Christian Education. He sought to develop strategies for doing Christian education that were consistent with the Invisible Institution and the Black church tradition; political realities of oppression today and yesterday; and African and folk cultural sources. He drew heavily on Black and liberation theologies to develop a model of Christian Education, which he referred to as an *Intentional Engagement model*[11] that sought to liberate African Americans from continued oppression.

Methods of Africentric Christian Education Enabling Liberation
The methodologies of Africentric Christian Education in the United States that are liberating in their educational outcomes are those that include: storytelling, root metaphors, praxis models (social action), event-centered experiences (such as holidays or special days), and role models (mentoring). These methodologies are utilized where most Christian education takes place including, but not limited to, the following: Sunday school, Bible study, special liturgical events, social action, preaching and worship.

Anne Wimberley's story linking method from her book *Soul Stories* is an excellent example of an African-centered Christian education approach in Sunday school: storytelling. Joseph Crocket's root metaphorical method in *Teaching Scriptures from an African American Perspective* provides a holistic African centered approach to Bible study. Charles Foster's events-centered education strategy in *Educating Congregations*, while not written for the African American church tradition, can be a strong congregational resource when formatted to highlight events and special days drawn from African culture and history. Again, Grant Shockley's *Intentional Engagement Model* describes a praxis methodology that is used in many congregations involved in social activism and advocacy.

Joseph V. Crockett in *Teaching Scripture: from an African American Perspective* employs four metaphors, Story, Exile, Sanctuary and Exodus as strategy for Christian education that is grounded in the experience of Africa's descendants. For Crockett, the metaphorical methodology allows an image to take on multiple dimensions.

> "Story" is the metaphorical reference for this strategy. The metaphor of story has at least three dimensions. One, story refers to the history of African Americans. Two, story is used to refer to particular passages from scripture. For example, we speak of the story of creation, the story of the Exodus, the story of Jesus, the parables, and so forth. The third dimension of story emphasizes its theological aspects. It refers to the drama of God's actions in history. Jesus of Nazareth is the story's main character and through the writing, witness, traditions, and actions of the Christian community, the drama continues to unfold."[12]

The metaphorical process ties together the African heritage and the Biblical story and, through the drama of God's actions in history, both are transcendent. The pre-slavery African heritage can be prefixed to the story of slave trade along with its oppression and discrimination and placed in the context of God's unfolding drama. This approach helps African Americans understand and experience their transcendence from freedom into the experience of historical oppression through a sacred historical perspective.

Anne Wimberley, in *Soul Stories: African American Christian Education*, utilizes a heroic story-driven metaphorical process:

Story-linking is a process whereby we connect parts of our everyday stories with the Christian faith story in the Bible and the lives of exemplars of the Christian faith outside the Bible. In this process, we link with bible stories by using themes as mirrors through which we reflect critically on the liberation we have already found or are still seeking. We also link with our Christian faith heritage by learning about exemplars who chose a way of living based on their understanding of liberation and vocation found in Scripture. By linking with Christian faith heritage stories, we may be encouraged and inspired by predecessors who have faced circumstances with which we readily identify.[13]

Story-linking is a metaphorical process that focuses on the heroic to provide a transcendent self-identity. Wimberley's story-linking, is a process for the heroic metaphorical representation of the "hope-bringer" of slave folklore for African Americans today. According to Robert Penn Warren, "To create a hero is, indeed, to create a self."[14] Warren makes the point that the hero/heroine is not just an expression of a pre-existing self, nor only a projection of that self, but instead belongs primarily to the process whereby the self emerges metaphorically. Africentric Christian education is a process for creating religious heroes and heroines that can bring hope to African Americans through this liberating metaphorical process of education.

Both Joseph Crockett and Anne Wimberley were impacted by the person and work of Grant Shockley and his influence can be seen in the liberation and world transforming focus found in both books. The metaphorical task of Africentric Christian Education is to mine the funded sources of biblical and cultural traditions of African heritage to find metaphors that are able to creatively carry and translate God's vision of liberation and human dignity for the present and future Black Church. Such a metaphor was effectively utilized in the educational ministry of Martin Luther King Jr. when he frequently employed the prophetic metaphor of the "Beloved Community".

Prophetic Africentric Christian Education of Reconciliation

Africentric Christian Education has prophetic Christianity as its primary source. Prophetic Christianity, according to Cornel West, is guided by a dialectical conception of human nature and human history that portrays what one is, what it is that one hopes for, and how one ought to act. Like Grant, West makes the case that at the heart of African American existential religious struggle is the dialectical tension of Christian faith and racism. Likewise, the primary source of African American's historical struggle is the dialectical tension between the white domination and the reign of God. An Africentric prophetic Christianity has as its telos the Reign of God (i.e. Martin King's metaphor, "the Beloved Community") that overcomes racism of every kind.

For West, prophetic Christianity rests on two norms, one existential (individuality) and two social (democracy).[15] The first norm of prophetic

Christianity is *individuality*: the principle of the self-realization of *individuality* within community. This can be understood both as penultimate liberation and otherworldly salvation. The second norm, *democracy*, requires accountability of institutions to the populace. Prophetic Christian Education builds on and moves beyond these existential and social norms via a theological hermeneutic of suspicion.

First, as West argues, a prophetic Christianity (and thus Christian education) promotes as an ethical norm the notion of individuality that stresses the value of community. West states that prophetic Christianity emphasizes:

> ...The importance of community, common good, and the harmonious development of personality... (and opposes a doctrine of individualism that) ...promotes human self centeredness, denigrates the idea of community and distorts the holistic development of personality. [16]

Further, according to West:

> The norm of individuality conceives persons as enjoyers and agents of their uniquely human capacities, whereas doctrinaire of individualism views them as maximizers of pleasure and appropriators of unlimited resources. [17]

A prophetic Christian education perceives individuality defined as of persons of faith, created in the image of God and capable of selfless acts of love. Africentric Christian education, therefore, affirms the individual in the context of and as part of a cohesive whole called the community. This is the prophetic aspect of Africentric Christian education in that it seeks to equip the student of faith with a self-understanding that is based in community. Reconciliation becomes the hallmark of this prophetic quality of Africentric Christian Education. It is in this that the function of reconciliation conceives of individuality also in terms of *ubuntu,* a characteristic Bishop Desmond Tutu explains as he describes how an individual *is* an individual *through* other individuals:

> We say, "a person is a person through other persons." It is not "I think therefore I am". It says rather: "I am human because I belong, I participate, I share." A person with ubuntu is open and available to others, does not feel threatened that others are able and good, for he or she has a proper self-assurance that comes from knowing that he or she belongs in the greater whole and is diminished when others are humiliated or diminished, when others are tortured or oppressed, or treated as they were less than who they are. [18]

Africentric Christian education is prophetic because it draws on Tutu's Ubuntu theology. It goes beyond survival and liberation toward the task of reconciliation in creating and affirming a Beloved Community.

Endnotes

1.   James D. Tyms *The Rise of Religious Education Among Negro Baptist*, (New York: Exposition Press INC. 1965), 85-89
2.   Benjamin Elijah Mays and Joseph William Nicholson *The Negro"s Church*, (New York: Negro Universities Press 1933), 1-5
3.   Paulo Freire, *Pedagogy of the Oppressed*, Banking education is form of education that disempowers the oppressed by pouring fact into their heads assuming they have no knowledge only their teachers do. So they do not learn to think for themselves or develop capacity for critical thinking necessary to struggle for freedom.
4.   Zora Neale Hurston, "Sometimes in the Mind," in Langston Hughes and Arna Bontemps, eds., The Book of Negro Folklore (New York: Dodd, Mead, 1958), 93, quoted in Riggins R. Earl, Jr. *Dark Symbols, Obscure, Signs: God, Self, & Community in the Slave Mind*, (Maryknoll, NY: Orbis Books, 1993), 133.
5.   John W. Roberts, *From Trickster to Badman: The Black Folk Hero in Slavery and Freedom*. (Philadelphia: University of Pennsylvania Press, 1989), 1.
6.   Theophus Smith, *Conjuring Culture: Biblical Formations of Black America*, (Oxford, 1994).
7.   Smith, 199.
8.   By Charisma I mean the personal traits or characteristics of person in a leadership position that is capable of eliciting popular loyalty, admiration, enthusiasm in followers or admirers.
9.   This social construction of charisma proposal is derived from Anthony J. Blasi"s book, *Making Charisma: The Social Construction of Paul"s Public Image*, (New Brunswick: Transaction Publishers, 1991), 11-12.
10.   See Grant Shockley, *Religious Education and the Black Experience* in Black Church, Vol. 2, n.1 1972, 91-111
11.   Grant Shockley, *Christian Education and the Black Religious Experience*. In *Ethnicity in the Education of the Church* (Nashville, Ten: Scarritt Press, 1987), 29-47 Charles R. Foster Ed.
12.   Joseph V. Crockett *Teaching Scripture: From an African-American Perspective*, (Discipleship Resources, Nashville 1990), 1-2
13.   Anne Streaty Wimberley, *Soul Stories: African American Christian Education* (Abingdon Press, Nashville 1994)
14.   Dixon Wecter, "Introduction" in *The Hero in America*, (New York: Charles Scribner"s" Sons, 1972), xiv.
15.   West, *Prophesy Deliverance: An Afro-American Revolutionary Christianity*, 16-20

16.   Cornel West, *Prophesy Deliverance: An Afro-American Revolutionary Christianity,*
17.   Cornel West, *Prophesy Deliverance: An Afro-American Revolutionary Christianity* 17.
18.   Desmond Mpilo Tutu, *No Future Without Forgiveness* (Random House, Inc. New York: 1999), 31

Building Community in a Multicultural Context: The Role of an Africentric Consciousness

Gloria J. Tate

As historically white Christian congregations have journeyed through the stormy waters of integration, the murky waters of pluralism, and most recently, the uncertain waves of multicultural and multiracial ministry, many of these congregations have had at least four similar characteristics. First, the consciousness of the predominantly or all-white congregation was awakened to the issues of inclusiveness, because the neighborhood around the church experienced racial change. This awareness surfaced as the congregation struggled with concerns about a declining membership and perhaps dwindling income. Some congregations experienced this "awakening" because persons of color began attending the church and it became necessary for the congregation to think more seriously about inclusiveness. Thus, the issue of diversity could be classified more as a response than an initiative.

Second, as the congregation was impacted by the presence of new people from differing racial backgrounds, the parameters and rules of inclusiveness in the changing congregation were set, either consciously or unconsciously, by the traditions of the pre-existing white congregation.

Third, generally efforts were made to assimilate people of other cultures and races into a Eurocentric cultural, behavioral and religious framework.

Fourth, if a racial/ethnic minister not of European origin was accepted or assigned to the pastorate of a racially and culturally mixed congregation, the church was then usually described as "transitional". The assumption, of course, was that eventually the Caucasian (and perhaps other) members would leave and new members would come only from the same racial or ethnic group as that of the pastor. This often proved to be the case since there still exists in many segments of society a belief that European culture is universally applicable, but an identity or ethos embraced by a non-European racial/ethnic person is only applicable to that person's racial or ethnic group. Some members of these previously all-white churches, therefore, found it difficult to believe that non-Caucasian pastors, especially African Americans, could effectively serve as their pastors. Furthermore, long time parishioners who remained were often older

Caucasians and as their deaths inevitably resulted in a congregation that was less diverse than when the racial/ethnic person became the pastor.

Given the above characteristics, it is understandable that, for most people, the concept of multicultural and multiracial ministry which has been promoted results from the exclusive and perhaps benevolent effort of the white church to extend hospitality. However, as neighborhoods, towns, and cities throughout the country experience greater racial diversity,[1] there is a genuine need for internal ownership of ministries that effectively witness the love of Christ in a manner that reflects the diverse cultures within the congregation.

Africentrism can indeed serve as a valuable resource to people of color as they seek to liberate themselves from the shackles of Eurocentrism. It should not be construed, however, as a cure-all or the only effective means for resolving the cultural conflicts within an ethnically plural congregation. My experience as an African American pastor in a church that was predominately white has informed my understanding of Africentrism's usefulness in a multicultural setting. I have found that my personal affirmation of Africentric principles has helped me as a pastor trying to assist persons in the African Diaspora, as well as people from non-African heritages, to embrace a sense of community that is affirming to participants from a variety of racial/ethnic backgrounds. Examination of the Africentric perspective reveals key principles that a congregation, even a previously all-white one, can utilize as it embarks upon a ministry that genuinely seeks to be multicultural. While not a social or cultural panacea, Africentrism does provide a valid tool with which to challenge Christians to think about the church's outreach, community involvement, and program development in new and different ways that recognize the value of a variety of cultures.

Moving previously white churches from perspectives that lock them in cultural orientations of the past and leave them incapable of embracing new perspectives is the task of multicultural ministry in neighborhoods that have experienced significant racial/ethnic change. How can diversity be affirmed rather than simply fitting differences into a pre-set mold? This is the challenge that faces our congregation.[2] In light of this challenge, our church's ministry sought to take into account three major factors: vision, leadership, and resources (both physical and spiritual).

Vision

As the current ministry of the church takes shape and form with an ever-changing membership, several questions must be addressed continually:

1. Given normal challenges and adjustments involved in congregational patterns of racial transition and current demographic trends, is the vision of a true multicultural faith community achievable?

2. What do the members envision when they speak of multiculturalism? Does it merely mean having a rainbow of faces displayed in Church photographs and during worship?

3. How committed are members to this multicultural vision? Is there enough commitment that energy will be invested in creating a community that affirms a spectrum of nationalities, ethnic groups, cultures, traditions, accents, economic levels and ages? Is assimilation into a European-oriented cultural and spiritual setting the expectation?

4. Is there an undying loyalty to the Eurocentric traditions and how will the new multicultural constituency deal with the church's ancestry?

5. Is there genuine openness to integrating the diversity of traditions and communal experiences brought by the populace? Is there a willingness to monitor leadership trends to insure inclusiveness?

In other words, do our actions, attitude and disposition match any stated multicultural vision? Somehow, bridges that are stronger than mere tolerance must be built between the various groups. This will take time. The work of bridging the gap between differing ethnic groups and cultures can sometimes be overwhelming. Just as we know all African Americans cannot fit into the same mold, so it is that Asian, African, and Hispanic members will have intra-racial and inter-ethnic barriers that come from long histories of suspicion, political divide, and animosity. The analysis of Kennon L. Callahan can easily be the reality:

> When you analyze the significant relational groupings in a church, you will discover distinctive subcultural groupings with distinctive goals and value systems; distinctive customs, habits, and traditions; distinctive language and communication networks; distinctive leadership and decision-making processes; distinctive sacred places of meeting; and distinctive vision of the future.[3]

Just as many congregations have experienced difficulty in building a bridge between the traditionalists and those who seek to "liven up" the church by adding gospel music and "non-traditional" activities (dance, videos, and instruments, etc.) to the worship service, or "different" social activities to the church's calendar, so it is that the process of expanding cultural boundaries can be undermined by the traditionalist whose mantra expresses a well-known sentiment, "we have always done things a certain way".

If there is true commitment to a multicultural ministry, the congregation must be led by a vision of multicultural community. To achieve the vision we must affirm each other's cultural identity as we mobilize the wealth of human resources that exist within the congregation. True community becomes possible within a new environment of openness. What will this multicultural community look like? Inasmuch as an authentic community is a reflection of the members that comprise it, there is no set pattern for its practices, traditions, and worship. It becomes a work in progress, ever-changing and growing as the Spirit leads us.

Leadership

In most church-based ministries, the pastor is influential, if not the key to defining the ministry of the church. The astute pastor, however, must always remember that it is God who shapes, molds, and guides the ministries that she or he is involved in, enabling movement from chaos to order. When the pastor or congregation relies primarily on their own vision and resources, taking insufficient recognition of God's role in shaping the new community, the conditions for chaos are set. When our lives are in partnership with all of God's creation, when we are governed by hope, trust, respect, and love, and are in fellowship with the will of God, we experience a sense of clarity that cannot be otherwise. I refer to this clarity as "order" because when one is clear about direction and purpose, there is a sense of orderliness in the process of change.

Whenever the institution called the Church is stagnant and impotent in its witness and work, its existence can be likened to chaos. In the area of finances, for example, institutional chaos has less to do with whether the congregation has operational dollars, than it has to do with how the dollars it has are designated. Chaos (lack of clarity) can also describe the state of having no discernible vision, or it can refer to having a vision but no discernible plan outlined for its implementation.

The pastor, as the chief administrator of the church, in addition to seeking order through planning, organization, and inspiration, is called to assist the congregation in breathing new life into itself. Together, pastor and the church leaders must address institutional chaos through effective management, leadership development, and the building of community.

The leadership must help the congregation develop a collective consciousness in order that they may move toward a new interdependence and appreciation of each other. Parishioners must be challenged to claim the creative energy of the Spirit, bring clarity to their vision, and maximize the potential that each person brings to the formation of a body that is in communion with each other and with the will of God.

Resources

What resources do we draw upon as we work to build community in a multicultural context? This is where I see the Africentric perspective as particularly helpful in providing a foundation for understanding what it means to live in community. As defined in the paper, *Is This New Wine?* Africentricity is:

> A perspective of the universe (or world view) that places Africa as the center for persons of African descent (as for Asians, an Asian-oriented center or Europeans, a European-oriented center). This perspective makes Africa the subject rather than object of all inquiry and investigation. Instead of using other cultural perspectives by which to evaluate/compare Africa, Africa becomes the standard by which other cultures, histories, and sociopolitical systems are compared.[4]

Africentrism encourages a perspective of communal ministry that can serve as fertile ground to nurture and nourish multiculturalism. There are three factors that define the means utilized by the Africentric perspective, which enable cultural and spiritual awareness and liberation. They are: (1) Molefi Kete Asante's concept of *consciousness before unity*, (2) the basic tenet of Africentricism which promotes an interconnectedness of all things, and (3) what Mercy Amba Oduyoye describes as the *Trinitarian life* or unity in diversity.[5] These three factors comprise a logical formula for reflection and exploration as one seeks to move toward the development of a true multicultural community.

I. Consciousness Before Unity

> Rather, speaking the truth in love, we are to grow up in every way into him who is the head, into Christ, from whom the whole body, joined and knit together by every joint with which it is supplied, when each part is working properly, makes bodily growth and upbuilds itself in love. (Ephesians 4:15-16)

This passage of Ephesians (similar to ideas reflected also in Romans 12), which speaks of different gifts, evokes from the maturing Christian certain questions: "What part of the body of Christ do I represent? What is my function? What are the gifts that I bring?" Most believers who dare to raise these questions generally think in terms of skills and talents as defined by North American or European culture[6] and as rated on the value scale of our society. Consequently, another question is raised for non-European, racial-ethnic theologians, as stated by Robert Hood, "Do Christians from Third World cultures have to become imitation European or North Americans before they can be considered fitting contributors to the formation and shaping of Christian thought?"[7] Is there no merit in the traditions and artistry of African Americans that have survived the Middle Passage, slavery, Jim Crow and post World-War II discrimination? Is there no merit in the customs and symbols of Native Americans that have survived invasion, massacre, and lives relegated to the reservation? Should these traditions, symbols, values, experiences and thoughts be regarded as a badge of shame in a global and multicultural world?

If the answer is yes, non-Eurocentric preachers must abandon their value systems. Native American and African preachers must reject their own culture's affirmation of being in community with nature and the ancestral spirits in order to be deemed biblically or theologically acceptable. Historical continuity is no longer endorsed nor are certain types of syncretism in terms of religious customs and symbols (except those identified with a supposedly superior European culture). However, Africentric Christians would answer these questions with a resounding no! The African American Christian who has an Africentric consciousness insists that the retention of an African culture and heritage is as important as her or his Christian affirmation. It is the primary means by which African Americans can effectively relate the gospel to the African American community. However, this principle has wider implications.

An awareness of one's heritage and identity is essential if it is to serve as the driving force, which empowers the congregation to engage in ministry. What significance does this awareness have if one's base of operation is a multicultural and multiracial setting? Does each group have to operate from its own racial perspective and minister to only their own racial group? How does this achieve true multicultural community?

Molefi Kete Asante's discourse on Africentrism expounds the belief that the pedagogical and phenomenological acquisition of consciousness precedes and even transcends any effort toward unity. He defines consciousness as that which "expresses our shared commitments, fraternal reactions to assaults on our humanity, collective awareness of our destiny, and respect for our ancestors."[8] In other words, there must be a focus on "getting each part to work properly" (Eph. 4:15-16) before the body can be considered sound. Others whose ultimate goal is not the development of a pluralistic community can also see the importance of understanding and affirming one's self before one can move into a broader context.

Elijah Muhammad taught that "a proper knowledge of self and kind" was a prerequisite for the achievement of black unity. Once blacks learned to love themselves as individuals, they would be able to show the proper love and respect for one another. . . "seek *first* the friendship of your own people and then the friendship of others (if there is any friendship in others)."[9]

What does it mean to be unashamedly African American in a multicultural context? In other words, to find no conflict in affirming the historic roots of all cultures, including one's own African roots? Molefi Kete Asante, in his discussion of collective consciousness, asserts that "consciousness precedes unity".[10] While he speaks about this consciousness as it applies to the African American community, I find this principle to be true about any human community. Callahan adds this further insight to our discussion:

> Some philosophical systems invite individuals to collapse their identity into the identity of the whole. The way beyond that is not to insist on an individualistic form of individualism. Some people focus only on individuality over against community, while others focus on

community as over against individuality. The way forward is not by occupying a middle ground. One must keep both significantly present. Individuality is found in community. Community is led forward by people's new discovery of individuality in the midst of roots, place, belonging, and sharing and caring.[11]

The implication then is that the journey toward "true community" begins with the raising of an individual's awareness. This awareness grows into a collective cultural consciousness, which prepares the individual for participation in the global community, with knowledge of the uniqueness he or she brings to the body of Christ, the Church. Therefore, it can be said that consciousness leads to personhood. Liberation theologians of previous decades understood that the process of transformation begins with the particular and culminates in one's relationship to the whole of humanity. One's own consciousness of self-in-community is the bridge to building a relationship with the whole human family.

II. Interconnectedness of All Things

When one knows the history, traditions, symbols, values, and experiences that establish a foundation for selfhood, one then becomes aware of his or her identity. This personhood, according to African teaching, is only found in the context of community. "To be human means to belong to a family or community … it is not enough to be a human being unless one shows a sense of, and participation in, community."[12] The biblical personalities of Moses and Esther stand as examples of those who came into personhood through a deep relationship with community.

Moses began the journey toward full personhood as a result of an act that stemmed from his consciousness of community. "He saw an Egyptian beating a Hebrew, one of his kinsfolk" (Exodus 2:11). The act of retaliation against the Egyptian was prompted by his sense of communal identification. It was this destructive act that ultimately had redemptive qualities, for it eventually placed Moses in position to discover God's will for him as a person.

Esther, although crowned a queen, lived in a world of anonymity. She had no real security of position and no affirmation from the community of which she supposedly was a member. The biblical account portrays her as a figurehead until she came into an awareness of the need to participate in the affairs of her people. Then comes her realization of interdependence. "Go, gather all the Jews to be found in Susa, and hold a fast on my behalf...After that I will go to the King, though it is against the law; and if I perish, I perish" (Esther 4:16). This realization becomes the turning point for Esther. She then takes on personhood in the eyes of the community and equally in the eyes of the king.

Not only does a particular consciousness lead to acts of identification with community, but the ultimate and individual salvation of both Moses and Esther is bound to the salvation of the community. This is coherent with African teaching:

A moral understanding of salvation, namely, deliverance from sin and death, is grasped by most Africans in a communal, rather than an individual, sense; that is, it is to be understood in terms of restoring communal stability[13].

The legacy of the black church is an understanding of a connection between individual and community; religion and politics; the sacred and the secular. From Native American and African religions we also learn that there must be community with nature as well as with people. This interconnectedness of all life and things is promoted by the Spirit.

The late Robert Hood, an African American ethicist, summarized the all-encompassing function of the Spirit in black religion as (1) active and acting, as experienced in worship; (2) refurbishing and fortifying in times of trial and tribulation; and (3) that which links black religion and black culture in the fine arts. Further, Hood described the functioning of the Spirit in this way:

(The Spirit) ...establishes solidarity during struggles for liberation and survival: solidarity within the temporal community and within the larger community of the ancestors and deceased relatives. It dispels weariness and faintheartedness. It connects ancestors with the living, mothers with sons, daughters with fathers, the uneducated with the sophisticated, and the impoverished with the affluent.[14]

This interconnectedness as promoted by the Spirit becomes our basis for understanding the concept of "true community". The basic concept of community is as relevant as our application would make it. Within the human arena we draw upon a variety of superficial and complex relations to establish transient communal bonds that serve our political and social purposes. Regrettably, some communal groupings that promise a sense of belonging provide little, if not negative, contributions to the moral and ethical health of the individual. However, what empowers the Christian individually and collectively is the development of authentic relations and bonds that transcend the barriers we construct. The term "true community" emphasizes a relationship that goes beyond the loose ties that exist now through the courtesy of Sunday morning worship and the emphasis we place on individual salvation. True community, therefore, exists when, according to David Brown, "a group of people function in such a way that they will not be submerged as individuals, but there will exist such a concerted atmosphere that one can live for all and all for one."[15]

This spirit of community has been the legacy of a number of cultures. In the not too distant past African Americans clearly practiced communal support. Because of the shared experiences of oppression, social and political exclusion, and economic deprivation, a genuine interdependence could be realized within family, neighborhood and church groupings. Families took in orphaned children without the benefit of adoption agencies. Adults took an active part in the raising of each other's children, and neighbors banded together in creative ways to provide assistance to each other. One does not lose identity in a communal context; rather true community is what makes us human, because true humanity responds to the divine call for a life of cooperation.

III. Unity in Diversity

Mercy Amba Oduyoye, in establishing a theological base for this understanding of human relations, uses the image of the Trinity. The way the Godhead operates reveals and also empowers us to develop the same cooperation in our human relations and in the building of community. Unity in diversity is a reflection of and finds its model in the integrated relationship found in the Trinity. It is not a difficult concept to understand when applied to African tradition and those of other indigenous cultures.

Oduyoye's position regarding the teaching of the Trinity is not isolated. At a meeting of the WCC Commission on Faith and Order (Bangalore, 1978), Metropolitan Mar Osthathios attempted to spell out the meaning and practice of the *sensus communis* as understood in traditional Africa:

> The unity of humanity is to be modeled on trinitarian unity . . . Ultimately all differences and separations between human beings have to be dissolved in a mutual *perichoresis* [embracing, penetrating, not merely sharing] where "thine and mine" are not different in case of property, purpose and will but different only in different personal and group identities with full openness to and penetration of each other. . . . The mystery of the unity of humanity in Christ, patterned on the mystery of the triune unity in the Godhead, has high significance for our social goals also. . . . Ultimately, parochialism, insularity, division, separation, class, ethnic conflict, political and economic injustice, exploitation and oppression have to be judged by this criterion [WCC 1978, 1-11].[16]

The Trinity reveals how these separate centers of consciousness are merged and linked to one another in a balanced and harmonious relationship. This relationship then informs our human families, institutions and nations of the importance of both unity and diversity within the community:

> The Unity-in-diversity of the Holy Trinity points to true community. God is One and Unbroken, yet has relationships among the three persons. God relates inwardly and outwardly. . . . Likewise human communities have unity, yet they must encompass diversity [WCC 1978, 1-11].[17]

So the body of Christ as the "true community" must go beyond a narrow focus of the privileged and the majority, in order to speak a word of hope to the marginalized, to cultures that have been dismissed and disrupted because of the influence of those hampered by the insensitivity of classical theology. Many view the "mainline" churches as grounded so deeply in a Eurocentric mindset that they continue to be insensitive to non-European cultures. If one is to find meaning in the Christian religion, non-European cultures must not only be tolerated or recognized by way of occasional ceremony, but must be affirmed as an integral part of the faith experience. This goes beyond the traditional understanding of the universal Christian goal of "the restoring of visible unity in one faith" among Christian churches.

Redefining community to affirm the inclusion of diversity in culture and theology frees us from the "ecclesiastical neo-colonialism" that continues to influence racial/ethnic persons who have bought into the belief that Christianity and European culture are one and the same. Redefining community as "unity in diversity" also opens our ears to a broadened interpretation of Scripture. For example, Romans 12 offers a formula for cooperation and harmony in the Church. Those who are in Christ and part of the body of Christ are encouraged to make a specific contribution to the well-being of the whole body (Church). What do we have to offer? What are the gifts of grace? They are the functions of prophecy, ministry, teaching, exhortation, giving and leadership as informed by heritage, culture, and nationality. Such functions open the door for a new set of parameters governing the way we do theology. The search for unity in diversity calls us to understand and implement the formation of ministry syncretistically.

Conclusion

As the congregation I serve sought to build community in our multicultural and diverse setting, we had first to assess our understanding of community. Second, we recognized a need to affirm all those who are a part of our current multicultural setting. Only then could we more clearly grasp "a vision of the new heaven and new earth" (Revelation 21:1) which the Author of our faith invites us to share. Finally, we set a short-range goal of simply laying groundwork upon which a multicultural sense of community could be achieved. This was done by utilizing three principles congruent with the Africentric perspective: *(1) that self-affirmation contributes to the affirmation of others, (2) that there must be an affirmation of interdependence and interconnectedness within the body, and (3) a belief that unity and diversity are not opposing forces.* Using these three Africentric principles of *consciousness, connectedness, and unity in diversity* as the framework for our ministry, we sought to challenge individuals within the congregation to interact and engage in dialogue with each other in more candid and open ways than they were accustomed to doing. We promoted intentional dialogue and conversations, focusing on understanding self, other cultures, views, traditions, the meaning of community, and transcending control and conformity.

Through our dialogue we began to identify elements of our collective consciousness; the common factors beyond our belief in Christ, that make for community cohesiveness within a multicultural context. Enabled by the utilization of Africentric principles, the process has led to more positive intercultural relationships, greater sensitivity to and affirmation of particular and widespread cultural expressions in worship, and openness to a variety of styles in all aspects of church life and work. We have not completed the journey. We will have to continue challenging ourselves in discovering how it is possible to strengthen our ties while recognizing, understanding, affirming, and appreciating the diversity of each culture.

How will we know when we have come close to our vision of a true community? We believe we will come closer:

- When we have satisfied more than a mere social or cultural concept of multiculturalism.
- When we have transcended the fleeting vision of physical diversity and have begun to operate as an authentic model of the Christian community described in Ephesians 4.
- When we are "joined and knit together", with each person using their gifts properly for the growth of the entire body.
- When individuals know that there is genuine appreciation in the community for what makes them unique.

At that point we will have become a fellowship where there is an enhancement of the spirit-filled, intercultural encounter that was experienced at Pentecost.

Endnotes

1. From April 1990 to July 1994 the African American population of the U.S. increased from 11.8% to 12%; the Asian increase was from 2.8% to 3.3%; and the Hispanic population increased from 9% to 10%. Respective statistics for the next period (July 1995 to November 2000) were from 12% to 12.2%; from 3.4% to 3.8%; and from 10.3% to 11.9%. (*Population Estimates of the U.S. by Sex, Race and Hispanic Origin*, U.S. Census Bureau, Washington, D. D. 20233, Release Date: January 2, 2001.) Racial statistics for the town of Teaneck, NJ in the year 2000 reflect a population that is 55% White, 28% Black, 7% Asian and 10% Hispanic.
2. The membership of the Presbyterian Church of Teaneck is a blend of African American, Caucasian, Caribbean, South American, Asian and African people. Each of these groups can be further sub-divided by more specific cultural and geographic origins.
3. Kennon L. Callahan, *Effective Church Leadership, Building on the Twelve Keys* (San Francisco: HarperCollins Publishers, 1990). 110-111.

4.   "Is This New Wine?", A paper addressing African American issues for discussion within the Presbyterian Church (U.S.A.), presented by African American Presbyterians for Study, and Action. August 22, 1993. Definition of Terms, iii.

5.   Mercy Amba Oduyoye, *Hearing and Knowing, Theological Reflections on Christianity in Africa* (Maryknoll, New York: Orbis Books, 1986). 139-142.

6.   Robert E. Hood, *Must God Remain Greek?* (Minneapolis, MN: Fortress Press, 1990). Robert Hood describes culture as ". . .the complex of all institutions, customs, beliefs, languages, knowledge, laws, oral traditions, habits, conventions, and morals that socialize and form persons and ideas within a given geographical space, but which also may move across national boundaries. Culture . . . fuels and nourishes the way persons, a community, or a people understand relationships within themselves (thereby touching upon matters such as self-esteem and purpose) and between themselves and their neighbors." 111.

7.   Ibid., 9.

8.   Molefi Kete Asante, *Afrocentricity* (Trenton: Africa World Press, Inc, 1988), 25

9.   Elijah Muhammad, *The Supreme Wisdom: Solution to the So-Called Negroes' Problem* (Chicago: University of Islam, 1957), vol. 2, 19; quoted in Mark L. Chapman, *Christianity on Trial* (Maryknoll, Orbis Books, 1996), 53-54.

10. Asante, 25

11. Callahan, 112.

12. Kofi Asare Opoku, cited in *African Roots: Toward An Afrocentric Christian Witness*, eds., Michael I.N. Dash, L. Rita Dixon, Darius Swann and Ndugu T'Ofori-Atta, (Lithonia, GA: SCP/Third World Literature Publishing House, 1994). 89.

13. Hood, 116.

14. Ibid., 210.

15. David Brown, *The Divine Trinity: Christianity and Islam*, (London: Sheldon Press, 1969), 60; quoted in Mercy Amba Oduyoye, *Hearing and Knowing*, (Maryknoll, NY: Orbis Books, 1986), 140.

16. Oduyoye, 142.

17. Ibid., 142.

CHAPTER ELEVEN

The Challenges of Africentric Ministry for Urban Theological Education

Warren L. Dennis

It is my conviction that the black community often embodies memories of God's providence and justice. The purpose of this chapter is to describe one way in which basic communal values of African and African American spirituality cohere in a distinctive principle of social cohesion to produce a core pedagogy of the African American religious experience. This core pedagogy and spirituality has been the sustaining element in the African American community. It can be discerned, if one is willing to look for it, in the most devastating conditions of urban living. It is out of this particular reflection that I want to frame a systematic understanding of how grassroots persons can give articulation to the providence and justice of God as a means of community building.

The Africentric approach to urban theological education and ministry that emphasizes grassroots leadership for effective ministry is a critical prerequisite for a North American urban ministry project that bridges the pedagogical and theological gap between the academy, church, and community for persons whose roots lie in West Africa. It is a process of teaching and learning about systemic change in both the church and the community. Such an approach treats the black belief system as a critical paradigm for understanding and transforming the black urban context as we enter the postmodern era.

I want to argue for the Africentric idea as a subject of public discourse—thus bringing together the theological academy, the black community—and Traditional African Religious thought ("which represents the religious heritage of our forebears in whose culture the spirit of God was an active agent"[1]) as a self-critical appraisal and core *instructional* response to the present crisis in the African American community. I underscore instruction because I believe there is an inherent pedagogy in the black community that comes from the liberating spirit of the people living in oppressed inner-city neighborhoods who are seeking authentication where they live. This pedagogy of African core spiritual beliefs and values is still evident after more that four hundred years of systematic distortion and dismantling of African culture even though most of the outer forms and materials of the ancestral culture were lost. A sufficient emphasis on core values has been retained to give credence to black religious thought that is rooted in an Africentric cultural orientation.

Numerous scholars, including Albert Raboteau, Melville Herskovits, Henry Mitchell, W. E. B. DuBois, St. Clair Drake, C. Eric Lincoln, and Gayraud Wilmore confirm the retention of these values and cultural traits as a basic strategy of survival.[2] They contend that African religious and cultural survivals are present in the black church and community today. Wilmore makes this point that:

> Scholars are now more confident than ever before the first slaves to become Christians, and many who followed them, held on to certain features of their old African beliefs. In Africa they had already recognized the existence of a supreme or high God. They had adopted baptism and believed in the power of prayer.... And where they adopted new ideas and practices they were similar to the old ones, the African forms were strengthened rather than weakened.[3]

Tracing the survivals of African religion in the development of African American Christianity, says James Evans, is a highly complex and controversial venture. He writes:

> The conflicting position of Melville Herskovites and E. Franklin Frazier have for decades framed the debate around African retention upon the black population of the United States. Herskovites argued that Africans maintained many of their traditions, customs, and beliefs in spite of the ravages of slavery. E. Franklin Frazier, on the other hand, believed that the experience of the Middle Passage, the brutality of slavery, and the irresistible influence of European-American culture prohibited the retention of the essential elements of indigenous African culture.[4]

On close examination of African core spiritual beliefs and values, through the anthropological lens of Herskovites, we can hear the voices our forefathers and mothers instructing us about the omnipresence and omnipotent power of God. By listening carefully to the way grassroots persons describe their every day reality we can tap into the teaching spirit about God's grace and mercy passed from one generation to the next. What these vestiges of African religious beliefs and survival techniques mean is that what Africa has to teach about principles of communal relations, respect of self and human life is still alive. The fact that black people still exist in America is an example of unyielding faith in a power greater than humankind. It means, moreover, that hope for the African American lies in reclaiming these beliefs and values as instruction arising out of the community itself.

My intention is to focus on urban theological education and faith-based community development and to merge the two as a basis for an African-centered urban theological education and ministry. I want to advance the role of faith, as understood from an African and African American perspective in the public domain, also to contribute to the ongoing conversation about the black church's role in our community life. Let us, therefore, consider the idea of the academy, the church and, the community creating together a public ethos of *teaching and learning* based upon a public dialogue about the core religious values and beliefs of the African American community. The idea of presenting our shared values in a public forum is the principle method I am advocating because of its potential to reconcile public differences and bring the community closer together.

Lastly, I want to contribute to the important question of the "Is This New Wine?" paper that made a controversial assessment of the crisis in the black community and the role of the African American Presbyterian Church in that crisis. The status of the African American witness to the love and liberation of Jesus Christ within the Presbyterian Church today is far from its potential to address the critical issues within the black community. The historic self-perception of African American Presbyterians (as being elitist and middle-class) and their perception of the African American community and vice versa, has complicated the task of engaging the crisis. Written didactically, dialectically and polemically to open up public dialogue and self-critical discourse about the nature of the African American socio-economic predicament, the "New Wine" paper achieved high visibility in a variety of church, community, and academic venues.

The Significance of the Public Dialogue

The New Wine paper is contextual theology framed anthropologically and pedagogically as a paradigm of praxis. It raises theological questions that come out of the Reformed tradition of the American Presbyterian Church. It upholds the teaching of the church concerning the centrality of scripture, the sovereignty of God, and our corporate responsibility in the socio-political structures of human affairs. It also challenges the Presbyterian Church to live up to these ideals with regard to its African American sisters and brothers.

This document of African American Presbyterians does not begin as a *tabula rosa*, rather it critically addresses and appreciates previous theses, antitheses, and syntheses. It is, most of all, a collaborative document designed to express solidarity with the African American grassroots community, and to put a premium on change, transformation, conversion, and future possibility. It is a visionary document that honors the past, respects the present, and values the future.

The current conversation concerning Africentric urban theological education and ministry is significant because it contributes to a larger dialogue about the role of religion in the public domain. It is an attempt to calling into question the ability of a 17th century European-centered theological discourse to deal with the realities of black urban communities in the 21st century. From the perspective of the black church, Africentrism has identified key cultural and religious issues that must be acknowledged if the black church is going to serve faithfully and effectively within the urban community. The emphasis on the *community* is important for this discussion because it implies a new approach to theological education that places a premium on where learning takes place and the public dialogue that is stimulated when we listen to the cultural and religious voice of grassroots persons in making their own contribution to the larger community conversation.

The Challenges of Africentrism as Ministry

Discussing Molefi Asante's use of the term, Ron Peters, analyzed the general meaning of Africentrism that has gained wide acceptance in the black academic and church circles:

> Africentrism refers to the practice of examining the historical validity of pre-colonial black Africa rather than the beginning of European Trans-Atlantic expansionism and colonial activity. Scholars are increasingly aware of the distortion of the Western aspects of the history of Christianity—that is the origin and development of ideas and institutions came to fruition in Europe without mention of other strains of Christianity that survived, for example, within the world of Islam. Black theologians and Womanist theologians have been helpful in exposing the misuse of the Bible and the Christian faith as tools in the oppression of African Americans throughout this nation's history... In its most generic form, "Africentricity" involves the notion that Africa and persons of African descent must be seen as proactive subjects within human history and in the evolution of world civilization, rather than as passive objects mentioned as an aside to a more central human drama of Western history. According to Asante, Africentrism regards Africa and its descendants as centers of anthropological value and critical partners in understanding the evolution of world civilization in a way that does not minimize the contributions of other people.[5]

By lifting up Africentrism as a method of exploration, the centrality of African ideas, beliefs, and values as valid frames of reference for acquiring and examining historical and biblical data is established. It, then, becomes the composite montage of specific ways of thinking, feeling, and acting, which is peculiar to African Americans as distinguished from other groups.

In the final analysis Africentrism as ministry is a public mandate for African Americans to dialogue about certain kinds of theological presumptuousness. It is a significant public challenge to Western theology, church history, and biblical interpretation. This public challenge takes seriously an examination of African American psycho-social self imagery, community spirituality, black male and female relationship, African ancestry and the whole history of the African continent. The fundamental role of this public challenge—I think—distinct from, yet building on, the indispensable work of academics, experts, and pundits—is to create and sustain high-quality public discourse addressing urgent community problems, which enlightens and energizes African Americans and inspires them to take public action.

African American clergy and laypersons cannot afford to stand by and observe the destruction of our communities from behind the walls and stained glass windows of sanctuaries, many of which contain decreasing numbers of folks from the community. We have a responsibility now, more than before, to take the sanctuary into the streets.

The challenge for theological education is to move from a traditional campus-based learning paradigm with its concentration on Greek philosophical presuppositions to an emphasis on non-campus based learning that value the faith stories and experiences of African American people.   Such guided reflection at a grassroots level reaches into the depth of African communal philosophy and religion and carries over into the African American religious experience as instruction dealing with how the community understands itself and its relationship to God.   In this instance, the community itself becomes the center of theological exploration and learning that is mutually beneficial to the church and the academy.   This folk-based pedagogy places a premium on community, linking the faith lessons of the past from one generation to another, as the major emphasis of theological education and ministry.

The community is significant for an Africentric ministry because it places a premium on listening, reflection and action, and moral discourse not only for an individual's well being, but also for the successful achievement of a communal consciousness. In this sense, the community is taking responsibility for the welfare of its members and addresses issues in a holistic and healthy manner. Such a view is advocated for in a curriculum of Africentric urban theological education and ministry.

Another challenge of Africentrism as ministry is to construct a theological framework dedicated to the temporal and eschatological liberation of poor and oppressed people. A theology that targets the needs and concerns of grassroots people is natural for an Africentric ministry that seeks to be liberating. Given the crisis state of the black community, the need to discern the capacity of its religious institutions to lead the people through the pressing problems of healthcare, urban dislocation, poor educational opportunities and unemployment is urgently necessary. Black theology (with its roots in the academy), has not adequately addressed the crisis nor has the contemporary black church. I think what is needed is a pedagogical movement with both the church and community to synthesize black theology, womanist theology, African theology and traditional African religions into an Africentric body of thought and praxis that can become entrenched in faith-based community development. I believe such a constructive movement that will fashion curricula emerging out of the urban context would have a transforming effect on the oppressive conditions of the black community. Moreover, the bringing together these of four theological approaches to the reality African and African American people must confront, will gives credence to our claim that the black experience is the lens through which we are able to discern the truth about God, nature and humankind.

The task of Africentric urban theological education and ministry is to uncover and make accessible an authentic articulation of faith in God in an urban context. In doing so, Africentric education and ministry will make it possible for the world to hears the prophetic voices of four centuries of a moral struggle to break the yoke of oppression and degradation, and the cries of those experiencing the contemporary agony and pain of systemic oppression. What I am advocating breaks with the academic approach of black theology by locating itself among the people; by making the people the subject of theological inquiry rather than the object of analysis. Africentric urban ministry is incarnational, relational, and holistic because it seeks to demonstrate how God is active in the lives of persons through their prayers, dreams, and stories of suffering, victory, and celebration. At the same time, it places a supreme value on the teaching capacity of the community as the basis of a liberating consciousness. The way that the lived experiences of the people reflect God's grace and mercy becomes the source of instruction for faith-based community development.

An Africentric urban ministry has a prophetic/public goal. The reflection and action method seeks to empower persons and communities, that have been victimized by systemic oppression and violence to speak to the realized presence of God's affirming acts in their lives, to collaborate with the church and the community and justice-seeking institutions on common, faith-based, community development concerns.   The goal is to transform the spirituality of the community by synthesizing the faith expressions of grassroots people with the insight of the academy with the consequence of producing an Africentric paradigm for liberating education and action.

Finally, the challenge for a more appropriate theology is to contextualize Africentrism as normal expression of the urban grassroots and to encourage greater involvement on the part of the black church and the academy in theological education within the boundaries of the community. "In the urban context," says J. Deotis Roberts[6] "it is now essential to take the seminary curriculum to the churches, community centers, and pastoral/church institutes where the people are."

The Curricula Relevancy of "New Wine."
The relevancy of the "New Wine" paper is its call for a revival of the historic mission of the black church in neglected inner-city neighborhoods, and its challenge to the church to begin radically new ministries among poor and grassroots persons. "New Wine" is a clarion call to reflect theologically and practically on a new urban reality. This new reality calls for a more appropriate biblical hermeneutic and contextual analysis that more vividly identified with the cultural concerns and interests revealed in African and African American history. The black church in the postmodern urban landscape must reclaim its biblical and pedagogical center in the African American community if it is to remain relevant. With its radical history the black church is in a strategic position to shape a new biblical understanding that will address the crisis

identified in the "New Wine" paper. It frames the moral discourse that is needed about matters of public importance. It will demonstrate its ability to deal with this crisis by recapturing its historic vocation to educate the community about its African and African American heritage, the truth and accuracy of biblical interpretation that emphasizes the Bible's liberating motif, and by inventing practical approaches to community building. The black church is in a position to debate publicly the conspiratorial disinvestments in the inner cities. This becomes the principle norm of curricula focus for an Africentric urban theological education and ministry.

The Contextual Relevancy of an Africentric Ministry

How do we as African American Christians understand the command to follow Christ into the 21st century? The point of raising the question, "Is This New Wine?" is the continuing crisis in the black community: black class distinction, high percentage of black female-heads of household, disparities in healthcare, school failure to educate, record rate of unemployment, and youth violent crimes. The crisis is precipitated by the new shifting global economic realities at the workplace and its effect upon dislocation from core inner cities, the shift of the political center to a dominating majority of white suburban areas, and an omnipresent technological world requiring advanced education and unprecedented diagnostic skills. Added to these pathologies and problems is the pandemic of HIV/AIDS (with the inherent code of silence that accompanied it), specifically among women and children; the emergence of a permanent African American underclass; African American men serving life sentences in prison; and a drug-infested culture that has the potential to virtually destroy an entire generation of young African Americans.

Africentric Ministry In The Making

Holding ministry and mission in balance is the vocation of the people of God. The focus of an Africentric ministry and mission is faithfulness to the black church tradition in the 21st century. That means carrying out Christ's work of healing the sick, opening the eyes of the blind, setting the captives free, and reconciling the world to God. In any definition of Africentrism as ministry, it is critical that we understand it as a lens through which we can assess the crisis of the black community and the black church's involvement in it. As such, Africentrism becomes an expression of faith in God that engenders a spiritual and missiological approach to the ordering of church life that includes celebration, education, pastoral administration, public participation and justice outreach.

Africentrism as ministry also emphasizes the centrality of African values and beliefs grounded in a strategy of "reflection and praxis" as a valid method for transforming of African American churches and communities. It teaches that the story of African Americans did not begin with the experience of enslavement in America, but rather with the culture and religious inheritance from ancient

Africa. Africentrism serves as a framework for uniting the black Christian story with ancient biblical story of liberation and freedom under God. Thus, Afrocentrism begins with a focus *in* community past, present, and future in which ministry and mission is discussed, affirmed and implemented.

An Africentric Ministry Model of Urban Theological Education and Community Building

One of the greatest needs in the African American community is to understand the socio-political dynamics that define how land is used in urban settings. An Africentric ministry of urban theological education starts with a grassroots pedagogical dialogue, between persons in the academy, the church, and the community that involves an analysis of the neighborhood. It is concern with such issues as school reform, tax equity, safe streets and adequate housing. The dialogue values people's experiences in ministry as equally important in the educational process with that of the clergy. Together, lay and clergy address issues of community building.

The model I am proposing for community building emerges out of my conviction that a practical and valid understanding of God is incarnated in the faith and practice of the people. They are empowered thereby to deal with the socio-political and economic problems through contemplation and dialogue with others in church and in the academy. I consider this as an Africentric workshop for Africentric community ministry. The purpose is to bring together the theoretical and the practical in a collaborative ministry at the grassroots level.

The Africentric workshop model, in contrast to ritual of public lectures and speech making, fosters community development from the inside out. The emphasis is placed on faith-based training, participation and interaction, follow-up and practical application, even in the most troubled areas of the black community. This model uses research and reflection, knowing and acting, faith and faithfulness, as the ways in which the African American community works for its own liberation. The idea is to bring together the best thinkers, scholars and activists to network with grassroots people in the interest of the community. Under this model, instead of holding conferences, when professional lecturers gives repetitive speeches, there would be workshops on networking, identifying resources, and improving the community's effort in such areas as: 1) community organizing techniques; 2) public policy debates and engagements, alternative schools, Africentric studies and educational programs; 3) classes for developing self-publishing enterprises; and 4) teacher training, research methodology, and the interpretation of history.

Conclusion

The African American community possesses a religious and teaching capacity that is rooted in its African heritage to define, sustain, and transform itself as it faces the most urgent crisis since our enslavement. In this essay, I have proposed that a curriculum of Africentric urban theological education and ministry focused at the grassroots level is an imperative for the African American Christian church and the black community.

I have lifted up the importance of *teaching and learning* from an Africentric perspective that incorporates the grassroots as the context of a ministry outside the bounds of traditional approaches to Christian ministry. The inner city is the place that is most appropriate for a distinctly African-centered ministry. It is where the African American church is called to teach AND discern what God is doing on its behalf. It is the place where that church needs to bring the message of the Kingdom of God in both thought and action. It is the place where we can examine transcontinental African religious and communal values, the past and present survival strategies, and where we can best experiment with a new theology.

The strength of the African American Church in this post-modern time is its ability to listen to the community and, through dialogic instruction, provide people with a strong moral sense of community. Historical analysis shows clearly that for the past 300 years the black church has been the mainstay of black community life. It has been the mediating institution in the African American community in times of crisis. The reclamation of traditional African values and beliefs would strengthen the black community's sense of civic responsibility, encourage the sharing and pooling of resources for community building, ensure the willingness of previously ignored and neglected people to work and contribute to the general health and welfare of persons and the community.

For urban theological education and ministry to be effective they must transcend the monastic tradition of power and control invested in one person. Instead they must adopt a non-traditional approach that is balance between collaboration with experts on one hand, and, on the other, respect the existing knowledge and capacity of grassroots persons. An Africentric urban theological education and ministry intent on bridging the gap between the academy and the church is most appropriate for addressing the pressing problems in the African American community. This has been the main argument of this essay.

Properly executed, Africentric urban theological education and ministry will run counteract the spurious culture that values structure over people and has no respect for inner-city neighborhoods and grassroots persons. Africentric urban ministry celebrates the possibilities of the community, while critically analyzing systems of apprehension and working against them with increasing sophistication.

Endnotes

1.   Kofi Asare Opoku, "African Traditional Religion: An Enduring Heritage"; *African Roots: Towards An Afrocentric Christian Witness*, ed. Michael I.N. Dash, L. Rita Dixon, Darius L. Swann, Ndugu, T'Ofori-Atta, (Lithonia, Georgia: Third World Literature Publishing House, 1994) 81.
2.   See Albert Raboteau, *Slave Religion: The "Invisible Institution" in the Antebellum South*. New York: Oxford University Press, 1978; Melville Herskovits, *The Myth of the Negro Past*. Boston: Beacon Press, 1958; Henry Mitchell, *Black Blief: Folk Belief of Blacks In America and West Africa*. New York: Harper and Row Publishers, 1975; W.E.B. DuBois. *Soul of Black Folks*. New York: Signet Classic, 1989; St. Clair Drake. *The Redemption of Africa and Black Religion*. Chicago: Third World Press, 1991; C. Eric Lincoln., ed. *The Black Experience In Religion*. Anchor Books, 1974; Gayraud S. Wilmore. *Black Presbyterian: The Heritage and the Hope*, (Philadelphia: Geneva Press), 41.
3.   Gayraud S. Wilmore. *Black Presbyterian: The Heritage and the Hope*, (Philadelphia: Geneva Press), 41.
4.   James Evans Jr. *We Have Been Believers: An African American Systematic Theology*, (Minneapolis: Fortress Press), 56.
5.   Ronald E. Peters. Associate Professor, Urban Ministry, Pittsburgh Theological Seminary, Pittsburgh, PA (1994). Unpublished manuscript entitled Africentrism and Mainline Denominations. pp. 3-4.
6.   J. Deotis Roberts. *Prophet Hood of Black Believers: An African American Political Theology for Ministry*, (Louisville: Westminster/John Knox, 1994.

CHAPTER TWELVE

Diaspora Ethics: "The Hinges Upon Which the Future Swings"

Katie Geneva Cannon

In 1970, as a Youth Advisory Delegate for the United Presbyterian Church's Fund for the Self-Development of People,[1] I underwent a transformative experience. My summer employment had ended for the day, so the Reverend Doctor James Herman Robinson (1907-1972)[2] invited me to tea in the main cafeteria at the Interchurch Center in New York City. As soon as we sat down, the conversation turned to Africa, and within eleven months from the time we sipped our cups of tea, Robinson helped me to make my first trek to the Motherland, traveling to Ghana, Liberia, and Cote d'Ivoire.[3] My Africentric consciousness was forever changed.

As a Presbyterian minister, Robinson founded the Church of the Master and the Morningside Community Center in New York City (May 1938).[4] He recruited students from nearby Union Theological Seminary, Columbia University, and Barnard College to volunteer in neighborhood projects in Harlem, such as cleanup efforts, housing programs, the cooperative store, etc. In the late 1940s, a wealthy couple heard about Robinson's efforts and donated 467 acres of land in Winchester, New Hampshire, to the Church of the Master. Robinson used the land to get children off the steaming, spirit-crushing city streets, and he recruited students from places like Mt. Holyoke, Amherst, Columbia, and Dartmouth to work during the summers at Camp Rabbit Hollow for boys and Camp Forest Lake for girls, as the land came to be known.[5] In 1957, Robinson applied the Camp Rabbit Hollow model to Africa, thus becoming the Founder/Executive Director of Operation Crossroads Africa, Inc.[6] In the past 45 summers, Operation Crossroads Africa, Inc. has sent over 10,000 persons in work camp teams to 35 African countries, 12 Caribbean countries, and Brazil. President John F. Kennedy called Operation Crossroads Africa the *progenitor of the Peace Corps.*[7]

It is significant that for a number of years Robinson worked as a Consultant on African Affairs for the United Presbyterian Church, a member of the State Department's Advisory Council on African Affairs, and a member of the Peace Corps Advisory Committee. It is also important to note that his courageous life of activism and leadership inspired him to serve as one of the founders of Sydenham, New York's first interracial hospital. In truth, James H. Robinson was in the vanguard of progressive, contemporary thinkers on Africentricity before it was fashionable. It is appropriate, therefore, to devote this pedagogical essay to an elaboration of Robinson's people-to-people diplomacy, *the hinges upon which the future swings*, that I employ in theological education.

In *Africa at the Crossroads,* Gayraud S. Wilmore offers two roughly equal and succinct summary statements addressing the most engaging concerns and operating principles that govern Robinson's Africentric ethics: [8] (a) to help us think theologically about some of the exasperatingly difficult problems of society; and (b) to provide the means by which we can develop methods of applying new knowledge to break economic, political, social, cultural, and even religious boundaries by which we are circumscribed. These two objectives are the fundamental principles in my signature course, *Resources for a Constructive Ethic: The Black Women's Literary Tradition.*

Theoethical Conscientization

I have been teaching Africentric ethics for 20 years: a critical reasoning process that opens up new cognitive realms regarding rules, ideals, guidelines, and values, by studying the various ways that African American people create moral agency in life-worlds where an aggregate of rigidly coded cultural imperatives bestows the status of superior normative humanity upon individuals at the top of the androcentric, material-means pyramid. In other words, Africentric ethics probes the complex cultural histories and social arrangements of slavery and colonialism in the past, and the globalization of capital in today's socio-political domain, the awesome dictatorial power of transnational corporations to invest in or withdraw economic resources from national governments. Africentric ethics then asks, what moral reflections come from Black folk who respectfully yearn to actualize the deepest possibilities of human existence? More than anything else, my specific work in Africentric ethics examines the themes and questions that emerge when people of faith draw our line of spiritual genealogy through the writings of Black women who debunk, unmask, and disentangle the composite reality of *man* as the universal norm, the taken-for-granted mode of being.

In 1983 as a Research Associate and Visiting Lecturer in Christian Ethics in the Women's Studies in Religion Program at Harvard Divinity School, I created my first set of lectures for what has become my signature course, *Resources for a Constructive Ethic: The Black Women's Literary Tradition.* For reading, I relied heavily on Black women's novels as required textbooks, necessitated by the fact that as a course of study, most students would not travel beyond the geographical boundaries of the Charles River. In order for students to become conscious of how existing systems of race, sex, and class affected them, they had to wrestle with the various ways that Black women's novels function as textual analogue to Robinson's travel work camp experience.

A glance back at my doctoral dissertation, published as *Black Womanist Ethics,*[9] makes me realize that the substance of that document is still my continuing thesis regarding critical truism in the work of Black women writers.

In other words, in *Resources for a Constructive Ethic,* I contend that the Black Women's literary tradition requires readers-students to constantly shift the territory of their normative gaze and the manner in which they see otherness as ordinariness as they journey through the allegorized terrain of racism, sexism, and classism that permeates the intriguing stories by African Americans, past and present.

> For the first time I am obliged to stay conscious, in an embodied kind of way, as I read across cultural lines. When I read and re-read the same sentence over and over again, I realize that I am being transported across unfamiliar territory. I am moving into another country, one that is not my home. Once I accept the foreign feeling of the novel's context, I no longer re-read every sentence, but instead, I read slowly so that all five of my senses can stay in tack as I move into larger understandings of the human experience.[10]

In the early 1980s, very few divinity students had ever read a book authored by a woman of African ancestry or ever had close contact with Black women in roles of intellectual authority, so in each assignment I required students to interface contestable issues in the texts with personal real-life contexts. Such interfacing assessment resulted in the following comment:

> I love literature, and even though I have not yet mastered the skills of literary analysis, I find each novel full of strategies for resisting unfathomable tragedy. This course gives me courage to stay conscious of how hierarchies of power establish favors only for a few. Black women's literature, like all good literature, is a parachute that carries me to many parts of the world, where I can see delicate, detailed mental pictures of the vast lay of the land, without tampering with the landscape.

The plots, characters and themes in novels like *Jubilee* by Margaret Walker; *Beloved* by Toni Morrison; *The Price of a Child* by Lorene Cary; *Dessa Rose* by Sherley A. Williams; *I, Tituba, Black Witch of Salem* by Maryse Conde; *Kindred* by Octavia Butler; and *The Wake of the Wind* by J. California Cooper, encourage students to transcend boundaries, inviting them to take mental leaps over rivers and through the woods to drastically different socio-cultural locations. The following comments by seminarians make clear how the external itinerary in historical novels oftentimes corresponds to internal journeys of self-discovery.

> African Americans must never forget the pain of slavery, the humiliation of bearing the children of rapists and the complete violation of the sanctity of the person that our foreparents endured. We must reclaim this legacy with pride and place the horrors that were executed on the history of the people who committed them. We

can only free ourselves from 'victim guilt' by calling the crime, a crime and pointing out the criminals.

Another one wrote:

> Homelessness and namelessness amount to beinglessness—a core ontological problem. The ghost in *Beloved* embodies re-memory, resulting in reincarnation as the key to all religious reflection. What does it mean to come back embodied as someone else's re-memory?

Beloved teaches us that we will face the terror in our past or the hunger of the pain will eat us alive.

Thus, Robinson's first objective, to help us think theologically about some of the exasperatingly difficult problems of society, is achieved immediately, and many times over, throughout each semester, as students read the unflinching examination of the historical, cultural, and personal atrocities and indignities wrought by the *isms* that infect protagonists in novels assigned in my course. Such novels also include: Ann Petry's *The Street*; Paule Marshall's *The Chosen Place, The Timeless People*; Toni Morrison's *The Bluest Eye*; Gayle Jones' *Corrigedora*; Alice Childress' *A Short Walk*; Toni Cade Bambara's *The Salt Eaters*; Ntozake Shange's *Betsy Brown* and Alice Walker's *The Color Purple*. Here is an assessment of this objective as spelled out in a student's notebook entry:

> Reading these novels makes me face African American women's history of accessibility to dominant men by recognizing that historical accessibility does not presuppose consent to sexual domination, humiliation and abuse. We must reject a *his-story* that excuses rapists who burned the brand of whore onto African American women. Retrieving the history of our sexual abuse will reveal the extent of the psychic damage done to our grandmothers, mothers, and us, and will enable us to see inconsistencies and weaknesses in what we thought we understood.

Africentric Methodology

The next year, 1984, when I moved across the Cambridge Commons to join the faculty of the Episcopal Divinity School (EDS), I discovered that in addition to the required reading of Black women's novels, I needed to include memoirs, autobiographies, biographies, and critical essays by African American women. So, over the years it has felt quite comfortable to shift the emphasis from the truth—telling in fiction to the inclusion of social inequities witnessed in non-fiction. For example, several students in a working group went to great lengths to show how reading *The Alchemy of Race and Rights: Diary of a Law Professor* by Patricia J. Williams made them realize that some things cannot be owned, no matter how extensive the consensus collaboration of the general public that says otherwise.

This book clearly unveils how the boundaries of private ownership are stretched in order to rationalize and legitimize the invasions of the rich and powerful and to protect the myths and interests of the dominant class. Realizing Williams' basic premise that some things are not commodities to be bought, sold and traded, frees us to no longer waste time and energy debating the distribution of ownership but to simply remove that which is not a commodity from a discourse on its proper, legal or just distribution.

Thus, our research question is this—If over 300 hundred years of African American labor (1520-1882) is a commodity for which payment is due, what reparations are owed for this labor, and what punitive damages are in order? From another student we can learn how the careful reading of biotexts, such as Maya Angelou's *I Know Why the Caged Bird Sings*; Nikki Giovanni's *Gemini*; Jamaica Kincaid's *My Brother* and Deborah McDowell's *Leaving Pipe Shop,* guided by judicious connections with existential reality, can lead to resonated centering points and common ground among people of various races.

> *Leaving Pipe Shop: Memories of Kin* by Deborah McDowell was a gut-wrenching book for me to read, partly because of a growing sense of empathy with the narrator: the powerful descriptive talents of Dr. McDowell, especially her ability to paint scenes and develop characters in ways that appeal to multiple senses, drew me in and glued me to the text. I too have lost most of my family of origin, some of the dearest ones having died much too early as well. I too know the machinations of kudzu, morning glories, and honeysuckle, their tremendous capacity to network and to survive in the worst environments along roadsides and in abandoned lots. I too lived in the Kennedy era, loved and feared my piano teacher, wore white gloves to church, had elders who mandated my attendance there and who observed my coming of age.

Lecturing weekly before feminist liberationist seminarians who tend to be imbued with justice-making activism, a desire to free both the oppressed and the oppressors, I developed an Africentric method for demystifying domination that proved most effective. I adjusted the syllabus to require seminarians to construct a cognitive map of the "logic" that sets the perimeters for the intelligibility of race, sex, and class exploitation. In other words, students learn how to debunk, unmask, and disentangle precise hierarchal mechanisms of subjugation, subordination, and alienation.

Throughout Black people's history in the Americas, doers-of-justice have consistently participated in a variety of literary undertakings and discursive interactions that identify benchmarks of deviation from the "legitimacy" of white supremacy. Understanding that this method of cognitive mapmaking sharpens their critical thinking skills for analyzing strategic actions, students early on attach a positive value to Robinson's second objective: to provide means by which we can develop methods of applying new knowledge to break economic, political, social, cultural, and even religious boundaries by which we are circumscribed. Long after the course ends, I get calls and correspondence from seminarians struggling to stay open-minded in their growing desire to live ethically as they identify the patterns that must be altered, and the accountable actions that must be taken in order for justice to occur. Here is a passage from a student's mid-semester inventory on insights gained from doing Africentric ethics collaboratively:

> I am learning so much more about violent repercussions in the work of justice, by studying the multitude of interpretative strategies in the cognitive maps of my classmates around the table. Their keen awareness of systemic oppression and willingness to ask hard ethical questions make me wonder if, sometimes, whether we are reading the same books. It is as if I have one piece of a tinker toy and together my colleagues help me make meaning by changing my toy into a motorized lego set.

In many ways, texts such as *In Search of Our Mothers' Garden: Womanist Prose* by Alice Walker; *Daughters of Anowa* by Mercy Amba Oduyoye; *The Black Women's Health Book* edited by Evelyn C. White and *Playing in the Dark: Whiteness and the Literary Imagination* by Toni Morrison, examine a series of contestable issues. In addition to highlighting racism, sexism, and class elitism, these non-fictional books by women of African descent highlight life-affirming possibilities in the struggle against ableism, ageism, lookism, heterosexism, specieism, colonialism, and imperialism.

The following brief statement suggests how one student starts to come to terms with the death-dealing everydayness of white supremacy.

> While the presence of Africans is duly noted throughout the canonical and normative American Literary Tradition, in *Playing in the Dark* Morrison exposes the misuse of African people and images in the imaginary landscape of Willa Cather, Edgar Allan Poe, Mark Twain, and Ernest Heminway. These writers use "literary blackness," to construct and validate the rightness of whiteness.

Several students underwent particular conscious-raising after reading *Sister-Outsider: Essays and Speeches* by Audre Lorde. One said:

> I have been troubled for some time now by the African American community's patent response to homosexuality, notwithstanding the tangible presence of gays and lesbians within our communit(ies), both in and out of the closet. Also, I fail to understand why homosexuality is deemed "more wrong" than adultery or sexism or dishonesty. For too long, homosexuals have been silenced in the

Black Church. Audre Lorde insists that we cannot put the weapon of silence in our enemies' hands.

Another wrote:

> Audre Lorde clarifies not only that the enormous anger that I have carried since I can remember is justified and natural, but that it is a powerful fuel. Although I realized even as I did it, that my straight A's in high school were achieved strictly out of spite and anger, I wanted the anger to disappear so that I could get on with a normal life. Twenty years later, I see the necessity and power of my daughters' anger, as nothing but a thin false calm over my own turbulence. Lorde says that we must learn to mother ourselves in order to lay to rest the bruised, hurt, weak girl-children we have been.

After a thorough reading of nonfiction prose by Bell Hooks, especially a line-by-line critique of *Black Looks: Race and Representation*, one student observes that Hooks deconstructs not only white images but also "race" productions generated within white supremacist western culture.

> From slave narratives to Micheaux's films, from black beast confections to Buffalo Soldiers, from revolutionary black women subjects to "renegade" connections between African Americans and Native Americans, from Anita Hill to Madonna—hooks challenges us to look critically as opposed to being spectators as we encounter images of blackness in all cultural contexts. Readers who want to decolonize our minds must consider the ideological content of images in order to move past the denial inherent in claims that we are merely being "entertained."

Most importantly, the cognitive maps based on non-fictional essays provided substantial resources in the development of each student's ethical voice. One student describes it this way:

> There are a number of "jaw dropping" passages in June Jordan's *Technical Difficulties: African American Notes on the State of the Union.* The book delves into the internally audible psyche; a place that records and plays back in our minds all the things that we don't say in public. Jordan has an incredible ability to effectively mix personal life experience with academic discourse. Her use of that which is intimate renders it public. She is able to make experiences that concern her, concern us.

Another ends her reflection paper with this comment:

> Reading June Jordan's brief description of a man raping her, and how she had no one to call, except by long distance, I thought of all the

African American women writers we have read this term and their deep love and dependence on other women. Even in *The Hottest Water in Chicago: Family Race, Time and American Culture* Gayle Pemberton, relied on her sister. Jordan's account saddens me. My resolution for this year is to reconnect with all of those women who have been vital to my life at various times. Since reading these books I've called Georgia and written letters to friends in Trinidad. There's a whole host of people who have seen me this far.

The impact of moving from Harvard Square to join the faculty at Temple University in North Philadelphia in 1992 coincided with my need to expand the core syllabus to include self-consciously constructed narratives about belief systems, cultural rituals, and kinship patterns by adherents of African Traditional Religions in the U.S. Sea Islands, the Caribbean, and Brazil. This expansion of the syllabus worked particularly well for students interested in African retentions in new world cultures. Within the context of this Africentric course, reading books such as *Mama Day* by Gloria Naylor; *Voodoo Dreams: A Novel of Marie Laveau* by Jewell Parker Rhodes; *Possessing the Secret of Joy* by Alice Walker; *Praisesong for the Widow* by Paule Marshall; *Baby of the Family* by Tina Elroy Ansa; *Changes: A Love Story* by Ama Ata Aidoo; *The Farming of Bones* by Edwidge Danticat; *The Bridge of Beyond* Simone Schwartz-Bart and *When Rocks Dance* by Elizabeth Nunez-Harrell helps students to keep in the forefront of their consciousness what values ought to be considered in making judgments about African realities on both sides of the Atlantic. After completing cognitive maps for the titles listed above, a working group summed up their learning in this way:

> We believe the biggest crime of the Maafa (the European enslavement of Africans) is the process of deculturalization of the Africans brought to the shores of America. The resources of African Traditional Religions were systematically suppressed. Most practices of Voodoo, Candomble, Santeria, Obeah, Rastafari, were labeled as heathenistic and treated as punishable offenses.

Students majoring in almost every discipline in the social sciences and the humanities who use this Africentric method acknowledge striking parallels that exist between the religion, art, music, dance, language and architecture in Africa and her Diaspora.

Conclusion

The city of Richmond is now the new venue for both me and my work as a theoethicist. In drawing up the course of study with colleagues in the Department of Theology and Ethics at Union Theological Seminary and the Presbyterian School of Christian Education, I did not propose *Resources for a Constructive Ethic: The Black Women's Literary Tradition.* Instead, this twenty-year march of time points to a growing accumulation of much new womanist scholarship. When I first began teaching at New York Theological Seminary in 1977, there were no books by Black women theologians. However, the primary materials now being published by Black women in the American Academy of Religion and the Society of Biblical Literature allow me to ask, and begin to answer, new questions about the ideologies, theologies, and systems of value of African American people. This pivotal shift is occurring as more women of all races, creeds, and colors earn doctorates from theological seminaries and departments of religion in universities. By asking heretofore undreamed and unfamiliar questions of every aspect of the theological traditions to which we are heirs, womanist, feminist, and mujerista scholars play a significant role in authorizing God-talk.

In essence, I have come full circle. As the Annie Scales Rogers Professor of Christian Social Ethics I am right back to where I began. *Womanist, Feminist and Mujerista Ethics* is my new Africentric course. Once again I am creating lectures from scratch but the required texts are no longer novels but publications by self-avowed, practicing womanist,[11] feminist, mujerista theologians. James H. Robinson's principles are still my overarching objectives because with each birthday I realize that the current students enrolled in my class, equipping themselves as leaders in church and society, are truly *the hinges on which the twenty-first century swings.*

Endnotes

1. See the article, "There's A Place for Us" in *Venture Magazine* (January 1971): 29.
2. James H. Robinson, *Road Without Turning: The Story of Reverend James H. Robinson* (NY: Farrar, Straus & Co., 1950).
3. Ruth T. Plimpton, *Operation Crossroads Africa* (NY: Viking Pr., 1962).
4. Frank T. Wilson, Sr., ed. *Black Presbyterians in Ministry: Living Witnesses Biographical Series* (NY: Consulting Committee on Ethnic Minority Ministries, Vocation Agency, United Presbyterian Church in the USA, 1972), 27-30; Louise E. Jefferson, *Twentieth Century Americans of Negro Lineage* (NY: *Friendship Pr., 1965).*
5. *Amy Lee, Throbbing Drums: The Story of James H. Robinson* (NY: Friendship Pr., 1968).
6. See Harold R. Isaac, *Emergent Americans" A Report on 'Crossroads Africa'* (NY: John Day Co., 1961); John David Cato, "James Herman Robinson: Crossroads Africa and American Idealism, 1958-1972," *American Presbyterian* 68 (Summer 1990): 99-107.
7. Gerald T. Rice, *The Bold Experiment: JFK's Peace Corp* (Notre Dame, IN: Notre Dame Pr., 1985).
8. Gayraud S. Wilmore, Foreword for *Africa at the Crossroads* by James H. Robinson (Phila.: Westminster Pr., 1962. See also, James H. Robinson, *Tomorrow Is Today*, (Phila.: Christian Education Pr., 1954); *Education for Decision* (addresses by James H.

Robinson and others) edited by Frank E. Gaebelein, Earl G. Harrison, Jr. and William L. Swing (NY: Seabury Pr., 1963); *Love of this Land: Progress of the Negro in the United States*. Illustrated by Elton C. Fax. (Phila.: Christian Education Pr., 1956).
9.   Katie G. Cannon, *Black Womanist Ethics* (Atlanta: Scholars Pr., 1988).
10.   All quotations in this chapter, unless otherwise indicated, were written by students enrolled in my courses at Harvard Divinity School (1983-84); Episcopal Divinity School (1984-1992) and Temple University (1992-2001). I owe a great debt to all the students, since 1977, who let me be a co-learner with them. They have been rigorous as well as generous in completing every aspect of course requirements. I offer special thanks to the women and men whose admirably nuanced words bear witness to the theoretical ideas in this paper.
11.   See the bibliography in the sample syllabus for a Graduate Seminar in Womanist Theology and Ethics in *The Womanist Theology Primer- Remembering What We Never Knew: The Epistemology of Womanist Theology* by Katie G. Cannon (Louisville: Women's Ministries Program Area, National Ministries Division, Presbyterian Church U.S.A.) 2001.

CHAPTER THIRTEEN

Africentricity:
A Missiological Pathway
toward Christian Transformation

Marsha Snulligan Haney

Africentricity is an essential, though often silent, dimension of missiological reflection, theory, and praxis within the North American context. The authors and their writings presented in this book suggest that the time has come to move Africentricity from the margin to the center of theological discourse. We claim not to have the final word on the subject, but serve as a guide with those who affirm the principles of Africentric (or African centered) Christian theology as authentic, relevant, and faithful Christian witness and mission to black public life in particular, and to human life in the post modern world in general.[1] After all what are the vision, the promise and the hope of Christian mission if it is not to create communities of dignity, integrity and just relationships that affirm human being as created in the image of God?

Each of the essays presented is grounded in the historical reality of the author. The issues raised emerge out of concrete experiences, and describe a specific approach for exploring Africentric issues, themes and influences. Each continues to operate in concrete historical contexts. We have been deliberate and intentional about applying the term 'model' to the essays presented because models are specific, not intended to translate from one specific context to another.

Therefore, to provoke a reframing of our thinking and action related to the Africentric models and approaches presented by the authors, I have selected missiological resources, data and analytical method to frame this concluding chapter. It is helpful first to briefly center our learning related to Africentricity first from a global perspective, then from the perspective of the USA. It is also helpful to recall that whether we are relating Africentricity to the thematic concerns of biblical hermeneutics, Christian theology, moral agency, ministry, worship, homiletics, social witness or multiculturalism, each one provides a trajectory for some understanding of how God intends to transform our families, society, the world, and us.

Africentricity from a Global Frame of Reference

Since the early 1960's, there has been a growing awareness of how diverse cultural contexts shape theology. From a global perspective, as countries throughout Africa, Asia and the Pacific, and Latin America began to claim political independence so too did their churches and church leaders. The growing voice of so many Christians in their local contexts began to express dissatisfaction with some inherited ways of doing theology; others rejected colonial and imperialistic ways of doing theology and living the Christian faith because they did not make sense within their own cultural patterns, thought forms, and worldview. Even as early as the 18th century it was not uncommon to hear that attempts to counter imperialistic and colonial Christian actions were met with hostilities, including death.[2] In Africa, as was true in other parts of the world, attempts to contextualize the Christian faith and make it culturally and theologically relevant were primarily through indigenization and enculturation. At the same time, the need to discover authentic theological expression motivated a growing number of Christians (as well as other religious persons) to embrace Africentrism as both a means and content of theological reflection and faith practice.

As humans worldwide were struggling, resisting and fighting for political and social independence, and global human rights, thematic issues were emerging, so too were persons motivated spiritually, theologically and missiologically to turn more and more toward Africentricity for theological and religious understanding. The current emphasis on and proliferation of ethnic studies, minority studies, post-colonial theological studies, and local church mission histories, help elucidate the key factors related to the growing synergy that characterized the need for an Africentric approach to life. The Africentric impact (or the need for it) is prevalent as a major aspects of global research identify common themes flowing through the worldview of Africans on the continent, and the African Diaspora in Britain, France and other European countries (including the colonies they ruled); in Central and South America (especially Brazil); the Caribbean and the West Indies; North America, including both Canada and the United States; and even as far as Asia, including India, Indonesia (including Papua New Guinea) and other Asiatic countries where African descendants lives as a result of enslavement and forced migration of Africans during the late 15th, 16th, 17th and 18th centuries.

In other words, wherever African peoples were, the African worldview was operable, especially in the face of the unknown, to help sustain life. As a result of the social protest historical mode of the 1960's, we have seen and will continue to learn how Christian theologians, church leaders, and seekers worldwide engage in efforts leading not only toward becoming self-propagating, self-governing, and self supporting, but also self-theologizing. This fourth factor, self-theologizing, was never a characteristic of the "three self-help" program of North Atlantic Christian missions (neither abroad or at home), and yet its occurrence was inevitable. The growing identity of local Christians in their various contexts, not only exposed the oppressive nature of older approaches and models of Christianity, but also contributed to the development of truly contextualized models of Christian theology.[3] Mission history research allows us to study critical growth and development of the phenomena of contextualization (contextual theology) not only within the ancient churches of Egypt and Ethiopia, but also in the phenomenal growth and development of African initiated and African independent congregations and denominations, both on the continent and beyond. Missiological research has suggested that sufficient Christian contextualization in the 3rd and 4th centuries accounts for the effective and faithful presence of the Church in Ethiopia and Egypt today, and lack of it contributed to the demise of the Church in ancient Nubia and North Africa (the church of St. Augustine).

Africentric Approaches Within A National (USA) Frame of Reference

Considering the African American religious experience in the USA, it is by examining the social history of the civil rights movement of the 1960's that we see with more clarity how vastly differing were the theological models used to motivate a particular people, African Americans, within a larger social and religious context. A closer examination of the sources and various approaches related to contextualization theory and practice are evidenced in the life and ministry of Martin Luther King, Jr. and Howard Thurman.[4] These two exemplars represent two distinct Christian models of public theological engagement in that era, and they are juxtaposed to the models of Elijah Muhammad (and Louis Farrakhan) and Malcolm X (El Hajj Malik Shabazz) which exemplify two distinct models of Islamic contextualization.[5] From the perspective of Missiology we are enabled to see how theological, spiritual, and contextual factors interact and converge differently through various models. What was not so clearly evident (with the exception of the Black Christian Nationalists) was a clear appreciation and articulation by a national leader, of the historical and theological contribution of Africentricity through the lens of a mainstream Christian faith.[6]

Yosef ben-Jochannan, Molefi Asante, Cain Hope Felder, Paula Hill Collins, Alice Walker, and Ronald Karenga are but a few of the voices who have assisted not only in the theoretic grounding and articulation of Africentricism and Afrocentrists, but also in the development of its ideological legitimacy. By building on Africentric antecedents and presenting diverse paradigmatic shifts, they have developed a variety of approaches that continue to inspire countless Christian women and men toward wholeness through Africentric Christian theological and religious education.

Prompted simultaneously in the 1960's by the critique of Black Christian nationalist movement and by the almost invisible but persistent voices of some church leaders and members, many congregations began to advocate for relevant and authentic Africentric models and approaches to ministry and theological education. As a dialogue in process, Africentricity continues to engage in a lively dialectic between theory and praxis, with some conversations more ecumenical than others. Some faculty members of historical black theological schools as well as lay church leaders involved in a variety of ministries, continue to demonstrate that predominantly westernized and Eurocentric worldview studies, liturgy, theological images, and biblical interpretations are meaningless in many Black (African American, African Caribbean, or African) contexts in the USA. (This reality is also being articulated with a new urgency throughout the Caribbean, Brazil, and South Africa.) As the Black Church is held more accountable for responding faithfully to the myriad of public challenges facing the black community, Africentric models and approaches, in all their variety, will continue to have a home situated in both the historic Black Church and within Africentric congregations in predominately Euro-American denominations.[7] To acknowledge the diversity of contextualized theology approaches at work among African Americans Christian thinking and action is to affirm the various ways in which Christians and Christian congregations seek to be faithful to God, and the *missio Dei*, and their response in light of a sense of vocational calling to mission as purposeful living. By focusing on humans and what is important to them within the their context, properly taught and modeled, contextualization takes us to the center of what God did in Jesus Christ—the Incarnation.

Africentricity: A Missiological Pathway to Christian Transformation
      By framing the discourse of Africentricity as a pathway of Christian transformation of the human person, we are better able to digest and interpret the need for the specific religious and theological insights provided by the authors of this book. Based on an understanding of Missiology as that interdisciplinary and critical reflection which researches, records and applies data relating to the biblical origins, the history, the anthropological principles and techniques, and the theological base of the Christian mission. The two primary dimensions undergirding this definition are theology and anthropology: theology because we begin with an understanding of God and God's purpose for humanity (expressed in the concept *missio Dei,* the mission of God), and cultural anthropology because God's intent and purpose must be communicated to humans (*imagio Dei,* (humans as created in the image of God) within human communities shaped by culture. Grounded in the understanding of both concepts is the belief that human identity, including ethnic identity, is a gift from God (divine origins), and what we do with it (human response) is our gift to God. Therefore, both the educational mission of the church, and the mission of social transformation are decisive.
      Missiology also acknowledges that, in fact, all theology is contextual, and that Christian theology is the product of a specific group of people in a particular time, place, and space seeking to respond faithfully to the God revealed in Jesus Christ and Jesus' self-understanding. It is as Christians in every context learn to depend on the triune God, and the reforming, revelatory spirit of God for

direction and guidance, that the universality of the Christian gospel is truly achieved and affirmed. How does this occur? Missiology affirms that the contextualization of theology- the process of making the Christian faith understood in terms of a particular context- is really a theological imperative and is in fact part of the vary nature of theology itself.[8] By paying attention to how we unearth five theological sources (the spirit and message of the Christian gospel, the social history of the Christian people, the nature of their encounter in Christian mission history, the culture in which they are to theologize, and social change in that culture) missiologists, theologians and mission advocates can better serve as a resource in helping to determine which of the six (primary) theological models is most appropriate.

While all five elements are found in each model, how they differ is related to which source serves as the point of departure for the theological inquiry. Based on the principle that each source serves as a kind of lens by which God's redemptive activity can be examined in greater detail, then as Deborah E. McDowell has suggested, even the experience of slavery (i.e., social history) can serve as a sacred text.[9] Just as first-century Christian theologians and church leaders had to answer questions that arose from women and men living in their cultural context, so too must contemporary Christians. We must engage in the process of answering questions posed by Christians themselves, nominal Christians, persons of other living faiths, and those who simply describe themselves as spiritual seekers.

It is only as theological educators, church workers and minister leaders grow in this understanding and knowledge that they are able to appreciate Africentric Christianity as a corrective to the current theological hegemony that persists.   This corrective reveals a broader range of attitudes and behaviors related to Africentricity within Christian thought, and acknowledges that there is more African centered Christian diversity than contemporary secondary literature suggests. By moving the issue of Africentricity from the margins of theological inquiry to the center, and by presenting Africentricity as a pathway toward Christian transformation, the following missiological themes are emphasized.

Africentric Missiological Themes

First, the **African American experience** (socio-political-religious) assumes the first and most important role in the doing of Africentric theology. This critical observation not only recognizes a biblical hermeneutics in an Africentric perspective, but also highlights the significance of Africentric biblical hermeneutics. It is also important to recognize that the theologians represented in this volume maintain that God's revelation is known not only through Scripture, but also through the human efforts that put God's love as revealed in Christ, into practice.

According to worldview theory, there is much similarity among African and African-American worldviews when the philosophical aspects of cultural differences are examined. Africentricity as embraced among African-Americans, takes as its point of departure the theological understandings of what it means for African Americans to journey through life with God beginning, not with enslavement in the USA, but beginning in Africa.[10] The goal is to help persons experience the transforming power of God, the call to Christian discipleship, and the call to the ministry of the Christian gospel as theology related to the whole of human life. The insights of the authors presented here demonstrate a deep awareness that in a rapidly changing world, Africentric Christian theological education has to express itself in everyday living if it is to be truly authentic. It must bear fruit on many fronts: in Africentric worship, liturgy, preaching, congregational leadership, theological education and the recognition of moral agency in all kinds of relationships with persons and systems within black public life.

Second, there is recognition that the encounter between **'Gospel and culture'** is at its core a lively and dynamic interaction of values, ethics, traditions, morality and discernment. How the socio-political-religious practices and religious faith implications come together in the life of an Africentric faith community often determines which theological source (experience, scripture, tradition, or culture) will serve as a point of departure for intelligent Christian reflection. The ongoing interface between the spirit and the message of the Gospel and social change issues within contemporary culture will help determine which of six primary models of contextual theology emerge as Christians seek to make their engagement in theological reflection, advocacy and action, both explicit and meaningful. Unfortunately, the current theological discourse on the nature and dynamics facing Gospel and culture within the context of North America has reminded primarily an exclusive Euro-centric monologue of like-minded persons and experiences. This posture will not assist North Atlantic missiologists nor their developing missiologies in addressing the crucial challenges facing present and future realities related to issues of both theological diversity, and human diversity in North America. Several aspects of contemporary culture create both opportunities and threats to a serious engagement of the Africentric approach.

Third, doing theology from an Africentric perspective requires an **interdisciplinary approach** which will help church members recognize how their lives relate to a wide variety of challenges and opportunities in the secular world. An interdisciplinary approach not only promotes a multi-dimensional Gospel for multi-dimensional human needs, it also communicates a holistic concern for whole persons: relationships that must be restored, bodies that are in need of healing, minds that must be taught, spirits that must be encouraged, and personalities that must be transformed. The contributors to this volume view an interdisciplinary approach as the only way to address holistically and authentically the complex challenges facing African American Christian women, men and children in the 21st century. The dialectical relationship between theology and other disciplines is particularly important today because of the complexity of critical issues now confronting persons, families, communities, societies, and nations.

Fourth, further **interreligious dialogue** between Christians and non-Christian Africentric believers is called for. Because of religious pluralism within the African Diaspora, interfaith and interreligious dialogue are mandatory. Rastafarians, the African Hebrew Israelites, the Black Jews, Black Christian Nationalists (such as Christians of the Shrine of the Black Madonna), Sunni Islamic Muslims, members the Nation of Islam, Santeria, Vondou, and other faith communities seek to witness "unapologetically" to elements of an Africentric worldview through sacred rituals, rites, writing, worship and sacred events. They, as well as Africentric Christians within mainline denominations seek to present their faith beliefs as capable of offering something valuable for the struggle for humanity. Perhaps the most important contribution of the diverse Africentric religious contexts is to highlight the significance and necessity of various types of interreligious dialogue. As individual faith communities communicate effectively about salvation and human liberation, truth and justice, and reconciliation and peace, they must do so in neighborhoods and communities where religious people of various faiths encounter one another in shared space: including the workplace, the market place, places of education, and places of entertainment and relaxation.

Fifth, the application of **Africentric theories and models of learning**, encourages public discourse on various levels. African centered theological thinking and practice (especially in urban centers) have contributed greatly to American discourse in the public arena as they communicate clearly their point of view through cultural arts and esthetics, educational institutes, economic self-development projects, holistic health emphasis and community development enterprises. At a time in history when our society is grappling with the question, "Can there be a public theology in the 21st century America in view of racial, ethnic and philosophical differences?" Africentricity is responding in the affirmative to both sets of critics: those within the Black church tradition who remain skeptical of an Africentric Christian witness that is based in part on a neo-orthodox reading of Galatians 3:28, and those within the Eurocentric Christian tradition who dismiss the value of their own ethno theological formation, and who dismiss Africentricity as narrow ethnocentrism or cultural romanticism. In spite of growing crisis and tensions around issues of ethnic diversity, certain public conversations provide opportunity to examine three specific conversation partners: gender differences, religious diversity, and issues of race and racism.

The application of Africentric theories and models of learning and their impact on gender issues, is demonstrated in the volume entitled *Living The Intersection: Women and Afrocentrism in Theology* edited by Cheryl Sanders. This work has been most helpful in examining and analyzing the intersection of the two most powerful theological perspectives among contemporary African American womanist theologians and proponents of Afrocentricism from a variety of viewpoints. The insights are especially helpful in chartering a future that is appreciative of the contributions of both movements and their synergy. The second factor involving Africentric theorists and learning models is that of religious diversity. The willingness, ability and availability of African centered religious believers to encounter and affect faith communities was alluded to earlier. Suffice it to say here that more research is needed on the part of those disciplines and practices that intersect both interfaith dialogue and the various forms of Africentric interreligious discourse.

It is equally important to observe the impact Africentric theories and models of learning have had on issues of race and ethnicity, especially within the academy. A key responsibility of Africentricism is to expose and critique the presuppositions of colonial, imperialistic and neo-liberal scholarship that continue to disregard, distort, and undermine the integrity and personhood of African Americans. Africentricity recognizes the crucial role of theological and religious education in providing insight and analysis of religious faith development, identity formation, theoretical scholarship, and applied theological education. The need to remain alert when facing these challenges is bests summed up by Christian ethicist Katie Geneva Cannon who made the following remark that originated with the Soledad Brothers, "We have to read and write even when the lights are off."[11]

Without a doubt, Africentricity has had a positive influence in prompting Eurocentric Christian theologians, scholars and practitioners to address race and racism as individuals and members of faith communities. This was most evident at the American Academy of Religion and the Society of Biblical Literature (AAR/SBL) annual meeting (Toronto, 2002) during a session entitled, "Theology and Whiteness: How can Traditional White Theologians Begin to Talk About Race". The following is a sample of the diverse issues raised by various panel presenters as they discoursed on the need for the construction of an anti-racist Christian theology for North America. They conceded the need to acknowledge Eurocentric theology as contextualized theology and "not as the theology by which all other flesh is measured and devoured"; an understanding of racism as the privilege of white supremacists based on flawed social and theological formations and systems; an understanding of white ideology and supremacy constructs operating as the norms for interpreting reality, divinity, and theology; the acknowledgement that the biblical mythology of Ham as the first form of white supremacy within in the Euro-centric Christian theologies of modern Europe and North America.; and, an understanding of contemporary globalization as imperialistic political economy and neo-liberal transnational polity which are both racist and imperial by design. As one of the Euro-American panel member stated:

> "White theologians must speak about the power of God to change; yet there is no change in racist powers and principalities. What good are white theologians if they can't address and challenge racism with theological resources? Jesus called and built life in radically

different ways, that today calls for a full challenge of the racist regime in this country. As more bombs, prisons, and executions are planned, we must deepen our resolve to fight anti-racism theology!"[12]

Clearly this type of awareness and articulation does not develop in a vacuum, but rather is the result of a lively dialectical encounter between diverse worldviews and theological understandings, including Africentric theology.

Sixth, in the **emerging global context,** where contextual theologies are becoming more pronounced and influential as they dialogue within the universal Christian church, Africentricity presents a lens for reading world realities at a global level. As the twenty-first century witnesses massive accessions to the Christian faith in Africa, Asia, Central and South America, more and more African American Christian scholars, especially young missiologists, leaders and congregations are already demonstrating an ability and willingness to engage global issues from the perspective of local efforts of contextualization.

Primarily, it is non-Eurocentric North American missiologists who are among the first to have acknowledged the new global missionary setting the Church now faces, the so-called "coming of the Third Church."[13]   In the first thousand years church history and mission history were under the auspices of the Eastern Church, including the North African Church, the Nubian Church, the Church of Egypt and the Ethiopian Church. In the second millennium, the leading church was the western, Eurocentric churches of Europe and North America, shaped by their cultural understandings and interpretations of divinity, humanity, and other worldview themes that supported ideological and theological justifications for slavery, colonialism and imperialism. Because of this reality Africans and peoples of African descent have had to wrestle with an array of problems deriving from slavery and colonization, specifically ideologies related to self-perceptions, the perception of others, and the kinds of practices African people have evolved in response to the incursion of North Atlantic Christianity. This is what makes the Africentric project so urgent.

The Church in the third millennium (often referred to as the 'Third Church') now clearly stands under the leadership of the Third Church, the Church geographically located in the southern hemisphere: in Africa, Asia and the Pacific, and Central and South America. It has been said that "...the most important drives and inspirations for the whole church in the future will come from the Third Church".[14] This is already apparent with the church in African growing more rapidly that in any other place in the world, and with Africentric forms of the Christian faith already contributing to this exciting development in substantive ways.

Africentricity not only provides a lens for reading world realities at a global level, but also Africentric forms, functions and meanings have had a great influence throughout the world. It has made for greater African American sympathy and understanding of the widespread resentment against the present USA hegemony over global forces, especially as they victimize the poor, oppressed, and marginalized. The influence of Africentricity as a global dynamic is much wider than it first appears. Consider the illustration taken from one single form of African American music hip-hop. Developed among urban youths, hip hop (in which secular, social, and economic factors become the main sources of cultural meaning and values for cultural formation) has crossed global boundaries and is now popular not only in Africa and Brazil, but is also a powerful form for communicating both Christian and Islamic religious messages. Trans-boundary realities such as this emphasize the epistemological and political intersections inherent in religious and social history.

Seventh, as **Christian partnerships** are formed with a greater sense of intentionally and specificity, Africentricity is proving to be a valuable theological resource. Limited sources of human energy, time, talents and finances require that Africentric Christian partnerships be approached from the perspective of good stewardship. Good stewardship requires that the myriad of opportunities for participation in and support of the various academic associations and societies, ministerial collaborations, and traditions ecclesiological partnerships (as well intended as they may appear) be evaluated in light of the value of the Africentric quest for healing, health and wholeness. Imposed, dichotomous, and other worldly theological perspectives (such as prosperity theology and dependence on television evangelists) are severely questioned and rejected.

The fact that some traditional theological paradigms are not meeting the felt religious and spiritual needs of a growing number of African Americans is apparent from the proliferation of Africentric church growth in both Protestant congregations and within Roman Catholicism, and the increased demand for Africentric Christian educational curricula. Children and youth are not receiving what they need from classical models based on traditional theological rhetoric and images of divinity, beauty, power, and individualism. Africentric philosophy, centered on persons at all stages of the life cycle, prepares and sustains young people creatively to live with faith, courage, and confidence in a violent capitalistic and often dehumanizing world, a world consumed by superficially and concerned only with the obvious and the shallow), and where quick fixes abound.

Persons in leadership positions that are poised for the kinds of partnerships required today must know how to function intergenerationally as well as cross-culturally. The role that theological education has made in encouraging such partnerships in the life of the Interdenominational Theological Center (Atlanta, GA) for more than forty years is chronicled in several volumes of the *Journal of the Interdenominational Theological Center (JITC)*. The Africentric orientation of the JITC and other publications of the ITC community is reflected in issues of the JITC such as *Stories About Ethiopia: An African Holy Land* (1998); *Reflections on the All African Conference of Church (1998);* and the book,

African Roots: Toward An Afrocentric Christian Witness (1994). The emphasis continues through the life and work of Africentric missiologists members of the faculty such as Josephus Coan, Ndugu G.B. T'Ofori-Atta, Darius L. Swann, Tumani Mutasa Nyajeka, Burgess Carr, and the author. Through the advocacy and promotion of projects involving seminarians and church leaders in global mission travel seminars throughout Africa, the Caribbean, Brazil, and India the importance of global partnerships and collaborations is being passed on to a new generation of scholars, pastors, mission leaders, and Christian educators.[15]

Eighth, Africentric theology is done from the **perspective of people,** laity and practitioners, as well as clergy and academics. A key factor that encourages this development is the Africentric adage that teaches, "I am because we are". This perspective understanding of what it means to be human ensures that a mission-conscious church is cultivated through emphasis on the communal nature of being--linking the past, present and future. In such congregations, denominations, and seminaries, Africentric theological insight and religious models of learning instruct people on the need to trust in the presence and spirit of God, and the manifestation of God's will and purpose within the community. The outcomes are two fold: not only will the Christian message make more sense for group of people and in each context, but also contextual models of theology allow people (women, men and youth) to utilize cultural elements that are consistent with the Gospel. The result is that the self-perception and self-worth of a people are elevated.[16]

Ninth, the **reign of God,** said to be the central theme in both the Hebrew Scriptures and in Jesus' life and message is also penultimate in an Africentric Christian theology. The essays in this book all affirm that Africentric theological understandings speak faithfully of the power of God to transform persons, culture and society in accordance with the gifts and requirements of the African American context. It has been demonstrated in the lives of both the "living dead" (those who are no longer among the living but who continue to inspire us with their words, actions and exemplary lives), and among the living, that the Christian faith contains a radical message of personal and social liberation and reconstruction. By emphasizing the redemptive role of Christ and Christian fellowship, bringing the individual Christian into union with others and into fellowship with Christ, Africentric theologians and ministry

leaders are better able to gain invaluable insight and discernment for effective living and faithful ministry.

An Africentric Christian identity based on the reign of God is a powerful spiritual and missional motivator. It stands as a corrective to the modern missionary movement described as being primarily linked to a traditionalist, colonialist and imperialistic interpretation of the Christian mission as one of "being sent". The major emphasis of an Africentric understanding of Christian mission and witness is not so much on "being sent" as it is "to **be** human as we go about daily living". The proclamation of this message in word, deed, and lifestyle is a missiological phenomenon that is already evident, but requires more research. The power of God to form, shape and empower Africentric Christian ministry is illustrated in the congregational mission statement of a growing and dynamic Africentric congregation: "[we] are an Africentric Christian Ministry that empowers women, men, youth and children to move from membership to leadership in the church, the community and the world."[17]

Finally, the tenth theme related to the intersection of Missiology and Africentricity that is foundational to the perspective of this book is the relationship between **spirituality and mission strategy**. An urgent question for Christian missiologists in North America has to do with how the spirituality of a religious person and faith community is absorb and overcome the massive changes that have transformed modernity but have left humans spiritually hungry and searching.

Missiology, from an Africentric perspective, suggests that there is no validity to our spirituality if it does not result in social action, in a vivid demonstration that faith in Christ makes a difference. The interconnectedness of spirituality and social responsibility, as we live and move in the tension of God's grace in the here and now, requires that our lives reflect contextually and theologically appropriate a sense of human responsibility and accountability to both God and our fellow human being.[18] This is the challenge of Africentric Christian faith- allowing personal and communal spirituality to inform and transform social, political, and religious realities in the single world in which we are called to live, move and have our being. Both spirituality and social responsibility are necessary and, with a correct biblical understanding the data of lived experience, they are inextricable.

Summary

The foregoing missiological themes summarize the learning presented by the authors of this book and accentuate the essence of the theological discourse that flows from Christian Africentric models and approaches. The various missiological themes assist the wider Christian community to obtain a greater appreciation of nature of the Africentric Christian worldview and its contribution to theological discourse and religious education. Working within US culture, as well as globally, Africentric understandings express and explicate the power of God at work reforming and transforming personal, cultural, and societal attitudes, behaviors and systems by utilizing the theological resources we should already possess as a result of our Christian baptism and confirmation.

Each author of this volume has contributed to a clearer understanding of the relationship between persons and faith communities (particularly the congregation and seminary), religion and culture, the spiritual and the secular, and our private and personal confessions of Christian faith by uncovering meanings embedded in a dynamic scholarship and applied theology formulated from an Africentric perspective. Our purpose in this work has been five-fold:

1) To force the reader to reconsider carefully the strengthens of Africentric theological and religious education as a pathway to the transformation of human persons and communities;

2) To uncover prevailing assumptions regarding the nature of theological inquiry, the variety of theological models, and the impact on our post-modern world of diverse Christian problems and solutions in this new world;

3) To encourage an interdisciplinary methodology based on the heuristic use of phenomenological approaches which permit an empathic and critical engagement with the subject matter at hand;

4) To help the reader to appreciate the value of ethnic cohesion as an endemic force within the history of Christianity that shows the contributions and benefits of the ethnic group and the importance of its solidarity and its security in the face of strains and stresses of the outside world, and the need for intellectual and spiritual satisfaction within itself.

5) To demonstrate that in view of the continuing and growing racial, ethnic and philosophical differences and conflicts over the possibility of a public theology in the United States in this 21st century, it is possible to appropriate from different ethnic groups theological and religious insight capable of informing and inspiring people in the public arena.

I believe that the authors have successfully presented both opportunities and challenges for further dialogue centered on the substance and shape of Africentric approaches and models. By focusing on Africentricity as the subject of academic inquiry into specific areas of human life, the assertions of the authors presented here make the case that theological education, advocacy and praxis must be relevant to daily living if the faith passed down to us by our ancestors, both before and after Christianization, is to be perceived as authentic for humanization and salvation.

Endnotes:

---

1.   The theory of Africentricity, or African centeredness used in this concluding chapter is my own representation and elaboration of ideas found in *Africentric Christianity: A*

Theological Appraisal for Ministry, by J. Deotis Roberts (Judson Press, 2000), and in Gayraud S. Wilmore's *(Black Religion and Black Radicalism.* Doubleday, 1972). Add to this, of course, the results of my own research and reflection.

2.   See "Attributes of Simon Kimbangu: Founder of the Kimbanguist Church" by Basile Akiele on the encounter of European missionaries and the death of prophetess Kimpa Vita and her son in the *Seventh Assembly of the All Africa Conference of Churches, Addis Ababa, Ethiopia, October 1997, The Journal of the Interdenominational Theological Center*, Volume XXVI, No. 2, Spring 1999.

3.   Stephen Bevans' *Models of Contextual Theology* (Orbis, 1996) is perhaps one of the most succinct, precise and thorough analyses of five models of contextual theology. While the counter-culture model is not included in his 1996 edition, it is included in the 2003 revised and expanded edition. From my perspective, the inclusion of this model is necessary in order to understand better both the growth of religious groups and cults within the USA that are anti-state and anti-government toward some laws, as well international Islamic attitudes and perspectives that facilitated the September 11, 2001 terrorist event and the aftermath.

4.   See Gilke's essay "We Have A Beautiful Mother: Womanist Musings on the Afrocentric Idea", *Living the Intersection: Womanism and Afrocentrism in Theology*, edited by Cheryl J. Sanders. It is important to observe, as Cheryl Townsend Gilkes has, that the Africentric vision as represented in Alice Walker's thinking, is greatly influenced by both Howard Thurman and Martin Luther King, Jr.

5.   For an in depth examination of Islamic models of contextual theology, see *Islam and Protestant African-American Churches: Responses and Challenges to Religious Pluralism* by Marsha Snulligan Haney (Lanthan, MD: International Scholars Publications, 1999).

6.   Jeremiah A. Wright, Jr. speaks to this matter as he states, "Hearing him [Cain Felder speak of Afrocentricity as a means toward achieving the end of Christocentricity] struck a resonant chord deep within the souls of many of the members of the Trinity congregation he pastors in Chicago because since 1972 this congregation has striven to embody that very philosophy. As a matter of historical fact, it was in 1972 that Trinity adopted as its motto the phrase, "unashamedly black and unapologetically Christian". See *Towards an Afrocentric Christian Witness*, edited by Michael I. N. Dash, L. Rita Dixon, Darius L. Swann and Ndugu T' Ofori-Atta (SCP/Third World Literature, Lithonia, GA, 1994).

7.   My use of the notion of the black community is based on the understanding as found in the *Harvard Encyclopedia of Ethnic Groups*, by Stephen Thernstrom, (Harvard University Press, 1980) which identifies the ethnic cohesion that exists as a result of a shared heritage and history, a common foundation and experience as a people bound together with collective self needs, and a common position and struggle within American society.

8.   Although Stephen Bevans makes this point most clearly in *Models of Contextual Theology* (see endnote 3 above), see also *Contextualization: Meanings, Methods and Models* by David J. Hesselgrave and Edward Rommen (Baker, 1989).

9.   See Deborah E. McDowell's essay entitled, "Slavery as a Sacred Text: Witnessing in Dessa Rose" in *Living the Intersection: Womanism and Afrocentrism in Theology*, edited by Cheryl J. Sanders, Minneapolis, MN: Fortress Press, 1995).

10.   Important insights are revealed when African and American-American notions and concepts are compared. For instance, *The Spirituality of African Peoples: The Search for a Common Moral Discourse* by Peter Paris (Minneapolis, MN: Fortress, 1995).

11.   Cited by Katie Geneva Cannon at the meeting of the American Academy of Religion/Society for Biblical Literature (AAR/SBL) in Toronto, Canada, 2002.

12.   Panel presentation on "Theology and Whiteness: How Can Tradition White Theologians Begin to Talk About Race." Annual meeting of the American Academy of Religion and the Society of Biblical Literature (AAR/SBL), Toronto, Canada, 2002.

13.   This reference is to "Gospel and Culture in a New Missionary Setting" by Samuel Escobar and his reference to W. Buhlman in *The Catalyst* (November 1997, Volume 24, No.1).

14.   Ibid., 1.

15.   Missiologist Darius Swann, having served as a young African American missionary to Uttar Pradesh, India, almost five decades ago, continues to encourage Indian and African American theological partnerships. "Dalits and African Americans: Can They Learn From Each Other?" is an example of one of his many articles on transnational discourse. "An analytical look at the two groups reveals striking similarities in situation and experience and also some important differences" is an important observation made by Swann in *The Dalit International Newsletter,* edited by John Webster (October 1996, Vol. 1, No. 3) 1.

16.   J. Deotis Roberts affirms the concept of Africentricity as useful for engendering a sense of worth in *The Prophethood of Black Believers: An African American Political Theology of Ministry* (Westminister, 1994).

17.   This is the mission statement of First African Presbyterian Church (Lithonia, GA), under the pastoral leadership of Rev. Mark Lomax.

18.   See Peter Paris, *The Spirituality of African Peoples: The Search for a Common Moral Discourse* (Minneapolis, MN: Fortress, 1995). 18.   The theory of Africentricity, or African centeredness used in this concluding chapter is my own representation and elaboration of ideas found in *Africentric Christianity: A Theological Appraisal for Ministry,* by J. Deotis Roberts (Judson Press, 2000), and in Gayraud S. Wilmore's *(Black Religion and Black Radicalism.* Doubleday, 1972). Add to this, of course, the results of my own research and reflection.

Selected Bibliography

Anderson, Victor Anderson. *Beyond Ontological Blackness: An Essay on African American Religious and Cultural Criticism.* New York: Continuum Press, 1995.

Angelou, Maya. *I Know Why the Caged Bird Sings.* New York: Random House, 1970.

Ani, Marimba. *Yurugu: An African-Centered Critique of European Cultural Thought and Behavior.* Trenton, NJ: New Africa Press, 1994.

Asante, Molefi Kente. *The Afrocentric Idea.* Philadelphia, PA: Temple University Press, 1987.

___. *Afrocentricity.* Trenton, NJ: Third World Press, 1988.

___. *Kemet, Afrocentricity and Knowledge.* Trenton, NJ: Third World Press, 1992.

Akiele, Basile, "Attributes of Simon Kimbangu: Founder of the Kimbanguist Church" in *The Journal of the Interdenominational Theological Center,* Volume XXVI, No. 2, Spring 1999.

Baker-Fletcher, Karen. *A Singing Something: Womanist Reflections on Anna Julia Cooper.* New York: Crossroad, 1994.

Billingsley, Andrew. *Climbing Jacob's Ladder: The Enduring Legacy of African-American Families.* New York: Simon and Schuster, 1992.

___. *Mighty Like a River: The Black Church and Social Reform.* New York: Oxford University Press, 1999.

Blasi, Anthony J. *Making Charisma: The Social Construction of Paul's Public Image.* New Brunswick, NJ: Transaction Publishers, 1991.

Brown, David. *The Divine Trinity: Christianity and Islam.* London: Sheldon Press, 1969.

Bevans, Stephen B. *Models of Contextual Theology.* Maryknoll, NY: Orbis, 1996.

Callahan, Kennon L. *Effective Church Leadership, Building on the Twelve Keys.* San Francisco: Harper-Collins Publishers, 1990.

Cannon, Katie G. *Black Womanist Ethics.* Atlanta, GA: Scholars Press, 1988.

___. *Katie's Cannon: Womanism and the Soul of the Black Community.* New York: Continuum, 2000.

___. *The Womanist Theology Primer-Remembering What We Never Knew: The Epistemology of Womanist Theology.* Louisville, KY: Women's Ministries Program Area, National Ministries Division, Presbyterian Church U.S.A., 2001.

Case, Sue Ellen. *Feminism and Theatre.* New York: Meuthuen, 1988.

Cato, John David. "James Herman Robinson: Crossroads Africa and American Idealism, 1958-1972." *American Presbyterian* 68 (Summer 1990): 99-107.

Chapman, Mark L. *Christianity on Trial.* Maryknoll, Orbis Books, 1996.
Cleage, Albert B. Jr. *The Black Messiah.* New York: Sheed and Ward Press, 1968.
Cone, James H. *Black Theology and Black Power.* New York: Seabury Press, 1969.
___. *God of the Oppressed.* Maryknoll, NY: Orbis, 1997.
___ and Wilmore, Gayraud S. *Black Theology: A Documentary History, 1966–1979.* Maryknoll, New York: Orbis Books, 1979.
Crockett, Joseph V. *Teaching Scripture: From an African-American Perspective.* Nashville, TN: Discipleship Resources, 1990.
Cruse, Harold. *Plural But Equal.* New York: William Morrow, 1987.
Dangarembga, Tsitsi. *Nervous Conditions.* Seattle, WA: Seal Press, 1989.
Dash, Michael I.N., Rita Dixon, Darius Swann, and Ndugu T'Ofori-Atta, eds. *African Roots: Toward An Afrocentric Christian Witness.* Lithonia, GA: SCP/Third World Literature Publishing House, 1994.
Drake, St. Clair. *The Redemption of Africa and Black Religion.* Chicago, IL: Third World Press, 1991.
DuBois, W.E.B. *Souls of Black Folk.* Chicago, IL: A.C Mclug & Co., 1903.
Earl, Riggins R. Jr. *Dark Symbols, Obscure, Signs: God, Self, & Community in the Slave Mind.* Maryknoll, NY: Orbis Books, 1993.
Eboussi-Boulaga, Fabien. *Christianity without Fetishes: An African Critique and Recapture of Christianity.* Maryknoll, NY: Orbis Books, 1984.
Ela, Jean Marc. *My Faith as an African.* Maryknoll, NY: Orbis Books, 1988.
Emeagwali, See Gloria T. *Women Pay the Price: Structural Adjustment in Africa and the Caribbean.* Trenton: Africa Press, 1995.
Emecheta, Buchi. *The Joys of Motherhood.* New York: G. Braziller, 1979.
Evans, James Jr. *We Have Been Believers: An African American Systematic Theology.* Minneapolis, MN: Fortress Press, 1992.
Fanon, Franz. *The Wretched of the Earth.* New York: Grove, 1963.
Felder, Cain Hope. *Troubling Biblical Waters: Race Class and Family.* Maryknoll, NY: Orbis Books, 1989.
___, Gen. Ed. *The Original African Heritage Study Bible.* Nashville, TN: Winston Derek Publishing Company, 1993.
___. "Afrocentrism, the Bible, and the Politics of Difference" *Princeton Seminary Bulletin* 15 (1994): 132-138.
___. Contrib. Ed. *The African American Jubilee Bible.* New York: The American Bible Society, 1999.
___. Co-Editor with Charles H. Smith. *The Jubilee Legacy Bible.* Nashville: Townsend Press, 2001.
Fiorenza, Elizabeth Schussler. *Rhetoric and Ethic: The Politic of Biblical Studies.* Minneapolis, MN: Augsburg Fortress, 1999.
Foster, Charles R., Ed. *Ethnicity in the Education of the Church.* Nashville, TN: Scarritt Press, 1987.

Frazier, E. Franklin. *Black Church in America*. New York: Schocken Book, 1964.

Freire, Paulo, Pedagogy of the Oppressed. New York: Continuum, 1984.

Gaebelein, Frank E., Harrison, Earl G., Jr. and Swing, William L., Eds. *Love of this Land: Progress of the Negro in the United States*. New York: Seabury Press, 1963.

Gates, Henry Louis. *Loose Canons: Notes on the Culture Wars*. New York: Oxford University Press, 1992.

Gardell, Mattias. *In the Name of Elijah Muhammad: Louis Farrakhan and the Nation of Islam*. Durham, NC: Duke University Press, 1996.

Gilkes, Cheryl Townsend *"The Role of Women in the Sanctified Church,"* The Journal of Religious Thought 43 Spring -Summer, 1986) 24-41, Journal of Social Issues 39 (Fall 1983) 115-139,

Grant, Jacquelyn. *White Women's Christ and Black Women's Jesus: Feminist Christology and Womanist Response*. Atlanta, GA: Scholars Press, 1989.

Gilkes, Cheryl Twonsend. "The Roles of Church and Community Mothers: Ambivalent American Sexism or Fragmented African Familyhood," *Journal of Feminist Studies in Religion* 2 (Spring 1986) 41-60.

Haney, Marsha Snulligan. *Islam and Protestant African-American Churches: Responses and Challenges to Religious Pluralism*. Lanthan: International Scholars Publications, 1999.

Herskovits, Melville. *The Myth of the Negro Past*. Boston: Beacon Press, 1958.

Hesselgrave, David J. and Rommen, Edward. *Contextualization: Meanings, Methods and Models*. Baker, 1989.

Hilliard, Asa G., III, L., Payton-Stewart and L. O. Williams, eds. *Infusion of African and African American Content in the School Curriculum*. Chicago: Third World Press, 1990.

Hood, Robert E. *Must God Remain Greek? Afro Cultures and God-Talk*. Minneapolis: Fortress, 1990.

Hooks, Bell. *Black Looks: Race and Representation*. New York: Routledge, 1992.

Hubbard, Dolan. *The Sermon and the African American Literary Imagination*. Columbia: University of Missouri Press, 1994.

Hughes, Langston and Bontemps, eds. *The Book of Negro Folklore*. New York: Dodd, Mead, 1958.

Isaac, Harold R. *"Emergent Americans: A Report on 'Crossroads Africa.'"* New York: John Day, 1961.

Jefferson, Louise E. *Twentieth Century Americans of Negro Lineage*. New York: Friendship Press, 1965.

Karenga, Maulana. *Kwanzaa: A Celebration of Family, Community and Culture*. Los Angeles: University of Sankore Press, 1998.

Kirk-Duggan, Cheryl. *Exorcizing Evil: A Womanist Perspective on the Spirituals*. New York: Orbis, 1997.

Kunjufu, Jawanza. *Restoring the Village Values and Commitment: Solutions for the Black Family.* Chicago: African American Images, 1996.

Lee, Amy. *Throbbing Drums: The Story of James H. Robinson.* New York: Friendship Press, 1968.

Light, Alan, ed. *The Vibe History of Hip Hop.* New York: Three Rivers Press, 1999.

Lincoln, C. Eric, *The Black Church Since Frazier.* New York: Schocken Books, 1974.

____ and Lawrence H. Mamiya. *The Black Church in the African American Experience.* Durham: Duke Univ. Press, 1990.

Lorde, Audre. *Sister Outsider: Essays and Speeches.* Freedom: Crossing, 1984.

Lyon, K. Brynoll and Archie Smith, Archie, Jr., eds., *Tending the Flock: Congregations and Family Ministry.* Louisville: WJKP, 1998.

Lucaites, John Louis, Celeste Michelle Condit, and Sally Cadill, *Contemporary Rhetorical Theory: A Reader.* New York: Guilford, 1999.

Madhubuti, Haki R. *Black Men: Obsolete, Single, Dangerous?* Chicago: Third World Press, 1991.

Marks, Shula, ed. *Not Either an Experimental Doll: The Separate Worlds of Three South African Women.* Bloomington: Indiana University Press, 1988.

Massey, James Earl, ed. *Designing the Sermon: Order and Movement in Preaching.* Nashville: Abingdon Press, 1980.

Mays, Benjamin Elijah and Joseph William Nicholson. *The Negro's Church.* New York: Negro Universities Press, 1933.

McClester, Cedric. *Kwanzaa: Everything You Always Wanted to Know But Didn't Know Where to Ask.* New York: Gumbs & Thomas, 1984.

McGrath, Alister. *The Future of Christianity.* Oxford: Blackwell Publishers Limited, 2002.

Meeks, Wayne A. *The First Urban Christians: The Social World of the Apostle Paul.* New Haven: Yale University Press, 1983.

Mitchell, Henry. *Black Belief: Folk Belief of Blacks In America and West Africa.* New York: Harper and Row Publishers, 1975.

Morgan, Joan. *When Chicken Heads Come Home to Roost: A Hip-Hop Feminist Breaks It Down.* New York: Simon and Schuster, 1999.

Morrison, Toni. *Song of Solomon.* New York: Alfred A. Knopf, 1977.

Mudimbe, V. Y. *The Invention of Africa: Gnosis, Philosophy, and the Order of Knowledge.* Bloomington: Indiana University, 1988.

Niebuhr, Richard H., *Christ and Culture* (New York: Harper & Row, 1951)

Njeza, Malinge. "Fallacies of the New Afrocentrism: A Critical Response to Kwame A. Appiah." *Journal of Theology for Southern Africa* 99 (November 1997): 47-75.

Norman Harris, *Afrocentric Visions: Studies in Communication and Culture*, ed. Janice Hamlet (Thousands Oaks: Sage Publications, 1998), 15.

Oduyoye, Mercy Amba. *Hearing and Knowing: Theological Reflections on Christianity in Africa.* Maryknoll, New York: Orbis Books, 1986.

____. *Daughters of Anowa: African Women and Patriarchy*. Maryknoll: Orbis Books, 2000.

____. "Troubled But Not Destroyed," Keynote address, All Africa Conference of Churches Seventh General Assembly, Addis Ababa, Ethiopia, October 1-10, 1997.

____. The Church of the Future, Its Mission and Theology. Resource Paper presented to the All Africa Conference of Churches Seventh General Assembly, Addis Ababa, Ethiopia, October 1-10, 1997.

Oglesby, E. Hammond, *O Lord, Move This Mountain: Racism and Christian Ethics* (St. Louis, MO: Chalice Press, 1998).

Opoku, Kofi Asare, "African Traditional Religion: An Enduring Heritage," *The Journal of the Interdenominational Theological Center* XVI, No. 1 & 2, (Fall 1988/Spring 1989): 14.

Patterson, Orlando. *Rituals of Blood: The Consequences of Two Hundred Years of American Slavery*. New York: Civitas:1998.

Payne, Daniel A. *Recollections of Seventy Years (The American Negro, his History and Literature)*. New York: Arno Press, 1969.

Presbyterians for Prayer, Study, and Action, *Is This New Wine?* (Louisville, Ky: Presbyterian Church (USA), 1993)

Pollard, Leslie, "Saga and Song: A Cross-cultural Primer in African-American Preaching," *Ministry* (May 1995): 5.

Paris, Peter. *The Social Teaching of Black Churches*. Philadelphia: Fortress Press, 1985.

____. *The Spirituality of African Peoples: The Search for a Common Moral Discourse*. Minneapolis, MN: Fortress, 1995.

Peters, Ronald E. *Is This New Wine?* In *Resistance and Theological Ethics*, edited by Ronald Stone and Robert L. Stivers. Rowman and Littlefield, 2004.

Plimpton, Ruth T. *Operation Crossroads Africa*. NY: Viking Press, 1962.

Roberts, J. Deotis, *A Black Political Theology*. Philadelphia: Westminster, 1974.

____. Roberts, J. Deotis. *Black Theology in Dialogue*. Philadelphia: Westminster, 1987.

____. *A Philosophical Introduction to Theology*. Philadelphia: Trinity Press, 1991.

____. *The Prophethood of Black Believers: An African American Political Theology for Ministry*. Louisville: Westminster/John Knox, 1994.

____. *Africentric Christianity*. Valley Forge: Judson Press, 2000.

Robert W. Funk, Roy W. Hoover and the Jesus Seminar. *The Five Gospels: The Search for the Authentic Words of Jesus*. New York: Mcmillan, 1993.

Roberts, John W. *From Trickster to Badman: The Black Folk Hero in Slavery and Freedom*. Philadelphia: University of Pennsylvania Press, 1989.

Raboteau, Albert. *Slave Religion: The "Invisible Institution" in the Antebellum South*. New York: Oxford University Press, 1978;

Robinson, James H. *Road Without Turning: The Story of Reverend James H. Robinson* New York: Farrar, Straus & Co., 1950.

____. *Africa at the Crossroads.* Philadelphia: Westminster Press, 1962.

Riggs, Marcia. *Arise, Awake and Act: A Womanist Call for Black Liberation.* Cleveland: Pilgrim, 1994.

Ross, Rosetta. *Witnessing and Testifying.* Minneapolis: Fortress, 2003.

Sanders, Cheryl J., ed. *Living the Intersection: Womanism and Afrocentrism in Theology.* Minneapolis: Fortress Press, 1995.

Shockley, Grant. "Christian Education and the Black Religious Experience." in *Ethnicity in the Education of the Church,* 29-47, edited by Charles R. Foster. Nashville: Scarritt Press, 1987.

Smith, Arthur [Molefi Asante]. *Language, Communication, and Rhetoric in Black America.* New York: Harper and Row, 1972.

Stallings, James O. *Telling the Story: Evangelism in Black Churches.* Valley Forge: Judson Press, 1998.

Smith, Theophus. *Conjuring Culture: Biblical Formations of Black America.* Oxford: 1994.

Smith, Wallace Charles. *The Church in the Life of the Black Family.* Valley Forge, PA: Judson Press, 1985.

Tienou, Tite. "Themes in African Theology of Mission." In *The Good News of the Kingdom* edited by Charles Van Engen, et al. Maryknoll: 1993.

Torrey, R. A. *The Power of Prayer and the Prayer of Power.* Grand Rapids Michigan: Zondervan Publishing House.

Townes, Emilie. *Womanist Spirituality.* Nashville: Abingdon, 1994.

Tucker, David M. *Black Pastors and Leaders: Memphis, 1819–1972.* Memphis: Memphis State University Press, 1975.

Tutu, Desmond Mpilo *No Future Without Forgiveness.* New York: Random House, 1999.

Tyms, James D. *The Rise of Religious Education Among Negro Baptist.* New York: Exposition Press, 1965.

Van Sertima, Ivan. *They Came Before Columbus.* New York: Random House, 1976.

Walker, Alice. *In Search of Our Mothers' Gardens: Womanist Prose.* San Diego: Harcourt Brace, 1983.

Washington, James M. *Testament of Hope: The Essential Writings of Martin Luther King, Jr.* San Francisco: Harper, 1986.

Washington, Joseph R., ed. *Black Religion and Public Policy: Ethical and Historical Perspectives.* Philadelphia: University of Pennsylvania Afro-American Studies Program, 1978.

Wecter, Dixon, "Introduction" in *The Hero in America,* (New York: Charles Scribner's' Sons, 1972).

West, Cornel. *Prophecy Deliverance.* Philadelphia: Westminster, 1982.

____. *Race Matters.* Boston: Beacon Press, 1993.

Wilmore, Gayraud S. *Black Religion and Black Radicalism.* Maryknoll: Orbis, 1973.

____. *Black and Presbyterian: The Hope and the Heritage.* Philadelphia:

Geneva, 1983.

___ . *Black the Christian Faith Through Africentric Lens*. Maryknoll: Orbis, 1998.

Williams, Delores. *Sisters in the Wilderness*. New York: Orbis, 1993.

Williams, Patrick and Laura Chrisman, eds., "Postmodern Blackness," *Colonial Discourse and Postcolonial Theory: A Reader* (New York: Columbia University Press, 1994), 421.

Wilson, Frank T., Sr., ed. *Black Presbyterians in Ministry: Living Witnesses Biographical Series* New York: Consulting Committee on Ethnic Minority Ministries, Vocation Agency, United Presbyterian Church in the USA, 1972.

Wimberly, Anne Streaty. *Soul Stories: African American Christian Education*. Nashville: Abingdon Press, 1994.

Wimbush, Vincent L. *African Americans and the Bible: Sacred Texts and Social Textures*. New York: Continuum, 2000.

Woodson, Carter G. *Mis-Education of the Negro*. Trenton, NJ: Africa World Press, 1993.

Wright, Jeremiah in Jini Kilgore Ross, ed. *What Makes You So Strong? Sermons of Joy and Strength from Jeremiah A. Wright, Jr*. Valley Forge, PA: Judson Press, 1994.

About the Contributors

Author's Biographical Information

Ronald Edward Peters

Ronald Edward Peters is the Henry L. Hillman Associate Professor of Urban Ministry and the first Director of Pittsburgh Theological Seminary's Metro-Urban Institute, an interdisciplinary program of religious leadership development for urban society. Prior to joining the Seminary faculty, Dr. Peters served as a pastor for eighteen years, including fourteen years as the founding pastor of Martin Luther King, Jr. Community Presbyterian Church in Springfield, MA, and four years in Miami, FL as pastor of the New Covenant Presbyterian Church. His work focuses on urban churches and public ministry both nationally and internationally.

A New Orleans, Louisiana native, Dr. Peters received his *Bachelor of Arts* degree from Southern University (Baton Rouge, Louisiana), the *Master of Divinity* degree from Gordon-Conwell Theological Seminary (Hamilton, Massachusetts), and his *Doctor of Education* degree from the University of Massachusetts at Amherst. He is an advisor to the Presbyterian Church (U.S.A.) on social witness policy, ethnic/racial ministry, and urban theological education. His interdisciplinary approach to theological education involves students in ministries related to public schools, social work, courts and prison systems, public health, faith-based community organizing, and cross-cultural courses offered in partnership with Trinity Theological Seminary, Ghana-West Africa.

Professor Peters' international experience includes research on the role of religion and the development of urban civil society in Namibia and Botswana as a Fulbright Scholar. He has conducted workshops on urban leadership development in Ethiopia, Ghana, Haiti, Kenya, and South Africa and observed urban theological education programs in Switzerland, Singapore, Thailand, and the Republic of China. Some of his writings include *Race and Toxic Waste* (Presbyterian Church, USA. Louisville, KY, 1994); *Gospel of Mark: A Men's Study of Christian Discipleship* (Men's Ministry Unit, Presbyterian Church, USA, 1996), and *"Is This New Wine?,"* in *Resistance and Theological Ethics*, edited by Ronald Stone and Robert L. Stivers (Rowman and Littlefield, 2004). Dr. Peters and his wife, Mary Smith Peters, live in Pittsburgh, Pennsylvania.

Marsha Snulligan Haney

Marsha Snulligan Haney is Associate Professor of Missiology and Religions of the World at the Interdenominational Theological Center, Atlanta, GA. Ordained in the Presbyterian Church (U.S.A.), she has served the church abroad with the Sudan Council of Churches (Juba, North Africa) as an educator and women's program staff developer, as a pastor and educator in Cameroon (Kumba, West Africa), and as both an urban community minister and mission personnel recruiter within the United States. She is currently serving as founder and director of the Urban Theological Institute, Interdenominational Theological Center, and is actively concerned with addressing issues related to urban theological education.

She holds master's degrees in Christian Education, Church Administration, and Missiology, and has engaged in Islamic studies in Birmingham, England. Her Ph.D. is in Intercultural Studies/Missiology from the School of World Mission, Fuller Theological Seminary, Pasadena, CA.

Professor Haney has taught, preached, lectured, and engaged in theological research in more than 30 countries. Her recent works include *Islam and Protestant African American Churches: The Challenges of Religious Pluralism* (International Scholars Publications, 1999); Guest editor with Darius L. Swann, *Seventh Assembly of the All Africa Conference of Churches, Addis Ababa, Ethiopia, October 1997*, published in the *Journal of the Interdenominational Theological Center*, vol. XXVI (Spring, 2001); "Toward the Development of a New Christian Missiological Identity" in *Teaching Mission in a Global Context*, Patricia Lloyd-Sidle and Bonnie Sue Lewis, editors (Geneva Press, 2001); and consultant editor, *The Journal of the Interdenominational Center*, *"Persons, Culture and Society: The Challenges of Transition and Transformation,"* vol. XXX (Fall 2002/Spring 2003); and "Congregational Ministry in Frontier Crossing: The Challenge of Religious Pluralism" in *Mission is Crossing Frontiers: Essays in Honor of Bongani A. Mazibuko,* edited by Roswith Gerioff (Cluster Publication, 2003). She and her husband, Willie C. Haney, Jr., reside in Decatur, Georgia.

Gayraud S. Wilmore has served on the faculties of New York Theological Seminary, Colgate Rochester Crozer Divinity School, and Interdenominational Theological Center and other institutions. Other works he has authored include *Black Religion and Black Radicalism* (Orbis, 1973), co-edited with James H. Cone *Black Theology: A Documentary History, 1966–1979* (Orbis, 1979), *Black and Presbyterian: The Hope and the Heritage* (Geneva Press, 1983; revised and enlarged edition, Witherspoon Press, 1998), and *Pragmatic Spirituality: The Christian Faith Through an Africentric Lens* (New York University Press, 2004).

Tumani S. Mutasa Nyajeka is Associate Professor, Missiology and Religions of the World at Interdenominational Theological Center. She is also author of "Shona Women and the Mutupo Principle" in *Women Healing Earth : Third World Women on Ecology, Feminism, and Religion (Ecology and Justice)* by Ruether, Rosemary Radford Ruether (Orbis Books, 1996).

Rosetta E. Ross is Chair of the Philosophy and Religion Department at Spelman College and is an ordained elder in the United Methodist Church. Among her other works are *Witnessing and Testifying: Black Women, Religion, and Civil Rights* (Augsburg Press, 2003).

J. Deotis Roberts has been a pastor, preacher, professor, lecturer, educator, administrator, and activist for social justice. He has served as visiting scholar, religion and theology at Baylor University, Duke Divinity School, Eastern Baptist Theological Seminary and various other institutions. Dr. Roberts' other works include *Black Theology in Dialogue* (Westminster, 1987), *A Philosophical Introduction to Theology* (Trinity, 1991), *The Prophethood of Black Believers: An African American Political Theology for Ministry* (Westminster/John Knox, 1994) and *Africentric Christianity* (Judson Press, 2000).

Richard C. Chapple, Jr. is Assistant Professor of Homiletics at Pittsburgh Theological Seminary. A full-time minister in the AME Zion Church, Professor Chapple has had supervisory responsibilities over pastors and congregations. An honors graduate of Howard University Divinity School from which he received the MDiv. degree, he also holds the M.Th from Princeton Theological Seminary. A regular speaker at AME Zion events, he has published articles on preaching and pastoral counseling in several publications.

Cain Hope Felder is Professor of New Testament Language and Literature and editor of the Journal of Religious Thought at the Howard University School of Divinity in Washington, D.C. Among his other writings are *Troubling Biblical Waters: Race Class and Family* (Orbis Books, 1989), general editor, *The Original African Heritage Study Bible* (Winston Derek, 1993), contributing editor, *The African American Jubilee Bible* (American Bible Society, 1999), and co-editor with Charles H. Smith. *The Jubilee Legacy Bible* (Townsend Press, 2001).

Johnnie Monroe is pastor of the Grace Memorial Presbyterian Church of Pittsburgh, Pennsylvania where he long been a leading figure in public ministries, focusing on social justice and public education issues. His pastoral experience of more than thirty-five years has included congregations in Philadelphia and Chester, Pennsylvania as well as administrative leadership within the Presbytery of Pittsburgh and Synod of the Trinity in the Presbyterian Church, USA.

Fred Douglas Smith, Jr. is the Associate Director of Practice in Ministry and Mission and Associate Professor of Urban Ministry at Wesley Theological Seminary. An ordained elder in the United Methodist Church, Dr. Smith has taught at Emory University, Pittsburgh Theological Seminary and has written extensively on Christian Education and urban ministry among African American youth.

Gloria J. Tate, pastor of the Teaneck Presbyterian Church of Teaneck, New Jersey. She holds the Doctor of Ministry Degree from United Theological Seminary and the Master of Divinity from Johnson C. Smith Seminary at the Interdenominational Theological Center where she also serves as Chair of the Johnson C. Smith Seminary Board of Trustees.

Warren L. Dennis is Professor of Metro-Urban Ministry at New Brunswick Theological Seminary in New Brunswick, NJ. He is an ordained Minister of Word and Sacrament in the Presbyterian Church, USA and received Doctor of Divinity Degree from United Theological Seminary, Dayton, OH. Among his other writings are "Comments on A Metro Strategy" in *Transforming the City: Reframing Education for Urban Ministry,* Eldin Villafañe, et al. editors (Eerdmans, 2002).

Katie Geneva Cannon is the Annie Scales Rogers Professor of Christian Ethics at Union Theological Seminary and Presbyterian School of Christian Education. Professor Cannon's work focuses on the areas of Christian ethics, Womanist theology, and women in religion and society. She has lectured nationally on theological and ethical topics and is the author or editor of numerous articles and seven books including *Black Womanist Ethics* (Scholars Press, 1988) and *Katie's Canon: Womanism and the Soul of the Black Community and Black Womanist Ethics* (Continuum, 2000).